LocoScript 2

Locomotive Software's
Word Processor
for the Amstrad PCW8256, 8512 and 9256

USER GUIDE

LOCOMOTIVE
SOFTWARE

9108

Locomotive Software gratefully acknowledges the advice and assistance on the design of the character set given by Victor Swoboda, Research Fellow, School of Slavonic & East European Studies, University of London.

Written by Jean Gilmour, Locomotive Software
Produced and typeset electronically by Locomotive Software Ltd
Printed by Ashford Colour Press, Gosport, Hants

Published by Locomotive Software Ltd
Dorking
Surrey RH4 1YL

First Published 1987
Second Edition Published November 1987 (Reprinted with corrections February 1992)
ISBN 1 85195 008 7

LocoScript 2 User Guide

Introduction

With an Amstrad PCW and Locomotive Software's LocoScript 2 you get a complete word-processing system. The PCW itself is a computer, designed to manipulate data of whatever type you like – numbers, text or even obscure codes. LocoScript 2 is a special type of computer program – called a word processor – that takes all the actions that the computer does well and puts these to work in producing professional-looking documents. (Unless this User Guide has been bought as a separate item, LocoScript 2 is supplied on the disc packaged with this User Guide.)

If you have used its predecessor, LocoScript 2's use of menus and keystrokes and the layout of the screen will all seem very familiar to you. LocoScript 2 is essentially the earlier LocoScript with a number of new features – but also with some important differences. Changes were inevitable to accommodate the new facilities, even to the LocoScript documents themselves. We explain how to convert LocoScript '1' documents – and yourselves – to LocoScript 2 in a special chapter (Chapter 2).

What is word processing?

Word processing, like typing at a typewriter, is all about preparing documents. However, there the similarity stops because, in word processing, you type your letter, article or whatever at the keyboard and this goes into your computer's memory, rather than straight onto a piece of paper. (The computer displays what it has in its memory on the screen so that you can see what you are doing.) Then later, you ask the computer to print out on paper the text you have typed in.

Why is this better? Well, imagine writing a letter. Almost inevitably, you will make a spelling mistake or change your mind about what you want to write somewhere along the line. Changing the data held in memory is something that computers are good at – so while your text is in your computer's memory, you can correct and revise it at will. When you come to print, you get a copy of the version that is currently in your computer's memory – a perfect 'clean' letter. Doing the same revision on a typewriter would involve lots of wasted paper and, more importantly, lots of re-typing – and, potentially, yet more mistakes.

In addition to this, while a typewriter only works with text characters which it processes one by one, LocoScript 2 also works with some special codes, which it uses to control how the text appears when it is printed – where the margins are, what type of characters are used, how far the lines of text are apart, etc. etc. So if you wanted your address at the top of the letter to be over to the righthand side of the page, you put in codes that say that this text should be at the righthand side of the page. Similarly, if you want to have 'Yours sincerely' centred at the bottom of the letter, then you put in a code that says that this is what you want. There's no need for you to work out the number of spaces you would need to type in order to get the text in the right position – you get the computer to do that arithmetic for you. These 'word-processing' codes can be revised at will, just like the text itself.

When you come to larger or more complicated documents, you may well want to make larger changes to the text – perhaps moving whole sections of text from one place in the document to another. This is no problem because, once again, this is something that computers do well. Alternatively, you might want each page to be numbered and to have some special text at the top and/or the bottom of the page. Special codes in LocoScript 2 arrange this, too.

There are lots of other jobs that you will want your word-processor to help you with. If you are a Secretary of a club, then you will want your word-processor to help you circulate details of forthcoming events or copies of the club newsletter to members. Or if you are preparing a report on something, then you will probably have one or more tables to prepare. Or you might have some sales literature to produce, which you want to lay out and style really nicely.

With LocoScript 2, there's essentially endless scope for revising and styling your text – so much so that you might get so carried away with producing the perfect document that you never actually get around to printing it!

Moreover, because you can save your work on disc any time you like:

- You can start and stop work on a document at will; you don't have to finish somewhere that is easy to carry on from – like the bottom of a page – as on a typewriter.
- You can make copies of the document stored on disc – making it very easy to produce different versions of the same document with very little extra effort.

LocoScript 2

LocoScript 2 is a very powerful word processor, providing a very wide range of word-processing 'tools' so that you can:

- prepare all sorts of documents – letters, contracts, invoices – very easily
- use different printers for your documents
- type text in a variety of foreign languages and in a variety of print styles and character sizes
- prepare tables
- centre headings; put addresses over to the righthand side of the page
- take pieces of text from one document and put them in another
- put special text at the top and the bottom of each page, put in page numbers
- have 'letter-head' documents with your address etc. ready set up in them
- link the chapters of a book together, etc. etc.

And to work alongside LocoScript 2, there are a range of 'add-on' programs – LocoSpell, LocoMail and LocoFile – plus several printer support programs. These are separate programs (and are sold separately) but they are fully integrated with LocoScript 2. (Be sure to buy the LocoScript 2 versions of these programs!)

LocoSpell checks your documents for spelling mistakes – drawing to your attention any word it can't find in its spelling lists. It also suggests a word that you may have meant to type and, as a side-line, counts the number of words in your document.

LocoMail lets you set up standard letters, invoices etc. and then helps you fill these out – both from the keyboard and from address lists and other records that you have stored on disc. It even helps you with working out such things as totals and the amount of VAT due – arithmetic is something else that computers are very good at!

LocoFile is a 'pop-up' database, based on the tried and tested principles of the card index but very much more powerful. Information can be entered faster, updated more easily, found more quickly and re-organised almost instantly. Moreover, it is fully integrated with LocoScript, allowing you to pull information from a LocoFile datafile and slot it straight into the document you are editing.

At every stage, LocoScript 2 guides you through the steps you need, not only to create documents and edit them, but also to get the best visual effect when you print them. You don't have to remember any complicated 'spells': there are menus of options and facilities to choose from and the keystrokes that will bring you the options you want are shown on every screen display. When you are more experienced, you may find these menus get a little in the way – so LocoScript 2 also provides some short cuts.

Learning to use LocoScript 2

LocoScript 2 provides a very wide range of word-processing facilities. But this doesn't mean that LocoScript 2 is difficult to master or that you have a lot to learn before you prepare and print your first word-processed letter. In fact, this is one of the very first things we show you how to do in the Tutorial that forms the main part of this guide.

The best way to learn how to use a word processor is through practice, and that is what the Tutorial provides – taking you through the different tasks you use LocoScript 2 for, starting with the ones that you will use every day. If you have used the earlier version of LocoScript (LocoScript '1'), you will already be familiar with LocoScript's screens and menus and so you won't need to study the Tutorial in quite such detail. However, there are a number of differences between LocoScript '1' and LocoScript 2 – so you do have some new things to learn. What these differences are and the parts of the Tutorial that cover them are explained in the chapter on Converting to LocoScript 2, which precedes the Tutorial. This chapter also explains what you need to do to use a 'LocoScript 1' document with LocoScript 2.

Throughout the Tutorial, we shall be taking advantage of the fact that you don't need to set such things as the size and style of the characters you will be using, the length of the page, the margins etc. before you start. Suitable settings are already provided. You may well want to change some of these settings to suit the particular job you want to do – and later we show you how to do this – but, as you will see, you can achieve a great deal without ever touching them!

But before you can get to work on the Tutorial, there's a certain amount of preparation that has to be done first.

Problems with LocoScript 2

If you are experiencing difficulty using LocoScript 2:

1 **Consult the User Guide.** The chances are that the solution to the problem is described somewhere in the manual. Our experience shows most problems are caused by trying to go too fast – moving on to the more advanced (and more interesting) topics, before completely mastering the (less interesting) basics.

The quickest way to solve your problem is almost certainly to follow the appropriate tutorial sessions. You may also find the index, glossary and quick reference handy.

2 **If that does not work,** or LocoScript 2 is demonstrably failing to work as described in the user guide, please write to:

> **LocoScript 2 Support**
> **Locomotive Software Ltd**
> **Dorking**
> **Surrey**
> **RH4 1YL**

When writing to Locomotive, make sure that you include the following details:

- Your name
- Your address
- The version number of LocoScript 2, eg. v2.00. This is shown on the first line of the Disc Manager Screen f1 menu.
- Details of your PCW (eg. 8256, 8256+extra memory, 8512)
- A brief summary of your problem, including sufficient details to enable our staff to repeat your actions. If you don't tell us how to repeat the problem, it's unlikely that we will be able to help you.
- If the problem concerns your printer, details of the interface and the printer (manufacturer and model number)

Please write to us, don't phone! We are unable to offer telephone support, and anyway, we find it easier to give good support with the facts and the problem written down. It makes **you** think more about the problem and lets **us** ensure that it is handled by the correct expert.

Note: The Screen Displays you see when using LocoScript won't necessarily match the Screen Displays shown in this User Guide. In particular, pictures of the Disc Manager Screen may not show the same range of files as you have on your discs. There is no need to worry unless what is described in the User Guide bears no relation to what is happening on the screen.

Contents

Appendices

Chapter 1

Preparation

Before you can start work on the LocoScript 2 Tutorial:

- Your PCW needs to be set up ready with a plug on the end of its mains lead.
- The PCW printer needs to be connected to your PCW and set up ready to print on single sheets of paper. In particular, there should be a ribbon in the printer.
- Last, but not least, you need to make what is known as a 'Start-of-day' disc. This is the disc that you will in future use to load the LocoScript 2 program into your PCW. You will also need to make an 'Examples' disc to use as you work through the LocoScript 2 Tutorial.

This chapter briefly describes how to set up your PCW and the printer (full details are given in your PCW user guide), then goes on to explain how to prepare a Start-of-day disc and an Examples disc. If your PCW is already set up for use, you can skip straight to the section on making a LocoScript 2 Start-of-day disc.

You will need two blank discs for this process. Mark Side 1 of one disc 'Start-of-day' disc; mark Side 1 of the other disc ' Examples disc'. (If you don't have any blank discs, you can always use an 'old' disc, provided you don't want any of the files on this disc any more.)

Setting up your PCW

To set up your PCW, you need to connect the Keyboard to the Monitor Unit and to attach a plug to the end of the mains lead on the back of the Monitor Unit.

To connect the Keyboard to the Monitor Unit, insert the 4-pin DIN plug at the end of the keyboard cable into the socket on the righthand side of the Monitor Unit.

When the keyboard has been connected, put a plug on the end of the mains lead. This plug must have a 5Amp fuse fitted in it: if you use a 13Amp plug, the 13Amp fuse supplied in the plug should not be used.

Important: The wires in the mains lead are coloured in accordance with the following code:

Blue   : **Neutral**
Brown : **Live**

The blue wire must be connected to the terminal marked N or coloured black: the brown wire must be connected to the terminal marked L or coloured red.

DO NOT PLUG YOUR PCW INTO THE MAINS SUPPLY YET

Finally, press the Eject button on each of your disc drives and remove the piece of cardboard that has been used to guard the drive against damage in transit.

LocoScript 2 User Guide: Introduction   **1**

Setting up the printer

If the printer is not already attached to your PCW, it is a good idea to set up the printer for single sheet paper and to insert the printer ribbon first.

Inserting the printer ribbon

The ribbon is contained in a cassette, so loading the ribbon is a matter of putting this cassette in position in the printer.

First gently lift out the dust cover at the front of the printer. This is hinged so you will have to release it from its hinges first.

Now hold the cassette with its 'fin' uppermost and the ribbon away from you. Turn the ribbon feed knob (to the left of the fin) in the direction of the arrow to take the slack out of the ribbon. Then slot the cassette into the position illustrated on the top of the cassette itself, taking care that the ribbon passes between the print head and the ribbon guide. Be careful not to twist the ribbon.

When the cassette is in place, press down gently on both sides of the cassette to ensure that it is properly located. Check that the ribbon is properly positioned in front of the print head and then gently turn the ribbon feed knob again to remove any slack.

Finally replace the dust cover.

Setting up for single sheet stationery

When you want to feed single sheets of paper through the printer, you just need to hinge back the paper tray at the back of the printer and clip the two paper tray extensions into the slots in this tray.

The tractor feed unit should only be attached to the printer when you want to use continuous stationery (see Appendix I).

Connecting the printer

First check that your PCW is not plugged into the mains supply.

Place the printer to the right of your Monitor Unit and quite close to it.

Now insert the 34-way connector on the printer ribbon cable into the 34-way 'PRINTER' socket on the back of the monitor unit. Be careful not to stretch the cable as you do this.

When the ribbon cable is attached, insert the plug on the end of the printer's other cable into the '24V DC' socket on the back of the Monitor Unit.

Your PCW is now fully set up.

8906

Making your Start-of-day disc

The first step is to protect the 'Master' disc(s) on which your new software has been supplied against being accidentally changed while you are installing your software. To do this, you need to look at the corners of these discs: you should notice either one or two holes with shutters that move over them. To protect your Master discs, these holes should all be open. (The corresponding holes on your new blank discs should, however, be closed.)

PCW8256/8512 disc

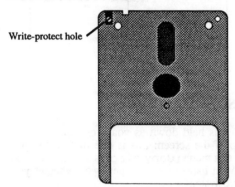

Write-protect hole

PcW9256 disc

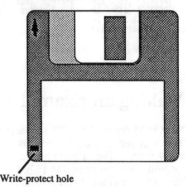

Write-protect hole

You then need to run the Installation program provided on the LocoScript 2 Master disc. How to run this Installation program is explained in the Update Information booklet supplied with your copy of LocoScript 2. This booklet contains separate sets of instructions – some for new users of LocoScript 2; others for people already using LocoScript 2. However experienced a user you are of LocoScript '1' (the LocoScript supplied with your PCW), you will still need to follow one of the sets of instructions for new users. Precisely which set of instructions depends on which LocoScript 2 pack you bought. All is explained in the Update Information booklet itself.

Be sure to follow the instructions in the Update Information booklet very carefully – particularly with regard to the option to select from the Installation program's "Initial Options menu". Otherwise, you may find yourself at odds with the program over the details of the system you are trying to set up.

At the end of the Installation procedure, you are told to press the [ENTER] key to load the software from the disc in the drive. You should then see the pattern of horizontal lines, followed this time first by information about your copy of LocoScript and then by a screen like the one shown overleaf (which shows a typical display on a PCW8512).

You have now both created your new Start-of-day disc and loaded LocoScript 2 from it. All that is left to do is to prepare an Examples disc to use as you work through the LocoScript 2 Tutorial.

```
                          Disc management.              Printer idle.  Using     M:
C=Create new document        E=Edit document      P=Print document       D=Direct printing
f1=Actions  f2=Disc  f3=File  f4=Group  f5=Document  f6=Settings  f7=Disc change  f8=Options
Drive A:                     Drive B:         empty    Drive M:
138k used   35k free  10 files  0k used    0k free   0 files  34k used  290k free    5 files

  group 0 138k      group 4    0k                   group 0   34k   group 4    0k
  group 1    0k     group 5    0k                   group 1    0k   group 5    0k
  group 2    0k     group 6    0k                   group 2    0k   group 6    0k
  group 3    0k     group 7    0k                   group 3    0k   group 7    0k

A: group 0   10 files  M: group 0    5 files
   0 limbo files          0 limbo files

 MATRIX  .#SS  11k    MATRIX  .#SS  12k
 MATRIX  .#ST  12k    MATRIX  .#ST  12k
 PHRASES .STD   1k       3 hidden  10k
 SETTINGS.STD   1k
    6 hidden  113k
```

Making an Examples disc

Now hold down the [SHIFT] key and keep this held down as you press the [f1] key. You will see a 'Menu' appear at the top of the screen: this is one of LocoScript's many menus. The option you want from this menu (Copy disc) is already selected for you – so just press the [ENTER] key. What happens next depends on whether you have a single-drive machine or a two-drive system.

Note: Throughout what follows, you will see messages on the screen about the 'Source' disc and the 'Destination' disc. The 'Source disc' is the Master disc you are copying and the 'Destination disc' is the new disc you are making the copy on.

Single-drive system

Before copying starts, LocoScript checks that you meant to select the Copy disc option – because if it just went straight ahead, you might accidentally copy the wrong information onto the wrong disc. Press the [↓] key once to move the highlighting to the 'Copy disc' option offered in this message and then press [ENTER]. LocoScript then tells you it is waiting for the Source disc.

Check that your LocoScript 2 Master disc is write-protected (as described at the top of page 3) and then insert this disc into the disc drive. (On an 8000 series machine, you will need to insert the disc with Side 1 to the left.) Push the disc in gently until it clicks home. Then press [ENTER] again. LocoScript now starts copying the data on the disc into its memory, track by track. The process of copying the disc is carried out in a number of stages, each requiring you first to put in the Source disc and then to replace this disc by the Destination disc. The message on the screen tells you how many stages your copy will take and records the progress of the copy through all the tracks on the disc.

Soon a message will appear telling you LocoScript is waiting for the Destination disc. When this appears, press the Eject button on the disc drive and withdraw the disc: insert the disc you labelled 'Examples disc' in the drive. (On an 8000 series machine, you again want to insert this disc with Side 1 to the left.) Press [ENTER] when you are ready. Again, you will see a message on the screen – this time, counting through the tracks as your PCW writes the copy onto the new disc. When it has written the section of the disc it had in memory, you will see the message prompting you for the Source disc again. Release your new disc from the drive and insert the LocoScript 2 disc again and press [ENTER]. Then when you see the message prompting you for the Destination disc, release the LocoScript 2 disc, insert your Examples disc again and press [ENTER]. And so on until the entire side of the disc has been copied and you see the following message:

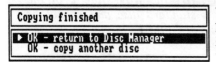

When this message appears, simply press [ENTER] and you are returned to the screen you saw immediately after LocoScript was loaded.

Two-drive system

The first thing that happens is that you see a message on the screen checking that you want to go ahead and copy a disc. On an 8000 series machine, this message also asks you which type of disc you want to copy – 180k or 720k. Press the [↑] key once to highlight the first Copy disc option, and then press [ENTER].

A new message tells you that LocoScript is waiting for you to put the Source disc in Drive B and the Destination disc in Drive A. Check that your LocoScript 2 Master disc is write-protected (as described at the top of page 3) then insert this disc into Drive B: push it in gently until it clicks home. Then insert the disc you labelled 'Examples disc' in Drive A. (On an 8000 series machine, you need to insert both these discs with Side 1 to the left). Press [ENTER] when you are ready. LocoScript then starts copying the data, track by track, from the disc in Drive B first into its memory and then writing this on the disc in Drive A. The message on the screen records its progress through all the tracks on the disc.

When the disc has been copied, you will see the message shown above. When this message appears, press [ENTER]. You are then returned to the screen you saw immediately after LocoScript was loaded.

Extra step for PcW9256 users

The Examples disc made thus far on a PcW9256 has a copy of the Installation program on it. To free the space this program occupies for your own work, you need to erase the file with .EMT as the second part of its name (full name something like INSTE232.EMT), together with any ENGLISH.F file on this disc.

In each case, use the Cursor keys [↑][↓][←][→] to move the highlighting to the name of the file, press [f3] to display the Files menu, press [↑] twice to highlight the Erase file option in this menu, and then press [ENTER] twice.

You have now finished all the preparation you need to do and are ready to start work on the LocoScript 2 Tutorial. But before you do this, put your LocoScript 2 Master disc (and any other Master discs) away somewhere safe. You won't need these discs in your general work but you will need them – undamaged and unaltered – when you want to update your system in any way, for example by adding other programs in the LocoScript family. (By the way, Side 2 of the PCW8256/8512 Master disc is not a standard disc and cannot be copied or used either with LocoScript 2 or CP/M.)

Chapter 2

Converting to LocoScript 2

If you have used the earlier version of LocoScript – LocoScript '1', you should find it very easy to adapt to LocoScript 2 because you will be used to using keystrokes and menus to pick out the actions you require.

However, there are still aspects of LocoScript 2 for you to learn – and not just the extra features LocoScript 2 has. Changes have also been made in other areas, principally to make it easier to use some of the more complex features of the system.

This chapter outlines all the differences between LocoScript '1' and LocoScript 2, picking out the sessions of the Tutorial you should pay particular attention to. It also explains what you need to do so that a document you prepared with LocoScript '1' can be processed using all the features of LocoScript 2.

Of course, all these changes do mean that you need to re-learn certain aspects of LocoScript – in particular, the names of the menus and the names of the menu options you need, and the keys to press to get certain actions. For example, in LocoScript 2, the key to press to tell LocoScript you have changed the disc in the drive is [f7].

Overall changes

LocoScript 2 is essentially LocoScript '1' with:

- Extra features – in particular, the ability to print on printers other than that supplied with your PCW and a much increased range of characters so that LocoScript could support many more languages
- Different menus and menu options

Most of the changes are in the parts of LocoScript that many users found difficult – especially handling different sizes of paper and Layouts, and changing the Document Header. For example, different Layouts now have names so that you can select the one you want by picking out its name. Another change is that the idea of the Document Header has gone and its place has been taken by Document Set-up, which explains very much better what this area of the word processor is all about.

LocoScript 2 also has a system of named 'Paper Types' so that instead of remembering that 11" continuous stationery is 66 lines long and that you like to set a gap of 5 lines at the bottom, you can just pick out the type of paper you have called 11continuous – and LocoScript does the rest from its store of information about the types of paper you like to use.

8809

Moreover, you no longer have to set up the printer as well as the document for the paper you want to use unless you want to print on a particular type of paper. Before it starts printing, LocoScript 2 checks which type of paper the document is set up for and asks you whether you want the printer to be set up for the same type of paper. If you say yes, then LocoScript 2 does all the setting up for you.

Another important change is that you no longer need to remember subtle variations in the way LocoScript menus work. There are now just three types of menu:

- **Commands menus** – which give a list of alternative actions and the one that will be carried out when you press [ENTER] is picked out by an arrow ▶ (or diamond ◆ when LocoScript will return to this menu after carrying out the command). You move the arrow to the option you require by moving the Menu cursor with the cursor keys or by typing the letters written as capitals – just as with LocoScript '1'.

- **Settings menus** – which give you a list of items that can be either 'set' (turned on) or 'cleared' (turned off). The ones that are set are picked out by a tick to the left of the option. To set an option, point to it with the Menu cursor and then press [+] or the Space Bar: to clear an option, point to it with the Menu cursor and then press [−] or the Space Bar – exactly as you did with LocoScript '1'. If what you do affects any other setting, then LocoScript will make all the necessary adjustments for you.

- **Selection menus** – which essentially show you the details that LocoScript is about to work with, in particular the details of the document you have picked out to process. These work in exactly the same way as they did in LocoScript '1'. So to change any of the details, you move the Menu cursor to the relevant line of the menu and then edit the current information as if it were text – with the added facility of clearing away text by pressing [−]

As in LocoScript '1', some menus display details, for example, of a document you have picked out to work on, a choice of settings to make and/or a choice of actions when you press [ENTER]. Such menus have a 'Selection' menu part, a 'Settings' part and a 'Commands' part.

Another overall change is that LocoScript 2 is much more geared to handling long documents than LocoScript '1'. Moving around a long document no longer means scrolling through the whole document on the screen: instead LocoScript jumps 'straight' to the new part of the document. In fact, all movements up and down a document are very much faster.

Some of the changes may catch you a bit by surprise. For example, differences in the character set for LocoScript 2 mean that you can no longer give your documents names that include ` ~ and ^ – but you can include ½, § and ◊. The names of documents (and other files) with these characters are automatically converted.

Many of these changes are for technical reasons, but others we hope you will agree make LocoScript better – for example, the way LocoScript 2 immediately gives you a fresh line to work on if you insert some text at the start of the line.

Major parts of the Tutorial to study

A number of aspects of LocoScript 2 are either totally new or radically different in the way they work from LocoScript '1'. The following gives a brief idea of the changes that have been made but to use these features you must work through the part of the Tutorial that describes them.

Formatting and copying discs (in Session 7)

Making back-up copies and preparing new discs for use can now be done from within LocoScript. This should be simpler to use and less error-prone than using DiscKit because you don't have to stop and load the CP/M operating system and then re-load LocoScript when you have finished.

Layouts (Session 11 and in Session 17)

Layouts still cover essentially the same details of how text should be laid out but they work in a very different way.

In LocoScript '1', all the details about each Layout were held in the Document Header: in LocoScript 2, this information is held in the Layout code itself. All that's stored in the Document Set-up are 'Stock' Layouts which are used as patterns for new Layouts you create. These Stock Layouts have both names and numbers to make it easy for you to pick out the pattern you want.

When you change a Layout, you generally only change the Layout for the piece of text you are actually working on at present – you don't automatically change other parts of your document. There's a special procedure to follow – described in Session 17 – when you do want to make such changes throughout the document.

A particular advantage of the new system is that you can transfer all the details of the Layout with text that you copy or move to a different document.

Using different types of paper (Session 19)

In LocoScript '1', you had to know and remember a lot of details about the paper you wanted to print on – unless all you ever used was A4 paper or 11" continuous and you were prepared to leave alone all the settings LocoScript made for you.

LocoScript 2 makes it much easier for you to use different sizes of paper by introducing the new concept of Paper Types. Each Paper Type holds a complete specification of a particular type of paper – its width, its depth, and whether it is single sheet or continuous, etc. – and it will have a name like A4, A5 or 2" Labels to make it easy to pick out the Paper Type you want. A number of Paper Types are provided for you: you set up any others you want.

LocoScript 2 makes the job even easier for you by automatically setting up the printer for the type of paper you have specified for the document – if you want it to. Whenever you ask it to print a document, it checks the type of paper you have

---

LocoScript 2 User Guide: Introduction 9

specified in the document against the type of paper the printer is currently set up for and displays a message if it finds these to be different. One of the options given in this message is to set up the printer to match the document. All you have to do is to select this option and press [ENTER]: LocoScript 2 does all the rest.

Session 19 is also important because it introduces LocoScript's store of information about the printer and paper you use on your system.

Using alternative printers (Session 20)

When you use LocoScript '1', you can only print your documents on the built-in printer and so you are restricted to the style of characters that this printer gives you. With LocoScript 2, however, you can set up your system to print in different styles on the built-in printer (an alternative Sans Serif style is supplied in the LocoScript 2 master disc). You can also print on an alternative printer. So if you have a 'daisy wheel' printer, for example, you could use that to give you true 'Letter Quality' instead of the 'Near Letter Quality' you get with the built-in 'dot matrix' printer. Session 20 describes how to set up LocoScript so that your documents are printed in your chosen typestyle or on your chosen printer.

You can print documents using LocoScript 2 on a wide range of different printers. The most straightforward to use are '630 compatible' daisy wheel printers and 'Epson compatible' matrix printers – that is, daisy wheel printers which obey the same printing commands and take the same daisy wheels as the Diablo 630 printer and matrix printers which obey the same commands as the Epson FX80 printer. The PCW Printers Guide gives a reasonably comprehensive list of the printers you might use.

Setting Header, Footer and Text Zones (in Session 17)

LocoScript 2 divides up the page in a different way to LocoScript '1'. Instead of dividing the page into three zones, LocoScript 2 divides it into five areas – Top Gap, Header Zone, Text Zone, Footer Zone and Bottom Gap. The Top and Bottom Gaps are the parts of the paper the printer cannot print on and are defined by the type of paper you are using.

This makes working out the depths of the Header and Footer Zones much easier. You now just have to work out how big to make the Zones so that these can accommodate your Header and Footer text. You no longer have to add in the parts of the paper that can't be used.

Another somewhat mind-bending task in LocoScript '1' was to work out the line number on which the Header and the Footer text was to start. You don't have to do this in LocoScript 2: instead the Header and the Footer automatically start at the top of their zones and you put in blank lines in the Header and Footer themselves to adjust the position of the Header and Footer texts. This is explained in Session 16.

Typing accents and special characters (in Appendix III)

The range of characters LocoScript 2 can handle is very much greater than in LocoScript '1', so that you can type text in a much larger range of languages – including those that use Cyrillic characters. There are over 400 different characters and symbols, each of which can be used in combination with 15 different accents. These characters include 16 characters that you can define yourself. (How to define these characters is described in the booklet on 'Designing your own characters.)

All of these characters can be produced on the built-in printer but it's only fair to warn you that you won't necessarily be able to print all of them on any alternative printer you use. The characters that can be printed always depend on the printer you are using.

The way many of these characters are typed on the keyboard is new. LocoScript 2 has a number of 'Super Shifts' – that is, key combinations which change the effect of keys pressed from then on. For example, to type some Russian, you first   select the Cyrillic Super Shift, and then use the keys as if each had a Cyrillic engraving. To return to normal you type another Super Shift.

Appendix III includes a complete listing of all the characters LocoScript 2 can handle, grouped under headings like Currency Symbols, Textual Markers, Accents, Mathematical Symbols. Beside each character are details of which keys you need to press to enter this character in your document.

Other parts of the Tutorial to work through

In addition to these major changes, a number of the word-processing features have been given important extra facilities. Again, we advise working through the relevant part of the Tutorial before you try to put these features to use.

Session 13: Refinements to Find and Exchange

This session tells you how to use the various options which have been added to Find and Exchange to make these features more powerful. These include telling LocoScript 2 to treat capital letters and small letters as the same when it is searching for the text you have given it, to search only for whole words and to set the case of the inserted text to match that of the replaced text. It is also possible to include 'wild cards' in the text being searched for.

Session 14: Extending the usefulness of Blocks and Phrases

Session 14 explains the changes in the way Blocks and Phrases now work.

Blocks are now remembered until changed, or until the PCW is turned off or reset. This means that blocks can easily be used to transfer text between documents, as well as around a document. There's no longer any need (or any facility!) to save a block of text to disc in order to insert the same text in another document.

In addition, LocoScript 2 displays the state of blocks and phrases in a different way. Instead of just getting a list of the names of the blocks and phrases that are in use, LocoScript 2 displays the name and the first few words of each of the blocks and phrases. These lists are brought onto the screen by two new menu options Show Blocks and Show Phrases. The list can also be used to clear the contents of a block.

Another new feature is that you can have several sets of phrases and switch between them.

Session 5: Moving straight to a page

Whereas LocoScript '1' moves very slowly through long documents, LocoScript 2 can move directly to a given page. All you have to do is to select the Find Page menu option, type the desired page number and press [ENTER]. LocoScript 2 will then display the text starting at the selected page.

Session 10: Special spacing between paragraphs

In LocoScript '1', spacing out your paragraphs meant leaving a blank line between them. Of course, you can still do this but LocoScript 2 also allows you to be more subtle – for example, leaving half-line spaces between paragraphs. This is done by specifying a new parameter called the CR Extra Spacing which defines the distance the printer is to move, in addition to the standard line spacing, after lines ending in a carriage return.

Session 18: Giving documents consecutive page numbers

One of the more laborious tasks when you are preparing a book or a long report is ensuring that the various parts you have prepared as separate documents have consecutive page numbers – so much so, that it is often tempting to keep the report as one large document rather than worry about setting individual first page numbers.

With LocoScript 2, however, you can get the program to set all the first page numbers for you – by using the new Set First Pages option. All you have to do is to pick out the documents in the right order: LocoScript 2 then uses a counter to work out what the first page number of each document should be and sets this number in the document. If you use the Page n of m type of page numbers, you can also set the total number of pages recorded for each document.

Session 4: Printing documents

The menu that appears when you print a document has been extended.

One new option allows you to print multiple copies. You can use this feature to give you multiple copies of both the whole document or just of certain pages.

Another change is that you now use this menu to specify whether you want High Quality or Draft Quality output. You don't set this up through one of the Printer menus any more.

Session 19: Fixing the Left Offset for different types of stationery

LocoScript 2 has a new approach to setting the Left Offset – that is, the shift in the printer's start-position so that your text is correctly positioned on the paper you put into the printer.

The Left Offset can still be set through one of the Printer menus, but you can also build the Left Offset you need for your continuous stationery into the specification of its Paper Type. This means that you can set up the Left Offset for your continuous stationery once and for all – provided you keep the tractors (that is, the paper holders on the tractor feed) in the same place, of course!

• The sections of the Tutorial we've picked out here are ones that are essential to read if you are going to use these new features of LocoScript 2. We would also encourage you to read other sections of the Tutorial as well – particularly those that cover features that you perhaps haven't been using to best advantage. We also recommend the Quick Reference section and the Postscript to the Tutorial which includes a series of example documents, illustrating the ways in which the features of LocoScript 2 can be put to use.

Converting a document from LocoScript '1' to LocoScript 2

A document that you have prepared using LocoScript '1' has to be converted before it can be processed by LocoScript 2. This conversion happens automatically the first time you edit the document using LocoScript 2 – so essentially all you have to do is to open it for editing. Conversion takes place as you work down the document – slowing down movements you make, but only for this first time. After you have worked through the document once, all the changes will have been made and movements up and down the document will become very much faster.

The conversion takes the details about the page size and layouts of the LocoScript '1' document and produces equivalent details for the new LocoScript 2 document. It does not change the layout and styling of the document, except where there are more than 30 tabs in a layout – LocoScript 2's maximum. In particular, the existing Layouts are re-specified as LocoScript 2 Stock Layouts, with Layout 0 becoming Stock Layouts 0 and 1; Layout 1 becoming Stock Layout 2; etc. However, if the original layout had more than 15 tabs, the Stock Layout won't have all the tabs. LocoScript 2 Stock Layouts have a maximum of 15 tabs.

Another part of the conversion takes all the details of the page length, Header Zone and Footer Zone and works out the Paper Type for the document. It's impossible to be certain precisely what type of paper you had set up the document for in every case, so the conversion program makes the following assumptions:

- If the page length is 70 lines, the document uses the A4 Paper Type
- If the page length is 66 lines, the document uses the 11continuous Paper Type
- If the page length is anything else, the Paper Type is a special type of continuous stationery which is temporarily given the document's name

It also sets Top and Bottom gaps based simply on the sizes on the Header and Footer zones and the position you set for the Header Text.

In general the conversion will give you the right results – but you could find that the footer, for example, is in a slightly different position. For this reason, LocoScript 2 starts by displaying a message telling you that you have opened a LocoScript 1 format document and suggesting that you check the Paper and Printer details. Press [ENTER] to clear away this message. The Pagination Screen (ie. the screen that shows your Header and Footer text) is then displayed, showing you that you have been put straight into the Document Set-up part of the system.

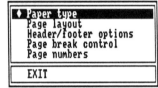

We strongly recommend that you press [f5] to bring the Page menu onto the screen, then select Paper Type and press [ENTER]. This displays a menu of Paper Types, with your 'special' paper type (if any) shown as *document-name?*.

If the paper you use for this document is A4, A5 or 11" continuous, move the Menu cursor to this option, press [+] and then press [ENTER] to select the Use Paper Type option at the bottom of the menu. You are then returned to the Page menu.

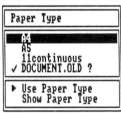

If the type of paper you use isn't one of the standard ones, move the Menu cursor to Show Paper Type and press [ENTER]. A second menu is then displayed:

Set the details in this menu so that they describe your paper and give this type of paper an appropriate name. In particular, ensure that it is correctly shown as single sheet or continuous (point to the correct option and press [+] to set this) and that the Height of the paper is given correctly as the length of the paper in inches times 6. For example, for 2½" labels, you will want the Height to be 15. (A full description of how to set up these details is given in Session 19.) When you have finished, press [ENTER], move the cursor to Use Paper Type and then press [ENTER] again.

8809

You should then use the Page layout option to check and, if need be, adjust the sizes of the Header and Footer zones as described in Session 17.

When you have finished setting the details of the paper and the page layout, press [EXIT] and then press [ENTER] to return to the Pagination Screen.

You can now set any other aspect of the Document Set-up you like. To return to the document itself, press [EXIT] and then [ENTER].

When you save this version of the document, you save a proper LocoScript 2 document. It will not need to be converted again. However, we should point out that you won't be able to edit or print it using LocoScript '1' any more. If you need a 'LocoScript 1' version, recover the old version of the document from Limbo before you go any further.

Using your current templates

Converting to LocoScript 2 doesn't mean that you have to set up the templates you use all over again. Instead, you simply need to convert the templates themselves to LocoScript 2.

To convert a template to LocoScript 2, you use exactly the same technique as you use to convert any LocoScript '1' document to LocoScript 2 – you use LocoScript 2 to edit the template and then save the result as a new LocoScript 2 document. Then you simply need to save the LocoScript 2 version of your template where it will be available when you want to create a new document to this pattern – for example, in one of the groups on your LocoScript 2 Start-of-day disc.

• **Do remember to convert each template you use to LocoScript 2. Otherwise, all the documents you create using the template will initially be LocoScript '1' format and will each have to be converted individually.**

Using saved blocks

Blocks of text that you saved using LocoScript '1' cannot be inserted directly into LocoScript 2 documents.

However, this doesn't mean that you can no longer use this text. All you need to do to make this text available in LocoScript 2 is use LocoScript '1' to insert them into a LocoScript '1' document and then convert this document to LocoScript 2.

You will then be able to insert the converted document into LocoScript 2 documents.

8809

Using LocoScript add-on programs

Add-on programs that you have used with LocoScript '1' must be upgraded to LocoScript 2 versions before they can be used with LocoScript 2.

In the case of LocoSpell and LocoMail (the spelling checker and the mail merge program for LocoScript), this upgrading happens automatically as part of the process of installing LocoScript 2. All you have to do is select the appropriate program(s) from the list offered by the Installation program and insert the original Master disc(s) when the program asks you for these.

In addition, there are (or will be) LocoScript 2 versions of third-party products which have been produced in consultation with Locomotive Software. However, where third-party products have been produced without reference to Locomotive, it is unlikely that these will work with LocoScript 2.

The LocoScript 2 versions of LocoMail and LocoSpell are basically unchanged from the earlier versions, though they do have some extra features. The main thing to note is that the old 'small' dictionary is unfortunately now too big to be used on Drive M on a PCW with just 256k of memory. Upgrading your machine's memory to 512k is recommended as this will allow you to use not just this small dictionary but also LocoSpell's 78,000-word dictionary.

LocoScript Tutorial

The tutorial that follows is divided up into a number of sessions, each one covering a different task. The first 'half' of the Tutorial is made up of sessions on the fundamentals of using your PCW to prepare and print documents, followed by sessions on the various ways in which you can use LocoScript 2 to style your document. The second half of the Tutorial looks at the more advanced word-processing features of LocoScript 2, such as Headers and Footers, using different types of paper and using different printers.

Later sessions of the tutorial will use techniques, etc. that have been introduced in earlier sessions – so we suggest you practise using LocoScript 2 in the way described in each session until you feel confident before going on to the next.

You don't have to work through the whole tutorial straight away – though, obviously, the more you know about how LocoScript 2 works, the better. Just work through as far as you want: then get some experience in using the techniques you have learnt before carrying on and seeing the other things that LocoScript 2 can do. As you work, follow the instructions carefully. If at any stage you are not sure how to carry out a particular instruction, just look it up in the index.

By all means, experiment a little as well. Don't worry about pressing the wrong key: if the key you press isn't right at the moment, all that happens is that your PCW will bleep – to tell you that LocoScript hasn't done anything with your keystroke. But do be careful to finish work on one session's document before starting on the next session – or you may get very confused.

The Tutorial is designed to gradually build up the range of LocoScript tools you know how to use. If you ever feel out of touch with real documents as you work through the tutorial, turn to page 243. Here, in a 'postscript' to the tutorial, we describe some examples of different types of documents – letters, reports, invoices, newsletters, books, etc. – that you could prepare using LocoScript. For each example we have noted the LocoScript features you might use in preparing these documents and what they would do for you.

LocoScript, like all other computer programs, doesn't understand English – it needs instructions that it understands. These have to be learnt but, in LocoScript, these instructions are almost all available through pull-down menus and so, much of the time, all that you need to do is select the menu option you want. The tutorial introduces all the options and explains what these can do for you.

In fact, many of the menus are just there to help you while you are learning how to use LocoScript. As you gain experience, pulling down menus can become tiresome – so LocoScript has lots of shortcuts as well, which we introduce alongside the menu options.

OK, learning how to use LocoScript takes some effort on your part but just remember all those advantages:

– invisible revisions and corrections

– perfect copies every time

– complicated layouts achieved with ease

– professional results

– different versions of the same document with little effort

...

First, though, a few pieces of essential information:

– the conventions used in this user guide

– how to load LocoScript 2

– how to configure your system to let you work with larger screen characters and/or "Sticky" Shift keys

– how to get back to the central point of all operations – the Disc Manager Screen

– how to abandon an action you've started

• If anything happens while you are working through the tutorial that isn't explained in the text, turn to Appendix V at the back of this guide. This is the troubleshooting section, which will tell you what has happened and what action to take.

Important: For this tutorial, you will need to have the PCW printer connected to your PCW **before** you switch on and load LocoScript. For details, see page 2.

Note: This tutorial assumes that you know the 'basics' of using your PCW – for example, how to handle discs and that you put a disc into a disc drive when you want to use the information and programs stored on it. Full details are given in your PCW user guide, but there is also a brief summary in Appendix I.

Conventions

The conventions used in this user guide are as follows:

• Messages on the screen and options in the menus are written in a special style of text. For example, the 'Copy disc' option is shown as Copy disc.

• Keys that you need to press are shown symbolically. As far as possible, the keys shown match the keys on the keyboard. For example, the key marked ENTER is shown as [ENTER].

• An italic (slanting) *n* is used to represent a number (one or more digits): the actual number depends on the document, etc. you are handling.

Loading LocoScript 2

Before you can use LocoScript 2 to prepare a document, you have to load the LocoScript 2 program into your machine and start it running. The steps are as follows, starting with your machine switched off.

1 Check there are no discs in the drives, then switch your machine on.

2 If your machine has two drives and the Installation procedure gave you a 'Drive B Start-up disc', insert this disc in Drive B.

3 Insert your Drive A Start-of-day disc in Drive A. If you have more than one Drive A Start-up disc, insert the first of these discs. (If you have an 8000 series machine, you will need to insert this disc with Side 1 to the left.)

The initial software is then read from this disc. You should see the familiar pattern of horizontal lines. If nothing happens, press the space bar: this prompts the PCW to start reading the disc.

4 If the message `Insert next disc` appears, remove the disc from Drive A, replace it by the next Start-up disc in the sequence and press ⌈ENTER⌉. Further files are then read from this disc.

Repeat this each time the message appears.

5 When loading is complete, the screen will change to something like this:

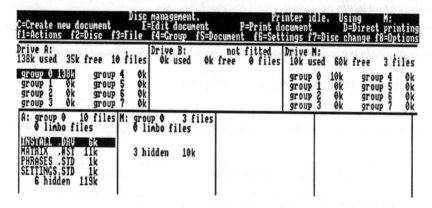

The appearance of this special screen – called the Disc Manager Screen – signals that the LocoScript 2 program has now been loaded and is ready to start work on letters and documents. If you see a very different display or the screen flashes or your PCW bleeps, you have not put a LocoScript Start-of-day disc in the drive – but

---

wait until your PCW has finished reading from the disc (ie. until the light on the disc drive stops flashing) before removing the disc and trying again with a different disc.

One thing remains to do. You must now release any discs currently in the drive(s) and withdraw them from the computer.

With LocoScript 2, you have a Start-of-day disc (plus one or perhaps two supporting Start-up discs) that you use to load the LocoScript 2 program into your computer's memory, and any number of Data discs that you store your documents on. Once the program has been loaded, the Start-of-day disc and the Start-up discs have done their job: they won't be needed again until you start using LocoScript 2 again. Indeed, this is precisely why they are called Start-of-day and Start-up discs.

All the rest of your work is with Data discs, which you use once LocoScript has been loaded into memory. You could use your Start-of-day and Start-up discs as a Data discs as well but this isn't advised. It is a lot easier to keep these purely as the discs you put in when you need to load the LocoScript 2 program.

Leave the Data disc that holds the document you are using in the drive all the time you are working on this document. Do not remove it.

• *If your machine is already on, you don't have to switch it off and switch it on again before you can load LocoScript 2. Instead, put your Start-of-day disc in Drive A and then use the special three-key combination* [SHIFT] [EXTRA] *and* [EXIT] *to 'reset' your machine. (Hold down the* [SHIFT] *and* [EXTRA] *keys and press the* [EXIT] *key without releasing the other two keys.) This is equivalent to switching off and switching on again but is better for your machine.*

Note: Resetting completely clears your computer's memory – so remember to check that everything important has been saved on disc before you reset your machine. This applies in particular to documents you have stored on the Memory disc (Drive M).

Special configuration options

LocoScript includes three special options that you might like to take advantage of:

• **Magnified text display** – in which documents are displayed in double-height, double-width characters as you edit them.

• **'Sticky' Shift keys** – which allows key combinations involving two or more keys to be typed by pressing the keys in sequence rather than together.

• **Disallow key repeats** – which can be used to stop the PCW from automatically repeating keys that are held down for any length of time.

To select Magnified text display, load LocoScript and display the Disc Manager Screen. Press [f8] to display the Options menu, use [↓] to move the Menu cursor (the band of highlighting) to the Large edit characters option, and press the [⊞] key (to the left of the Space bar). This puts a tick beside the option. Then press [ENTER] to leave the menu and return to the Disc Manager Screen.

Note: The magnification only affects text that is being edited. Messages on the screen, menu options, document names etc. remain their normal size. The text is also printed at its normal size.

To select Sticky Shift keys, simply hold down the [SHIFT] key as you load LocoScript from your Start-of-day disc. A * should appear in the top righthand corner of the screen to show that the 'Sticky Shift keys' option has been selected. Alternatively, you can press [f8] to display the Options menu, use [↓] to move the Menu cursor (the band of highlighting) to the 'Sticky' shift keys option, and press the [⊞] key (to the left of the Space bar). This puts a tick beside the option. Then press [ENTER] to leave the menu and return to the Disc Manager Screen.

As you type a key combination, you should see a * followed by letters representing the Shift keys you have press (S for [SHIFT], A for [ALT] etc.) in the top righthand corner of the screen – unless this part of the screen is already showing some other message such as Num or Gre.

To select the 'No repeat' option, press [f8] to display the Options menu, use [↓] to move the Menu cursor to Disallow key repeats and press the [⊞] key to tick this option. Then press [ENTER] to leave the menu and return to the Disc Manager Screen.

Returning to the Disc Manager Screen

The central point for all operations is the Disc Manager Screen, which shows you which documents and files you currently have available. It might, for example, look like this:

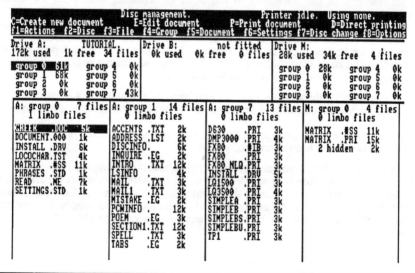

The Disc Manager Screen is automatically displayed immediately after you have loaded LocoScript 2.

As a general rule, you need to return to the Disc Manager Screen between, say, editing one document and editing a different document or printing the same document.

Wherever you are in LocoScript, what you do to get back to the Disc Manager Screen is finish whatever you are doing at the moment (for instance if you have a menu displayed on the screen, close this up by pressing [CAN]) and then press [EXIT]. This signals to LocoScript 2 that you want to leave the job you're currently doing. LocoScript puts up an Exit menu from which you select an option and then it returns you to whatever task you were doing before. If this doesn't return you to the Disc Manager Screen, then press [EXIT] again.

Abandoning an action

Mistakes are always possible. The ways out of trouble are as follows:

• If you call up a menu you don't want (or you have got to a stage in the process at which there is a menu on the screen that you want to get out of), press [CAN]. This closes up the menu. However, don't press [CAN] when there is an error message on the screen: **always** select one of the options listed in the error message.

• If LocoScript has started an operation you don't want – for example, moving you from one end of the document to the other or replacing one word for another throughout your document – the general procedure is to press [STOP], wait for LocoScript to pause and then press [STOP] again. The first [STOP] makes LocoScript pause; the second abandons the action. If however you want LocoScript to stop printing, the key to press is [PTR]. Pressing [PTR] halts printing and puts you into LocoScript's Printer Control State from where you can sort out paper jams, abandon printing etc. etc. (Details are given in Session 4.)

• If you want to abandon the changes you have been making to a document, press [EXIT] to finish work on the document and then select the Abandon edit option in the Exit menu. The new version is then thrown away: it doesn't replace the previous version stored on disc. LocoScript doesn't touch the version stored on disc until after the new version has been successfully stored.

In fact, all is not lost if you change your mind about discarding the old version after saving the new version – or accidentally select the wrong option in the Exit menu. LocoScript doesn't actually erase discarded documents from the disc until it needs the space to store a new document: instead it puts them into a special 'Limbo' state. This gives you the chance to recover any documents you discard accidentally (see Session 7).

Session 1

Fundamentals

The complete newcomer to computing often finds doing anything with a computer a bit of a daunting prospect. Lots of things about the computer are strange. Then to cap it all, people 'in the know' insist on talking in their own incomprehensible jargon.

This session is for people who don't feel at all at home with a computer. If you are thoroughly familiar with the ins and outs of storing files on disc, you can proceed straight to Session 2 – though we recommend you to glance through this session to see what is covered here.

The components of your PCW

Your PCW has three obvious components – a Monitor Unit (with the screen and disc drives), a Keyboard and a Printer – but the way to think about it is as a processor, which actually does all the computing, to which are attached a number of electronic 'Devices' whose job is either to supply the processor with information and instructions, or to receive information from the processor, or in some cases, both.

In the case of your PCW, the processor is housed in the Monitor Unit and the devices are a Keyboard, a Screen, a Printer and Disc Drives. Your PCW also has a connector on the back which can be used to attach further devices. For example, we will be describing later how you can use this connector to attach another printer to your PCW.

The Keyboard

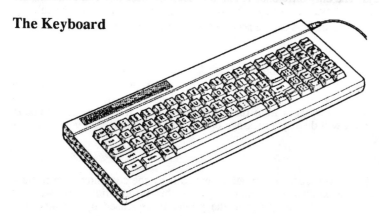

8809

The Keyboard's role is purely to take information and instructions from you and pass these on to the processor. When you want to give your PCW an instruction or some information, then you type this on the keyboard.

If you look at your keyboard, you will see that you have a number of keys with letters, numbers and other characters on them – rather like the keys you have on a typewriter. These are known as the Character Keys.

But, in addition to these, you have a number of keys with strange legends like f1, Paste, EOL, Enter, and DEL→. These are keys that are used to give specific instructions to the computer – though, just to complicate matters, the instruction that is given often depends on which task your computer is doing at the moment. We will be seeing in this tutorial what instructions these keys send the processor while you are using LocoScript 2.

As well as pressing the keys on their own, you may also need to press them in combination with the keys marked Shift, Extra and Alt. These keys don't do anything when pressed on their own: what they do is modify the effect other keys have when they are pressed at the same time as one or more of these special keys.

The Shift key has very much the same effect as the Shift key on a typewriter. In other words, when you hold down the Shift key and press a letter key, you get a capital letter. When you hold down the Shift key and press a key with two legends on it, you get the character or action corresponding to the upper legend: without the Shift key, you get the lower character or action. (Pressing the Shift Lock key gives you the effect of holding down the Shift key with every Character Key you press – until you press the Shift Lock key again or the Shift key.)

The Extra and Alt keys work in a similar way to the Shift key. You either get a special character or a special action depending on the key you press in combination with these keys. The only difference is that the result of these key combinations are not engraved on the keys – instead you have to look up the details in the manual.

Further effects and characters can be accessed by holding down both Shift and Alt.

The Screen

The Screen's job is to display information.

What's shown on the screen is organised by the processor. As a rule, you will usually see everything you type – basically, just so that you can see what you are doing. You also see messages from the computer to you. Whenever the computer spots a problem, it will display a message on the screen – telling you what it thinks has happened.

The Printer

The Printer's job is to transfer information sent to it by the computer onto paper – giving you what is known as a 'Hard copy' of this information. The way the information is laid out on the paper in the printer is organised by the processor before it is sent to the printer.

A word processor like LocoScript 2 makes extensive use of printers, because the whole point of word processing is to produce 'Hard copies' of documents which you can give to other people to read!

The Disc Drives

The Disc Drives' job is to help you store and retrieve information – rather like you store and retrieve information when you use a tape recorder.

The discs you put into these drives have storage areas on them in which information can be stored in an electronic form. The data stored on disc is 'permanent' in the sense that it will still be there when you use the disc again – however long after you first stored the data. However, it can also be 'erased' when you have finished with it or it can be replaced by new information.

When you want to keep some information, then you get the computer to 'save' this on one of these discs. Later, when you want the computer to use this information, you put the disc back in the drive and get the computer to 'read' the information from the disc into its memory – by taking a copy of the information stored on the disc.

Disc Drives work much faster than tape recorders. It is also very much easier to find the individual recordings on a disc than it is on tape.

How the computer processes information

The computer processes the pieces of information you give it by following a series of instructions known as the computer program. The program organises every aspect of the job you want to do. The facilities you can use at any time depend on the computer program you are using. When you use LocoScript 2, you are using the facilities provided by the computer program known as LocoScript 2.

To use any computer program, you have to put a copy of the program into the computer's memory – this is called 'loading' the program. Then you have to start the program working – or 'running'. What you do to load a program and run it varies from computer system to computer system and from program to program. LocoScript 2 is loaded and run as part of the process of switching on the computer.

Once the program is running, what happens to information and instructions that you type at the keyboard is firmly in the control of the program. Some programs ignore what you type completely. LocoScript 2, however, spends essentially all its time taking information and instructions that you type in, processing these and then displaying the result on the screen. And it does this so fast that it seems to you that you are actually typing in and altering text on the screen – whereas, in fact, you are adding to and changing information held in an area of the computer's memory.

When you are not used to using a computer, you may well be worried about typing 'the wrong thing' in case you damage the program or damage the computer. Such fears are groundless. For a start, you always work with a **copy** of the program – so the

---

only way you could destroy the program itself is by erasing it from your program disc – and most programs are quite strongly protected against that.

The worst you can do by typing 'the wrong thing' is lose the document you are currently working on or, in some very rare cases, you can make the program stop running. You can always tell if you have stopped LocoScript because it won't react to any of the keys. If LocoScript does stop, all you need to do is to reload LocoScript again – either by resetting your PCW (see page 20) or by switching off, waiting a few moments and then switching back on again. If you lose a document, then this can sometimes be recovered, as you will see later – but sometimes it will be gone for good. Losing important documents in this way can be very frustrating, which is why we show you how to make 'Back-up' copies of your discs and encourage you to save your work frequently.

About disc drives

Another thing to understand about is the different types of disc drive you can have and how they are used.

The disc drive(s) behind the slots on the PCW Monitor are called Floppy disc drives – and the discs you put in these are called Floppy discs. (Despite appearances, these discs are indeed floppy. They just don't seem floppy – thanks to their rigid outer casing!)

Floppy discs are used one at a time in a Floppy disc drive. The computer 'locks on' to each disc as it is used and so, while you can readily use different discs in a drive, you need to tell the program you are using that you have done this. You also need to be very careful about when you change over from using one disc to using another: you must never remove a disc that LocoScript is currently working on – for example, because you are editing or printing one of the documents on this disc. LocoScript tells you which discs you can't touch at the moment by always showing Using, followed by the names of the drives that contain discs currently in use (or 'none'), in the top righthand corner of the display.

Because you are able to put a sequence of different discs in a Floppy disc drive, LocoScript (and other programs) always refers to information as being on the drive – when it means that the information is on the disc that is currently in this particular drive – and it gives the drive a name to identify it by. If you have just the one Floppy disc drive, this is called Drive A; if you have two Floppy disc drives, one is called Drive A and the other is called Drive B.

If you have an 8000 series PCW with two floppy disc drives, there is an important difference to remember between Drive A and Drive B: Drive A is a 'normal-capacity' disc drive but Drive B is a 'high-capacity' disc drive. Another important difference is that Drive A only reads from one side of the disc at a time (the side nearest the screen) and so you need to turn the disc over to read from the second side: Drive B reads from both sides of the disc and so the disc is only ever inserted with Side 1 to the left.

Discs you use in these drives are both CF2 discs – but they will have been set up either as 'normal-capacity' discs or as 'high-capacity' discs. As a general rule, 'normal-capacity' discs can only be used in Drive A and 'high-capacity' discs can only be used in Drive B – so they are often referred to as 'Discs for Drive A' and 'Discs for Drive B'.

Floppy discs are not the only type of disc you have – because in fact you also use part of the computer's memory as a special type of disc, known as the Memory disc. This 'disc' is used by LocoScript 2 to store certain files that it needs to have access to. However, it can also be used as a temporary storage place for documents – temporary because it is wiped clean when your PCW is switched off or there is a power cut or you reload LocoScript by 'resetting' your machine (see page 20).

The Memory disc operates in exactly the same way as your Floppy discs (except much faster), so LocoScript 2 gives the Memory disc a Drive name too – Drive M. Of course you can't take the disc in and out of Drive M the same way you can take discs out of Drives A and B.

(There's another type of disc that you can add to your PCW and that's a Hard Disc. This is essentially an extra piece of electronics to add to your computer, complete with storage for very great amounts of information – typically 50 times as much as you can store on one floppy disc. If you do fit such a disc, then LocoScript will call it Drive C – and again you won't be able to take the disc in and out of the drive. However, this disc doesn't get wiped clean when you switch off.)

Word processing with LocoScript 2

LocoScript 2 is a special kind of computer program called a word processor. This means that it has the specific job of processing text – helping you to make whatever changes you want to the text you type and to embed special codes in your text that specify how it should be laid out and styled when you come to print it.

Computers are good at manipulating the information in their memory – and LocoScript 2 lets you take full advantage of this by helping you:
- delete text that is no longer wanted
- re-order your text
- change the codes
- embed new codes and new text in the existing text

etc. etc. In fact, you can change and change again interminably.

As it does this, you naturally want to see the current state of your text. So LocoScript 2 further processes the text and the codes so that you see an 'image' of the document on the screen.

Because you will want to make changes in any part of the text, you need a way of pointing at the place in the document where you want to make your change. Pointing with your finger at the screen is no good because the computer can't 'see' you do this.

What you need is something that you can point with by pressing keys on the keyboard.

The pointer LocoScript 2 gives you is an oblong shape on the screen called a cursor. This cursor can be moved by pressing four special keys on the keyboard called the Cursor Keys – ⊡, ⊡, ⊡ and ⊡. The position of the cursor always shows where you are working – ie. the place in the document that any text you type will be inserted or where the next instruction you give will start to have an effect.

LocoScript 2 also organises the display on the screen so that as well as seeing the text you are preparing, you also see lots of other information about what you are doing and the facilities that are available to you. In particular, LocoScript 2 shows you the names of keys to press that bring menus of other options on the screen from which you can pick out the action you want – by moving another pointer, again with the Cursor keys.

When you are happy with your text, you tell LocoScript 2 to print it. Then, LocoScript sends a copy of the sequence of characters and codes that it has been carefully preparing to your printer – which faithfully carries out the instructions and produces a perfect 'clean' copy.

Storing documents

The PCW only keeps the information about one document in its memory at a time. What is more, the PCW's memory is automatically wiped clean every time you switch it off – or when there's a power cut.

To stop all your hard work being lost, you can save an 'electronic' copy of the document on one of your computer discs – and you can do this any time you like. You don't have to have completed the document before you can save it. Later, you can 'read' back into memory a copy of the document as stored on disc – and then carry on working on it as if you had never stopped.

After carrying out further changes, you can store a copy of the new version on the disc. This effectively replaces the old version – but it doesn't actually write on top of it. In fact, the new version is written first and the old version is erased only after this has been completed.

Each document is stored on disc as a unit known as a 'file' and typically you will have lots of files on each disc. The maximum amount that you can store on a disc depends on the type of disc. A 'normal-capacity' ('Drive A') disc on one of the 8000 series machines lets you store about 90 pages of text in up to 64 different files, but there's room for four times that amount of text – in up to 256 different files – on either a 'high-capacity' ('Drive B') disc or on any of the discs used with a PcW9256.

(The amount of storage space on a disc is always given as a number of k where k stands for kilobyte and 1 kilobyte is 1024 bytes. Each byte can hold one character – so each kilobyte holds about 1000 characters. 'Normal-capacity' discs have a storage space of 180k; 'High-capacity' discs and PcW9256 discs give you 720k.)

So that you can pick out the one you want to use, each file is given a name and details of the file's name and where it is on the disc are held in the disc's 'Directory'.

Even where you can only have up to 64 files, you could still have a lot of searching to do to find the file you wanted – particularly if you have a number of discs in use.

To make it easier to find the document you want, LocoScript 2 gets you to allocate each document to one of its eight groups – each of which LocoScript 2 displays separately, listing the documents in the group in alphabetical order. If you are organised about which disc you use and which group you use for each document, you will find it very easy indeed to find the documents you want – especially as you can choose names for the document, the group and the disc that are descriptive of the sort of information you are storing in them.

Backups

Having one copy of each document you prepare on a disc is fine – provided nothing happens to the disc. However, there are lots of disasters that just might happen to the disc:

- – it could get scratched
- – it could have coffee spilled on it
- – it could accidentally be left too close to the magnet in your TV
  etc., etc.

and then all your hard work would be lost.

The way to guard against such disasters is to make what are known as 'Backups'. These are copies of 'working' discs that have valuable information on them – and that means anything that you don't want to lose or to have to type in again.

A Backup is typically just a separate disc on which you make a straightforward copy of all the information on the original disc – and which you then store somewhere safe. OK, this means buying extra discs – but, as many people have learnt from painful experience, new discs are a lot cheaper than re-typing all the documents etc. you've lost through a problem with a disc!

Session summary

That's basically all that is important to know about computers – and certainly all you need to know to appreciate what LocoScript 2 is doing for you.

Along the way, we deliberately introduced a number of jargon words – partly because there is no need for these to be incomprehensible but partly because, as you will discover, they give you a very powerful way of describing what you are doing. Any moment now, you too will be blinding others with jargon!

9108

Session 2

Running off a letter

In this first practical session of the tutorial, we shall go through all the stages of preparing and printing a very simple letter using LocoScript 2. The idea is to give you an overview of how to use LocoScript to produce a document and to get you accustomed to the way LocoScript works.

If you have used LocoScript before, you can skip this session of the tutorial altogether.

Preparation

Before you can start, you have to load the LocoScript 2 program into your machine and start it running. So, if you haven't already done so, work through the loading procedure described in the introduction to this tutorial (page 19), finishing when you have removed your Start-of-day disc from the drive.

Note: For this tutorial, you will need to have the PCW printer connected to your PCW **before** you switch on and load LocoScript. For details, see page 2.

Getting started

The first step is to put a Data disc in Drive A (the upper disc drive if your machine has two) and press ⌐f7⌐. A Data disc, you will remember, is a disc on which you store your documents.

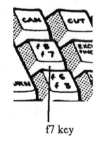

f7 key

The Data disc we are going to use here is the Examples disc that you prepared in the preparatory session (pages 4–5).

Insert the Examples disc into Drive A. (On an 8000 series machine, you will need to insert this disc with Side 1 to the left.) When the disc has clicked home, press ⌐f7⌐. *You press* ⌐f7⌐ *each time you either change the disc in a drive or turn it over – to tell LocoScript 2 that you have done this.*

The first screen

What you have on the screen at the moment is LocoScript's Disc Manager Screen. This shows you what files and documents you have available and where they are to be found.

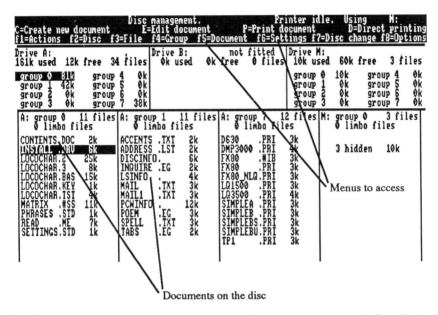

Documents on the disc

The Disc Manager Screen is the central point for all your work with LocoScript. You begin work on each of your documents from here and you are automatically returned here when you finish.

Notice the three 'Information lines' at the top of the screen. *All the different screens that LocoScript displays have three Information lines at the top, giving you details of the job you are doing at present and outlining the actions and menus that are currently available.*

Starting a new letter

Press the 'C' letter key. This tells LocoScript to create a new document, ie. give you the equivalent of a blank sheet of paper.

LocoScript's immediate reaction is to put up a short 'Selection' menu, suggesting where to store the new document and what name to give it. You can change any or all of the details in the menu, as we shall describe later, but at this stage, just press [ENTER] to accept all the details LocoScript suggests. [ENTER] *is always the key to press to tell LocoScript to go ahead with the current information.*

The new document

The screen now changes completely to this:

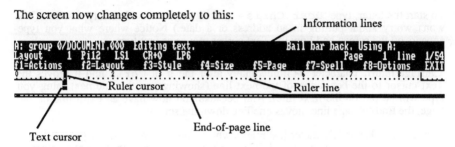

Information lines

Ruler cursor

Ruler line

Text cursor

End-of-page line

There are a number of features of this screen to pick out.

- Three Information lines at the top of the screen – exactly as there were three Information lines at the top of the Disc Manager Screen we displayed earlier.
- A 'Ruler' line immediately below the information lines: This line is very like the paper bail on a typewriter; it lets you know where your margins and tabs are.

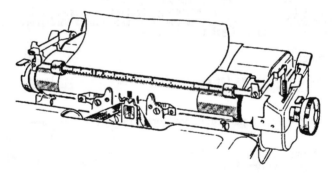

- The special line – part broken, part solid: This is the End-of-page line and it always appears immediately below the last line of text to appear on a page. At the moment, there isn't any text on the page – so the End-of-page line is right up the top of the screen. You will see it move down as you type.

The rest of your screen is your (electronic) piece of paper. Positioned on this electronic piece of paper is an oblong shape – the 'Text cursor'. This is used to mark where in the text you are working – in particular, where anything you type will appear on the screen.

Typing

To start the letter, type `Dear Chris` – exactly as you would on a typewriter. (We won't worry about putting in an address or a date.) Notice where what you type appears on the screen and how the Text cursor moves as you type.

Now press [RETURN]. Pressing the [RETURN] key does two things: it puts the special 'Carriage return' character ↵ immediately after the s of `Chris` and it moves the Text cursor to the beginning of the next line (showing you that the next thing you type will be put on the next line). And because you now have an extra line on the page, the End-of-page line moves one line down the screen.

The Carriage Return character just marks where you have pressed the [RETURN] key to start a new line: it is never printed. You don't have to work with these characters on the screen (we show you later how to stop them being displayed) but most people find them helpful.

Now press [RETURN] again – to move the Text cursor to the beginning of the next line. This gives you a blank line under `Dear Chris`.

The next thing to prepare is the first paragraph of the letter. The text we shall use is:

```
Many, many, many thanks for recommending AMSTRAD's PCW and Locomotive
Software's LocoScript 2. I'm absolutely thrilled to bits. Here I am, a
positive duffer with computers as you know, producing a word-processed
letter the same day as I got the program.↵
```

Start by typing:

```
Many, many, many thanks for recommending AMSTRAD's PCW and Locomotive
```

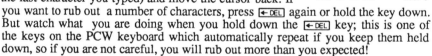

Type just these words: in particular, don't press [RETURN]. If you make any mistakes in typing this, press the [←DEL] key.

This will rub out the character before the Text cursor (ie. the last character you typed) and move the cursor back. If you want to rub out a number of characters, press [←DEL] again or hold the key down. But watch what you are doing when you hold down the [←DEL] key; this is one of the keys on the PCW keyboard which automatically repeat if you keep them held down, so if you are not careful, you will rub out more than you expected!

When you have typed this, look at the screen. This shows you that you are now nearing the righthand margin of your page.

Now watch carefully what happens as you type `Software` letter by letter – in particular, what happens as you type the letter a

8809

The screen flashed and `Softwa` moved onto the next line because LocoScript worked out that the word was too long to fit on the first line. When you use a typewriter, you have to work out where to start each new line but with LocoScript, you don't have to do this – LocoScript does the calculations for you. The only time you have to press the [RETURN] key is when you specifically want to start a new line.

This feature of LocoScript is called Word Wrap, and it is one of the many ways in which a word processor is very much better than a typewriter. You never have to worry about whether the word you are typing is going to fit. All you have to do is just type the words. Carry on typing the rest of the paragraph and you will see Word Wrap work again for you when you get to the words `positive` and `letter`.

Where LocoScript shows one line stopping and another beginning is precisely where the lines will break when your document is printed out. Similarly, LocoScript automatically moves onto a fresh page (with its own End-of-page line) at precisely the point at which the text will move onto the next page when you print your document out.

Correcting your mistakes

The second paragraph of the letter is a special piece of text we have set up for you. Add this to your letter by pressing the [PASTE] key and then typing the letter Z. (We explain this particular piece of LocoScript magic in Session 14.) Your letter should look like this:

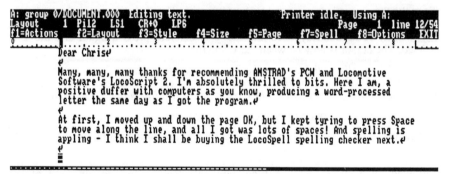

This paragraph contains a number of deliberate mistakes which need to be corrected. To do this, we have to move the Text cursor to each mistake in turn and then make the necessary correction.

You move the cursor by pressing the ⬅, ➡, ⬆ and ⬇ – the four 'Cursor' keys.

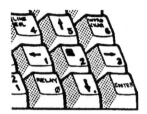

(LocoScript has a number of cursors that it uses at different times to pick out items on the screen. The Cursor keys are always the ones to use to move the current cursor.)

If you are used to working on a typewriter, then you will have to 'unlearn' the techniques you know for moving around a document – in particular, you can't use the Space Bar to move along a line of text, because pressing this inserts 'space' characters.

The first mistake is tyring, so start by moving the Text cursor to the y of this spelling mistake. Press the ⬆ key until the cursor is over the A of At (Don't worry if you overshoot; just press ⬇ to get back to the right place.) Then press the ➡ key until the cursor is over the y. (This time, press ⬅ to get back again if you overshoot.)

The Text cursor now appears to be on the y but actually it is just before this letter. The Text cursor is really a very thin line, after one character and before the next: the oblong shape is only used to make the cursor visible. The real position of the cursor is marked by the lefthand edge of the oblong. It is important to remember this – as you will see.

To make the correction, you need to delete the yr. These characters are immediately after the Text cursor – so the key to press is the DEL→ key. (This is just next to the ←DEL key.) Press this key once and the y is deleted: press it again and the r is deleted. The cursor is now between the t and the i.

(You could equally well have put the Text cursor after the yr. Then the characters you want to delete would be immediately before the cursor and so to delete them you would press the ←DEL key twice. The cursor would still finish in the same place.)

Now type ry, and there on the screen is the word trying.

The second mistake is spelling on the second line of the paragraph. This should have been my spelling. Once again, use the four Cursor keys to position the Text cursor – this time over the first letter of spelling and then type my, followed by a space. As you type, you will see the text to the right of the cursor moving right. Suddenly, as the end of the line reaches the right margin, the line splits into two halves. Rather than push the end of the line out of sight off the righthand side of the screen, LocoScript opens up a space and moves the end of the line onto the next line.

Many, many, many thanks for recommending AMSTRAD's PCW and Locomotive Software's LocoScript 2. I'm absolutely thrilled to bits. Here I am, a positive duffer with computers as you know, producing a word-processed letter the same day as I got the program.↵
↵
At first, I moved up and down the page OK, but I kept trying to press Space to move along the line, and all I got was lots of spaces! And my ▊
                                              spelling is
appling - I think I shall be buying the LocoSpell spelling checker next.↵

OK, the paragraph doesn't look very tidy at present but that is easily remedied – just press the [RELAY] key when you have finished typing. This lays out afresh the paragraph you are working on, taking away the broken lines.

The other mistake is appling, instead of appalling. To correct this, move the cursor to the l of appling and then type al. Again, the line you are working on becomes too long and LocoScript opens up a space, but this time don't tidy it up – because we are going to see LocoScript do this for you.

Relay key

Assuming that the first paragraph is correctly spelt, all that's left to do is add Thanks again and your name at the bottom. (We won't worry about adding an address at the top, because that will only delay us before we can print out the finished letter.)

Moving the Text cursor down to the bottom of the page is one of LocoScript's built-in actions. This one is known as Page and it is the lower option on the key marked DOC/PAGE. So just press this key.

The Text cursor moves right to the end of your current text. But, more interestingly, look what has happened to the second paragraph that you left a little ragged – LocoScript 2 has tidied it up for you. *By pressing* [PAGE], *you have changed where you are working to the bottom of the page and LocoScript 2 always makes sure that everything is properly laid out up to the point you are working.*

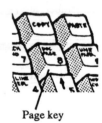

Now type:

Page key

[RETURN]

Thanks again [RETURN]

[RETURN]

[RETURN]

[RETURN]

Fred [RETURN]

8809

After the corrections have been made

Finally, check the whole letter over for mistakes. This is unfortunately something that LocoScript can't automatically do for you. (However, if you find checking documents for typing mistakes tedious, then make a note to find out about LocoSpell – the spelling checker that works with LocoScript.)

When you are sure you're happy with it, press the [EXIT] key. *(Throughout LocoScript, you press the [EXIT] key whenever you want to finish what you are currently doing and go back to the previous task.)*

LocoScript responds with a menu of 'Commands' – Finish edit, Save and Continue, Save and Print, and Abandon edit – with Finish edit highlighted.

We will look at what all these options are in Session 3. For now, we will just take the Save and Print option. This is LocoScript's shortcut to making a printed copy of the letter we have prepared. (Printing is really a separate task from preparing a document. We look at printing properly in Session 4.)

LocoScript always pre-selects one of the options in any menu that gives you a choice of commands. The option that is selected is picked out by the arrow. To select a different action you need to move the arrow to the option you want. You do this by moving the band of highlighting – the Menu cursor – to this option. The arrow automatically moves as you move the cursor. *(This is how you pick out the action you want in any 'Commands' menu in LocoScript 2.)*

In this case, you want to move to the Save and Print option. The Menu cursor, just like the Text cursor, is moved by pressing the Cursor keys – which, you will remember, are ⬅, ➡, ⬆ and ⬇. So the way to move the Menu cursor down to Save and Print is to press ⬇ twice.

(We will see later a shortcut for moving straight to the option you want, but you can always move any cursor in LocoScript by pressing the Cursor keys.)

Note: If the Save and Print option isn't included in the menu, you haven't got a printer connected to your PCW or the printer is not connected properly or it is busy printing something else. In this case, select Finish edit instead: then when you return to the Disc Manager Screen, press the [PTR] key and see whether this says you have 'No printer' (ie. the printer is not connected properly) or Printer: Active (ie. it is busy printing something else – the READ.ME document, perhaps – and probably waiting for another sheet of paper.) Turn to the Troubleshooting section (page 298) for further advice.

Now press [ENTER] – just as you did earlier to tell LocoScript to go ahead and create the new document outlined in the Selection menu. That time, pressing [ENTER] told LocoScript to go ahead with the current information. This time, the instruction is to carry out the action picked out by the arrow.

LocoScript now closes up the screen you have been working on and returns you to the Disc Manager Screen. The light on your disc drive flashes on and off a few times, as LocoScript saves your document – the first part of the combined task.

Next, you will see another menu on the screen – rather like the Selection menu you saw when you were creating the document at the beginning of this session, but with different options. Ignore these options for now: just press [ENTER]. The following message will then appear:

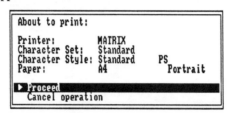

This message is just a reminder that LocoScript is expecting you to use A4 paper – rather than any other size of paper. It only appears the first time you print a document after loading LocoScript 2. Press [ENTER] to tell LocoScript to proceed.

The letter cannot start to print until you have paper (and a ribbon) in your printer. Load a sheet of A4 paper as described in your PCW manual and in Appendix I. When you press [EXIT] at the end of this process, your letter will start to print. When it is finished, you can just lift it out.

If you look at the Disc Manager Screen, you will see that there is now the entry DOCUMENT.000 in one of the columns in the lower part of the screen. This is the copy of your letter that LocoScript made on disc when it saved your work. You can produce new versions of the letter and/or reprint it by working with this copy – as we shall see in later sessions of this tutorial.

Session summary

In this session you have worked through all the stages of preparing and printing a very simple document. By the end of the session, you had a really quite professional-looking product – certainly better than you could produce on a standard typewriter.

But you haven't used any of LocoScript's facilities for presenting text really well and when you look at the Disc Manager Screen in a few days time, you may have trouble remembering what you stored in DOCUMENT.000. To do better, read on.

8809

Session 3

Preparing a new document

In the previous session, we showed how easy it is to prepare and print a simple document using LocoScript – but we did this without bothering about where the document was stored, what it was called or what LocoScript was telling you about the document you were creating.

In practice, it is best to pay attention to all these. So in this session, we are going to look at the process of preparing a new document again but this time we shall go through the steps you take to ensure the finished document is stored where you want it and called by a name that will help you remember what is stored in it. We shall also look at the information LocoScript is displaying on the screen as you prepare your document.

Creating the new document

Before you can create a new document you must display the Disc Manager Screen – that is, the screen on which the names of documents on your discs are displayed. If this is not on the screen at the moment and you are not sure how to display it, turn to page 21.

You must also have the Data disc on which you want to store the new document in one of your disc drives. *(Remember the difference between your Start-of-day disc and other discs you use while you are working with LocoScript. Your Start-of-day disc is the disc you use right at the beginning to load the LocoScript 2 program into your computer; the other discs are Data discs on which you store your documents.)*

For this tutorial session we are going to use the Examples disc as the Data disc, and this should be put in Drive A (the upper disc drive if you have two). If necessary, replace the disc in the drive by the one you want to use, but if you do this, remember to tell LocoScript 2 that you have changed the disc by pressing [f7]

Picking where to store the document

The next job is to pick out where you want to store your document. But first, a word about how LocoScript organises documents into groups.

LocoScript lets you have up to eight groups of documents on any disc. The idea is that you use these groups to keep similar documents together. When you first use LocoScript, you may be tempted to keep all your documents in one big group but, as you will soon discover, splitting your documents into groups makes them very much easier to find. There are also some other benefits of keeping similar documents in the same group as we shall see later (Session 21).

What you group together is up to you. If you are using LocoScript at home, you might decide to keep letters to friends in one group, letters to your bank etc. in another group, and, say, articles you write for your club magazine in a third. At the office, you might use the different groups for, say, letters, memos, reports and invoices.

The Disc Manager Screen shows you which of your disc drives have a disc in them, what groups are available on those discs and how they have been used so far.

The disc drives are referred to by their names. Drive A (and Drive B if you have one of these) is the disc drive that you can put your compact floppy discs in. Drive M is a special part of your PCW's memory that is used like a disc drive. LocoScript uses it to store a number of special files which it needs to have available while it is working. These files are also stored on the Start-of-day disc but LocoScript works with the copies it makes on Drive M so that you can use your disc drives for your Data discs. These files mustn't be deleted.

If you like, you can store documents on Drive M, exactly as if it were another compact floppy disc – but you should only use Drive M as a temporary home for any document. If you want to keep something, then you must store it on one of your floppy discs because Drive M is wiped clean the moment you switch off.

The three boxes towards the top of the Disc Manager Screen summarise the eight groups on each of your drives. Each of the columns in the lower part of the Disc Manager Screen lists the contents of a different group. Which group is displayed is written at the top of the column.

```
                          Disc management.              Printer idle.  Using      M:
          C=Create new document       E=Edit document       P=Print document       D=Direct printing
          f1=Actions  f2=Disc  f3=File  f4=Group  f5=Document  f6=Settings  f7=Disc change  f8=Options
          Drive A:               .    Drive B:         not fitted  Drive M:              .
          162k used  11k free  35 files  0k used   0k free  0 files  10k used  60k free   3 files
          group 0   82k     group 4   0k                         group 0  10k    group 4   0k
          group 1   42k     group 5   0k                         group 1   0k    group 5   0k
          group 2    0k     group 6   0k                         group 2   0k    group 6   0k
  Group Cursor  group 3    0k     group 7  38k                  group 3   0k    group 7   0k
          A: group 0    12 files  A: group 1   11 files  A: group 7   12 files  M: group 0    3 files
           0 limbo files           0 limbo files           0 limbo files          0 limbo files
          CONTENTS.DOC   2k    ACCENTS .TXT   2k   D630    .PRI   3k
          DOCUMENT.000   1k    ADDRESS .LST   2k   DMP3000 .PRI   4k     3 hidden   10k
          INSTALL .DRV   5k    DISCINFO.       6k   FX80    .#IB   3k
  File Cursor  LOCOCHAR.TST   4k    INQUIRE .EG    2k   FX80    .PRI   3k
          MATRIX  .#SS  11k    LSINFO  .       4k   FX80_NLQ.PRI   3k
          PHRASES .STD   1k    MAIL    .TXI   3k   LQ1500  .PRI   3k
          READ    .ME    7k    MAIL1   .TXI   3k   LQ3500  .PRI   4k
```

Picking out a group

You pick out the group you want to work with by moving the band of highlighting in the top part of the screen – the Group cursor – over the name of this group. The Group cursor is yet another of LocoScript's cursors and so it is moved by pressing the Cursor keys. However, in this case, you have to hold down the [SHIFT] key at the same time as pressing the Cursor keys. *(The way to remember that you have to hold down* [SHIFT] *as well is to think of moving from one group to another as a big movement of the cursor – because there are other places in LocoScript where holding down the* [SHIFT] *key at the same time as pressing a Cursor key produces a bigger movement than just pressing the Cursor key on its own.)*

For this exercise, you want the third group on Drive A – group 2. So hold down the [SHIFT] key and then press [←], [→], [↑] or [↓] until the Group cursor is on this group. As you do this, you will see the band of highlighting in the bottom part of the screen move as well. This is the File cursor and it is 'tied' to the Group cursor in that they always pick out the same group of documents. If, as in this case, there isn't a column for the group the Group cursor is on, then the File cursor becomes a vertical bar – showing you that the group is currently empty.

Creating the document

When the Group cursor is in place, press the 'C' letter key to tell LocoScript that you want to create a new document – just as you did in Session 2. (C for Create is quite easy to remember but if you are ever unsure which key to press, just look at the second of the three Information lines at the top of the page. There you will see C=Create new document – to remind you.)

As before, LocoScript then puts up a Selection menu, giving details of the group and the drive you have selected and suggesting a name that you could use for your new document. *(LocoScript always displays a Selection menu of this sort when you ask to do something with a document.)* The name LocoScript suggests for a new document is always DOCUMENT.*nnn* where *nnn* is a number.

If the Selection menu shows that you didn't pick out the group you meant, press [CAN]. This clears away the menu and returns you to the Disc Manager Screen as if you had never pressed C. Re-position the Group cursor and then press C again. *([CAN] is always the key to press when you want to clear away a menu that you have brought onto the screen by mistake.)*

Cancel key

Giving the document a name

Now think up a name for the new document. The name you choose must have a main part which is between one and eight characters long; to that you can add an 'extension' of up to three characters which you separate from the main part by a full stop. There are a number of characters you can use in the name (see Appendix III) but in general it is best to use just the capital letters A...Z and the digits 0...9. You can't put any spaces in this name.

It's a good idea to choose something that will remind you about the contents of the document. For example, you might call your account of the treasure hunt your club held in May TREASURE.MAY or TRHUNT.MAY. The name we are going to use here is SESSION.3

Make sure the Menu cursor is on the Name line of the Selection menu and then type this name. (If the Menu cursor is over a different line, what you type will appear on that line – and not on the Name line.)

Don't worry about typing the letters in as capital letters – *whenever LocoScript needs something to be in capital letters, it automatically translates any lower case letters you type into capital letters.*

What you type writes over the DOCUMENT. *nnn* name. You will see a small cursor move along the line as you type. When you type the full stop, LocoScript automatically makes the rest of the main part of the name blank and transfers the small cursor to the extension so that the next thing you type is the first character of the extension. Finally, press the Space bar once or twice to clear the remaining characters of the DOCUMENT.*nnn* name.

If you spot a mistake in the name you have typed, then correct it exactly as you would correct text. In particular, you don't have to rub out all the way back to the mistake – you can just position the small cursor with the Cursor keys where you need to make the change and make the correction in the normal way.

• When you have the correct document name, press ENTER to tell LocoScript to go ahead with these details. LocoScript then clears away the Disc Manager Screen and opens up its Editor Screen, ready set up for the document you are going to create.

The Editor Screen

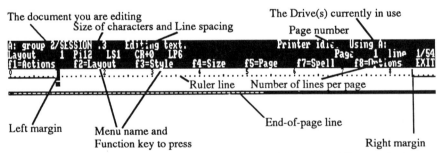

This is exactly the same screen as we saw in Session 2: the only difference is that we are now working on a different document.

A couple of the features on this screen need a bit more explanation.

The Ruler line: As we said before, the job of the Ruler line is to tell you where the left and right margins and the tab positions are. At the moment, it is just showing you the margins because no tabs have been set. The Ruler line you have here has been set up for use on standard A4 paper. The margins are approximately ¾" from each side of the page.

The Ruler line is marked out in such a way that it counts characters of a particular size – called the Scale Pitch. The Scale Pitch you have here is 12 characters per inch (to match the size of characters we've given you to use). From the numbers on the Ruler, you can work out the maximum number of characters of this size you can fit on each line or the number of these characters you can fit between two tab positions.

The oblong on the Ruler line is the Ruler cursor, which is used to tell you how far across the page you are working. As you type, you will see the Ruler cursor keep in step with the Text cursor.

The End-of-page line: This marks the point in your text where one page ends and another begins. A long document will have a number of End-of-page lines spread through it, but when you have just created a new document or your document is only very short, you will just see one End-of-page line – immediately under the last line that has been typed.

The End-of-page line has a special pattern to it to let you see how many blank lines there are left at the bottom of the page it finishes. This comes in useful, for example, when you want to see whether you could fit in a short paragraph on one page without moving any of the text over to the next or you want to work out how many blank lines to put at the beginning of a short letter so that it is neatly centred on the page.

The End-of-page line

Lines of text on the page

Blank lines at the bottom of the page

Spend some time getting used to the layout of this screen – because you will find the information it shows very useful, especially when you are refining how a document looks. By all means, try pressing some of the f-keys to see what menus appear – but when you have got a menu on the screen, just press [CAN] to clear it away again. Don't press [ENTER] at this stage or you might see some strange effects!

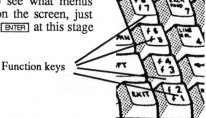

Function keys

Typing in text

Typing in text is just like typing on a standard typewriter. You simply press the key or the combination of keys for the character you want and this character is entered in your document and displayed on the screen.

LocoScript 2 handles a very wide range of characters, including Greek and Cyrillic letters – all of which can be printed on the dot-matrix printer supplied with the PCW8256 and 8512 machines.

Typing the different characters

All the common 'Roman script' characters – like the characters this manual is using here – are typed by pressing the key with the character engraved on it, either on its own or with [SHIFT] held down at the same time. If you are about to type a number of 'Shifted' characters, then it's best to start by pressing the 'Shift Lock' key. This key 'holds down' [SHIFT] for you until you press the Shift Lock key again or [SHIFT] – exactly like the Shift Lock on a typewriter. Alternatively, if what you are about to type is a number of capital letters, you can lock into Capitals by holding down [ALT] and pressing [ENTER]. LocoScript then converts any lower case letters you type into capital letters – until you hold down [ALT] and press [ENTER] again. (It also shows Caps in the top righthand corner of the screen.)

There are a number of other characters – including ©, various arrows and \ – that you can type in addition to the ones engraved on the keys. These characters are typed by holding down either [ALT] or [EXTRA] at the same time as pressing the key, some of them with [SHIFT] held down as well.

When you want to type text in a foreign language that uses Greek or Cyrillic letters or you want to use some of the special symbols, what you do is slightly different. Before you start typing this text, you hold down the [ALT] key and press one of the f-keys, depending on which set of characters you want to use. This special key combination puts the keyboard into a special mode called a 'Super Shift', in which the keys produce different characters. The keyboard stays in this mode until you hold down the [ALT] key and press [f1] whereupon the keyboard goes back to producing Roman Script characters.

When you are using one of the special Super Shifts, this too is shown in the top righthand corner of the screen – as Gre, Cyr or Sym.

The full range of characters you can type and which keys you need to press to type these are explained in Appendix III. Turn to page 263 and spend some time seeing what characters are available and what you need to do to type them. However, it is only fair to point out that the only printer on which you can guarantee being able to print these characters is the PCW's built-in printer. Other printers won't necessarily be able to handle the full range of characters. (For further details, see the Session 20 and your printer's own manual.)

Putting in accents, footnotes etc.

If you want accents on letters, LocoScript can do that as well. You can give any letter any one of 15 different accents by typing first the accent and then the letter. (If you just want the accent on its own, type the accent and then press ⌷ENTER⌷.) Do try this out: the key combinations for the accents are also given in Appendix III. For example, you will see that an acute accent is typed by holding down ⌷EXTRA⌷ and pressing E; an umlaut is typed by holding down ⌷EXTRA⌷ and pressing W.

The accented letter will be displayed on your screen and entered in your document as a single character. It will also appear as one character on the PCW printer – but this won't necessarily be the case if you print your document on a different printer. Many of LocoScript 2's accents aren't available on every printer.

LocoScript also includes a variety of raised numbers in its set of characters but if you plan to type mathematical or chemical formulae or if you want to have numbered footnotes in your documents, you may need another of LocoScript's facilities – Superscripts and Subscripts. Putting these into your text is covered in Session 9.

Practising – and correcting

Practise typing text into a LocoScript document. You can do this in a variety of ways. For example, you can simply type away at whatever comes into your head or you can open a page of a book at random and just copy it. Either way, you should soon get used to the feel of typing and to LocoScript wrapping words from one line to the next for you.

As you type, do keep one eye out for how LocoScript is keeping track of what you do. Watch the Ruler cursor move along the Ruler line in line with the Text cursor. Notice how the line number at the top of the page clocks up and how the middle section of the End-of-page line gets smaller as you add extra lines to your text. Being thoroughly familiar with what these markers do, will help you when you come to make changes to your document. Also notice how LocoScript automatically moves on to the new page. (But don't worry for now about when it decides to move onto the next page: that's covered in Session 15.)

If you make any mistakes or you want to change anything, correct these exactly as you did in Session 2 – by using the Cursor keys ⌷←⌷ ⌷→⌷ ⌷↑⌷ ⌷↓⌷ to position the Text cursor where you want to make the change (again, notice what happens to the Ruler cursor and the page and line numbers as you do this) and then using ⌷←DEL⌷ and ⌷DEL→⌷ to rub out characters you no longer want, before typing in fresh characters. Remember when you are moving the Text cursor that its true position is marked by the lefthand edge of the Cursor blob.

Notice how LocoScript continually re-adjusts your text as you work so that your document is always correctly laid out up to where you are currently working – even taking back words onto the previous line when there is now room to fit them in.

8809

Saving the new document

When you have typed in all the text you want and made any corrections, the time has come to save (and perhaps print) your new document.

Press [EXIT]. (Remember, [EXIT] is always the key to press to tell LocoScript that you want to finish the current task. The word EXIT at the end of the third Information line is to remind you that this is the key to press.) LocoScript then puts up its Exit menu:

The four options give different results.

Finish edit saves your document on disc so that you can open it up and change it or print it sometime later. You are returned to the Disc Manager Screen.

Save and Continue saves your document on disc but immediately returns you to the Editor Screen with this showing the same part of the document as it was when you pressed [EXIT]. The Text cursor also goes back where it was.

This option is most useful when you are doing a lot of work on a document and you don't want to lose the work you have done if your PCW fails, because of a sudden power cut, for example. If you resume work on a document after a failure of this kind, you start again with the last version you saved. (We suggest saving your work often – at least about once an hour – to avoid accidentally losing it.)

Save and Print saves your document on disc and then puts you straight into the menu that is used to print it out. This is useful when you want to print a copy of the document – for example, as a proof copy. You are then returned to the Disc Manager Screen. Save and Print isn't the only way – or the best way – of printing a document. We show you in Session 4 how to print a document without first editing it.

Note: The Save and Print option isn't included if there isn't a printer connected to your PCW or the printer isn't connected properly – or it is already printing.

Abandon edit throws away all the work you have done, then returns you to the Disc Manager Screen. Nothing is saved on disc. This is the option to take when you want to return to the version of the document you had before you started editing.

The Exit menu is a 'Commands' menu – which, you will remember, means that you select an option from this menu by pointing the arrow at the option you require (if necessary, by moving the Menu cursor to this option) and pressing [ENTER].

There are two ways of moving the Menu cursor: you can either use the Cursor keys or you can type the letters written in capitals in the option you require. *(This is true for most of LocoScript's menus.)* For example, you can move the Menu cursor from `Finish edit` to `Save` and `Print` either by pressing ⬆ twice or by typing SP.

In this case, we are going to select `Finish edit`. This will often be the option you want because this simply saves a copy of the document on disc, and so to make things easier for you, LocoScript pre-selects this option for you. If you have changed this selection, then simply type F — the capital letter in the menu option. Then press ⌜ENTER⌝

As LocoScript saves your document, you will see the light on one of your disc drives flash on and off as your document is written onto the disc. Unless, that is, you have chosen to save your document on Drive M, the Memory disc: then you won't see your document being written onto the disc but you will see a message like this on the screen:

```
┌─────────────────────────────────────┐
│ WARNING: Files saved on drive M      │
│ Before switching off, copy :         │
│ the result of your edit              │
│ ▶ OK                                 │
└─────────────────────────────────────┘
```

This is one of the 'Alert' messages LocoScript uses to 'alert' you to what is going on. A number of these let you know when an error has occurred (so it is a good idea when you see an Alert that you don't recognise to look it up in the Troubleshooting section — Appendix V).

This particular Alert reminds you to copy the document you have saved on Drive M to one of your discs as soon as possible. Drive M is wiped clean the moment your computer is switched off or reset and anything stored there is lost. Even the briefest of power cuts will lose any work stored on Drive M — so never put off saving anything important on disc.

Press ⌜ENTER⌝ to clear the message off the screen.

• Notice when you return to the Disc Manager Screen how the Group cursor is still on your chosen group and the File cursor is on the document you have just created. LocoScript always leaves these cursors in place so that you can easily use the same document again.

Session summary

In this session you have seen:

- How to pick out a particular group on the Disc Manager Screen
- How to create a new document and set its name and the group it is stored in
- How the Editor Screen is laid out and what information is displayed on the screen
- Where to look to see what character size, line spacing, margins etc. you are using
- Where to look to see whereabouts in your document you are currently working
- How to type the full range of characters LocoScript 2 provides, including accented letters
- What all the choices are when you want to finish editing and how to select the option you want

Session 4

Printing

Producing documents on a word processor is pointless unless you also know how to print them out, ie.

- how to get the printer ready for you to start printing
- how to tell LocoScript which document you want to print out
- and last, but by no means least, what to do when you run into problems, such as the paper becoming jammed. (Printers are, unfortunately, very prone to problems – particularly when you are not very experienced in using them.)

In this session, we describe how to print out documents on the printer supplied with your PCW and what to do when things go wrong. We will show you how to print a single copy or multiple copies of a document and how to print individual pages, rather than the whole document.

At every stage in printing, LocoScript helps by setting up everything in advance for the type of paper it expects you to use. At the moment, this is A4 sheets of paper: we show you how to prepare for using different sorts of paper and how to use a different type of printer later (in Sessions 19 and 20). Until then, keep using A4 paper and the PCW printer – because this makes printing quite straightforward.

In this session, you will again be using your Examples disc as the Data disc.

• If you follow the instructions given here but nothing is printed or the paper becomes jammed in the printer, turn to the section called 'What can go wrong' on page 57 and follow the instructions there. This should cure the problems for you.

Note: None of the actions described here will be available if you don't have a printer properly connected to your PCW. The printer should be plugged into your PCW before you switch on. See your PCW manual for details.

Printing a document

There are two ways in which you can print out a document.

If you have just been working on a document, then you can print out copies of this document by selecting the Save and Print option from the Exit menu, and pressing [ENTER]. We saw this in action in Session 2.

But the only document you can print out using Save and Print is the document you have just been working on. The general way to print out documents is from the Disc Manager Screen (that is, the screen that lists all the files and documents).

The two methods are actually very similar, so what we shall look at here is printing from the Disc Manager Screen. The Save and Print option in fact just takes you into the process of printing out from the Disc Manager Screen with the document already selected. The first step is therefore to display the Disc Manager Screen: if you are not sure how to do this, turn to page 21.

The next step is to put the Data disc with the document on it into one of your disc drives. For this tutorial session, the disc you want is your Examples disc. If necessary, replace the disc in the drive by the one you want to use: remember to press ⌷f7⌷ to tell LocoScript 2 that you have changed the disc.

The document we are going to print is called PCWINFO and it is stored in group 1 on your Examples disc. To tell LocoScript that you want to work with this document, you have to pick it out with the File cursor – the band of highlighting in the lower part of the screen. As we have said before, all cursors in LocoScript are moved with the Cursor keys – ⌷←⌷ ⌷→⌷ ⌷↑⌷ and ⌷↓⌷. So to start with, move the File cursor to the column you want by pressing the ⌷←⌷ and ⌷→⌷ cursor keys. (You will see the Group cursor towards the top of the screen move in tandem with it.)

Don't worry if the group isn't displayed at the moment, just keep pressing ⌷→⌷ – or ⌷←⌷ if pressing ⌷→⌷ doesn't bring the column onto the screen – until the column you want is displayed. The groups are displayed in the order Drive A (first to last), Drive B (first to last) and then Drive M (first to last). You will see the lower part of the display scroll across your screen as you keep pressing these keys. The only reason the group you want won't be displayed is if you didn't put the right disc in the drive!

Once the File cursor is in the correct column, use the ⌷↑⌷ and ⌷↓⌷ cursor keys to position it over the document you want to print – PCWINFO in this case.

Printing one copy of the whole document

When the File cursor is over the document you want, press the 'P' letter key. (You should find P for Print easy to remember, but if you are ever unsure, there is P=Print document on the second Information line to remind you.)

LocoScript now puts one of its Selection menus on the screen. (If instead you see a message saying the printer is Active, you still have some of the last document to print.) This is the same menu as you see when you take the Save and Print option – only here, we are going to look at the options in detail.

```
┌─────────────────────────────┐
│ Print document              │
├─────────────────────────────┤
│ ▐Name:    PCWINFO ▪         │
│ Group:    group 1           │
│ Drive:    A                 │
├─────────────────────────────┤
│ √ High quality              │
│   Draft quality             │
│   Number of copies:    1    │
├─────────────────────────────┤
│ ▸ Print all of document     │
│   Print part of document    │
└─────────────────────────────┘
```

The top part of the menu shows you which document you picked out. Normally this will be the one you want, but if not, you have two choices:

– either press ⌷CAN⌷ (to abandon the menu), pick out the right document and then press **P** again

– or change the information in the 'Selection' part of the menu until it is correct

8809

Editing the information in the menu isn't as difficult as it might sound but it is usually even easier just to press ⌜CAN⌝ and try again.

The lower part of the menu gives you a number of choices about how you are going to print this document. It already has a number of choices selected for you so that you can tell LocoScript to print one copy simply by pressing ⌜ENTER⌝ – *LocoScript menus are always set up ready to carry out the task you are most likely to want.* We shall look at these options in turn.

Setting High or Draft Quality

On a dot-matrix printer like the one supplied with the PCW8256 and 8512 machines, you have a choice of producing good quality output slowly or less good quality output about three times as fast. These are referred to as High Quality and Draft Quality, respectively. In general, you will choose High Quality output for finished documents but Draft Quality for print-outs while you are still working on the document.

The Quality part of the Selection menu is used to set the type of print quality you want. At any time, the option that is set is the one that has the tick beside it – so High Quality is selected at the moment.

When you have a choice of two settings as here, there are a number of ways of selecting the other option:

– you can move the Menu cursor to the option you want and press either the ⌜⊞⌝ key or the Space bar; or

– you can move the Menu cursor to the option that's currently set and press either the ⌜⊟⌝ key or the Space bar.

Pressing the ⌜⊞⌝ key 'sets' the option you are pointing to; pressing the ⌜⊟⌝ key 'clears' the option you are pointing to; pressing the Space Bar 'toggles' the option – ie. sets the option if it is currently clear and clears the option if it is set.

You will see these keys in action in other LocoScript menus that give you a choice of settings. What is special here is that, because you can only have one option or the other, setting one option automatically clears the other option and, similarly, clearing an option automatically sets the other.

(Don't worry about learning how this works from this description – learn by trying it out. You will find it a lot easier than it seems at first glance!)

So if you decide to set Draft quality, move the Menu cursor to this option and press the ⌜⊞⌝ key. This ticks Draft quality and, because the print quality can only be either High or Draft, it also 'clears' High quality.

And printing

The rest of the menu is already set up for printing one copy of the whole document, so simply press [ENTER] to tell LocoScript to go ahead. Before it starts printing, you may well see a message on the screen. In particular, you will always see a message when you are printing your first document since loading LocoScript 2.

This is just a reminder about the type of paper LocoScript is expecting you to use in your printer. Other messages will appear when you start to use different types of paper for your documents (see Session 19).

When you have finished reading (or acting on) this message, press [ENTER]. Your document will now be printed – provided there is paper in the printer. If not, load a sheet of A4 paper as described in your PCW manual (or in Appendix I): then the document will start to print. (Remember to check that the bail-bar is back and to press [EXIT] after loading the paper.)

What you are printing is a three-page document. When it gets to the bottom of the first page, LocoScript will release the finished page and then wait for you to put in a fresh sheet of paper. Load another sheet of paper as before, push the bail-bar back and press [EXIT] to tell LocoScript that you have finished adjusting the paper. LocoScript will then begin printing the second page. Similarly, when it gets to the bottom of the page, you will need to load another piece of paper.

• You can use LocoScript for other jobs while the document is printing. You could, for example, create a new document or edit a document you prepared before. However, the disc holding the document you are printing must be left in the drive.

Printing part of the document

When all the document has been printed, check that the File cursor is still over PCWINFO (you will remember that LocoScript always leaves the File cursor where it was so that it is very easy for you to work with the same document again); then press P again. The same menu appears, and as before it is ready set up for printing one copy of the whole document. This time, we just want to print page 2 of the document – ie. we want to print part of the document rather than all of it.

Move the Menu cursor down to Print part of document – either by using the Cursor keys or by typing PP once you have moved the Menu cursor out of the top section of the menu. You have to move the Menu cursor out of this area first because otherwise your typing will simply replace the name of the file you have picked out to print. You must always check that the Menu cursor isn't over a part of the menu in which you can type a name or a phrase before you use this shortcut to moving the Menu cursor.

Notice how the arrow marking the selected option automatically moves to Print part of document *as you get there. You will see this again in other menus.*

Now press ⌈ENTER⌉ to say 'go ahead'. LocoScript then displays a second menu, with slots for the page numbers of the first and the last page you want printed. It also tells you what the first and last page numbers of the document are. (The first page number is usually 1 but it doesn't have to be: we will show you ways of setting the first page number in Sessions 17 and 18.)

As we just want to print page 2, the page number of both the first page we want printed and the last page needs to be set to 2.

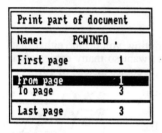

Put the Menu cursor on From page, type 2 and then press ⌈ENTER⌉. This sets the first page to be printed as page 2. Now move the Menu cursor to To page, type 2 and then press ⌈ENTER⌉. This sets the last page to be printed as page 2.

Notice how pressing ⌈ENTER⌉ after the number hasn't made the menu disappear. The job ⌈ENTER⌉ does here is to 'enter' the number – ie. to tell LocoScript that you have finished typing this information. You have to press ⌈ENTER⌉ again to tell LocoScript to go ahead.

When all the details are correct, press ⌈ENTER⌉ and, provided there is paper in the printer, LocoScript will then start to print page 2.

(As before, you can do other work while your chosen section of the document is printing – provided that you don't change the disc in the drive.)

Printing multiple copies

When the page has been printed, check that the File cursor is still over PCWINFO and press **P** again – exactly as before. Once again the Selection menu when it appears is ready set up for printing one copy of the whole document.

This time, we want to print two copies of page 1. (You could print up to 99 copies if you wanted, but we will just print two.) Start by moving the Menu cursor down to Number of copies.

Type 2 – the number of copies we want to make – and then press ⌈ENTER⌉ to 'enter' this number of copies. As before when you entered the first and last page numbers, the menu stays on the screen.

If you wanted to print this number of copies of the whole document, you would now press ⌈ENTER⌉ again (this time to tell LocoScript to go ahead), load a sheet of paper and start printing as before. But as we only want two copies of page 1, move the Menu cursor to Print part of document and set the first and last page number as before – only setting both of these to 1, rather than to 2.

When these details are correct, press [ENTER]. Now put a sheet of A4 paper in the printer as before and LocoScript will then start to print page 1. When it has finished, load another sheet of paper, push the bail-bar back, press [EXIT] – and the second copy of page 1 will be printed. (As before, you could edit another document, say, while this is going on.)

• LocoScript prints one copy of all the pages you selected before printing the next set. It doesn't print all the page 1's and then all the page 2's etc. etc.

Abandoning printing

It is always possible that after setting LocoScript off printing, you decide either that you don't want to print this document or that you don't want so many copies after all. For example, you may decide that you only want eight copies instead of 10.

To see what happens, use the steps described above to start printing three copies of PCWINFO.

The first step in abandoning printing is to press the [PTR] key.

If you have decided that you don't want to print this document at all, do this immediately; if you have decided that you don't want all the copies you asked for, wait until LocoScript starts printing the last copy that you want and then press [PTR]. Pressing [PTR] interrupts the printing by putting LocoScript into its Printer Control State. LocoScript stops printing the document as soon as it can: the built-in printer will stop at the end of the current line, but other printers may go on printing for some time. Press [PTR] now.

While LocoScript is in its Printer Control State, all your actions are to do with controlling the printer. At first glance you might not notice that the screen has changed at all but if you look at the Information lines at the top of the screen, you will see that these have changed a lot:

State of the printer

Printer control menus   Type of paper

Note: If you look at the screen while you are loading paper into the printer, you will see that the Information lines change to this pattern then as well. LocoScript automatically goes into Printer Control State when you load paper in case you want to make any special printer settings – and to give you time to get the paper straight.

The Printer Control menu you need in order to abandon printing is the Document menu. If you look at the Information lines at the top of the screen, you will see that this is brought onto the screen by pressing [f7]. Press [f7] now. The following menu should appear:

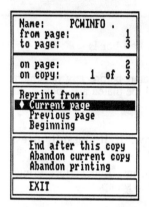

If you want to abandon printing altogether, the option you want is Abandon Printing. If you want to continue printing the current copy but you don't want any more copies after that, then the option you want is End after this copy. (The third option, Abandon current copy, is typically used when you have run into a problem such as the paper jamming in the printer: see below.)

The Document menu is another 'Commands' menu but it is subtly different from the Exit menu you have used in previous sessions to finish work on the documents you were preparing. In the Exit menu, the option that is currently selected in a 'Commands' menu is the one picked out by the arrow. Here it is picked out by a diamond. We will be looking at this type of menu more closely later (Session 12).

When the Document menu is displayed, the option that is selected for you is the first of the Reprint options. So move the Menu cursor to the Abandon option you require and press [ENTER] to tell LocoScript to carry out this action. If you have chosen to finish the current copy, the menu will remain on the screen in case you want to select one of the reprint options (see page 59). To continue, move the cursor to the EXIT option and press [ENTER] again.

Important: Before you can print any more of the current document or select another document to print, you must leave Printer Control State. Do this by pressing [EXIT]. As you will remember, [EXIT] is always the key to press when you want to stop doing one type of task and go back to what you were doing before.

What can go wrong

This section is mainly of help when something actually does go wrong as you try to print a document. However, read through it now and follow the instructions. Then you will feel much more confident that you can cope when you run into a problem.

• Nothing is printed

A printer needs to have everything set right before it will start to print a document. Normally, LocoScript automatically looks after all these settings for you and, provided you follow the instructions correctly, all should be well. However, it is very easy, especially when you are inexperienced, to miss out a step or press a key that you didn't mean to – and then your printer may refuse to print anything.

There is no need to panic. All you need do is go through the following check list, checking and putting right anything which is not set correctly.

Note: If you do all these checks correctly and still nothing prints, consult your dealer because it is likely that the printer itself is faulty.

1. Check that there is a ribbon in the printer

2. Check that there is paper in the printer and that the bail-bar is pushed back

The bail-bar must be holding the paper against the platen before any document can be printed. (If you are not sure what the bail-bar and the platen are, look at the picture of the printer either in your PCW guide or in the printer's own user guide.)

3. Press [EXIT]

*** Your document may well start to print now. If it doesn't, press the [PTR] key to the right of the Space Bar. Do this now.

As we explained above, pressing the [PTR] key puts you into LocoScript's Printer Control State through which you control how your printer is set up.

4. Check that the printer is ready to print

The printer can't print anything while:

– it has 'No paper' in the printer

– it is 'Waiting for paper' – typically because you told the printer to expect single sheets of paper but you actually loaded continuous stationery, or

– printing is 'suspended'

Check the second Information line to see which of these states your printer is in. If you see 'No paper', just load some paper in the printer – that should clear it. If you see 'Waiting for paper' or 'Printing suspended', press [f1]. Press [f1] now. This brings the Actions menu onto the screen, which will look either

like this: or this:

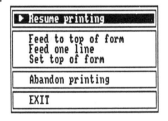 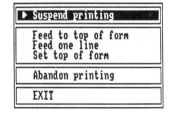

When the printer is either 'Waiting for paper' or printing is 'suspended', the top option in the menu is Resume printing. When the printer is ready to print, the top option in the menu is Suspend printing.

In either case, the top option is automatically selected for you (shown in the usual way by the arrow next to this option). So when you want to make the Printer ready to print, simply press [ENTER] to select Resume Printing. If the printing wasn't suspended, just press [CAN] to clear away the menu.

5. Press [EXIT]

Note: You can also resume printing from Printer Control State by pressing [⊞]. This both clears 'Waiting for paper' and leaves Printer Control State. Similarly, you can suspend printing and exit from Printer Control State simply by pressing [⊟].

- **The paper jams in the printer (or you suddenly realise that you are not printing on the right sort of paper)**

1. Press [PTR] – to put LocoScript into its Printer Control State. (Do this now.)

Printing will stop **as soon as possible – usually at the end of the line.**

2. Clear out the old paper, reload with fresh paper, but don't press [EXIT] yet.

3. Press [f7]. This brings the Document menu onto the screen.

The Document menu normally gives you a choice of three places in the document at which to re-start printing – the beginning of the document; the beginning of the current page; and the beginning of the previous page. (The Previous page option is only available when it is appropriate.)

Note: Some printers print a large number of characters between you pressing the [PTR] key and it actually stopping. For this reason, it is always a good idea to check the page number of the 'current' page, rather than assume that this is automatically the page that was being printed when the problem happened.

The first option – Reprinting from the beginning of the current page – is pre-selected for you. You can see this from the diamond beside it. As always, move the Menu cursor to the option you want – moving the diamond as well – then press [ENTER]; then move it to the EXIT option and press [ENTER] again to leave the menu. Alternatively, abandon printing either altogether or the current copy (see page 57).

When you leave this menu after selecting one of the Reprint options, LocoScript 2's first action is to display an Alert message.

Don't clear the Alert off the screen yet. First, load paper into your printer and/or adjust its position so that printing will start at the top of the page. If you are using single sheets of paper, the paper should automatically be positioned correctly: with continuous stationery, you may have to turn the Paper Feed Knob on the side of your printer until the paper is in the right place. When you are ready, press [ENTER]. The paper's position is then recorded as the position to be used for the first line of text.

4. Press [EXIT]

LocoScript then starts reprinting the document from the point you picked out.

• The printer suddenly stops printing

The chances are that the printer has spotted the end of the paper you are feeding into it, and has stopped so that there is no risk of accidentally printing on the platen.

Don't replace the current page with fresh paper yet – because there is still some of the current page waiting to be printed. First, press [PTR] to enter Printer Control State and then press [f1] to bring the Actions menu onto the screen. This menu now has an extra entry that you won't have seen before – Finish current page. Move the Menu cursor to this option and press [ENTER]; then press [EXIT] to leave Printer Control State. LocoScript now finishes printing the current page before stopping again.

When it stops again, load fresh paper into the printer. When the paper is in position, press [+] to resume printing. (Loading the paper has automatically put LocoScript back into Printer Control State.) LocoScript then carries on printing your document.

Session summary

In this session, you have seen:
- How to print out a document from the Disc Manager Screen
- How to print just part of a document
- How to print out multiple copies of a document
- What to do when your printer apparently refuses to print anything
- What to do when the paper gets jammed

Session 5

Changing a document – I: Small Changes

In this session and the next, we shall edit a document – that is, we shall take a document that is already stored on disc and change it. In this session we shall:
- see how to start editing a document
- look more closely at the small-scale insertions and deletions introduced in Session 2
- and see how to move from one place in your document to another efficiently.

In the next session, we will see how to make more drastic changes to your document, for example, by moving whole paragraphs from one place in your document to another.

We will again be using the Examples disc as the Data disc in this session.

Note: While you are editing a document, you should leave the disc you are using in the drive, because LocoScript will be reading it and writing to it while you work.

Starting to edit a document

The starting point for editing a document is always the Disc Manager Screen, that is, the screen that lists all the files and documents that are available. If you are not sure how to display this, turn to page 21.

In addition, you must work with the disc holding the document in the appropriate disc drive. This is only a problem on an 8000 machine with two disc drives: then, if the document is stored on a 'normal-capacity' disc, you must use it in Drive A; if it is stored on a 'high-capacity' disc, you must use it in Drive B. If necessary, replace the disc in the drive by the one you want to use. Remember to tell LocoScript you have changed the disc by pressing ⌜*f7*⌝.

The document we are going to edit in this session is called LSINFO and it is stored in group 1 on your Examples disc. Insert this disc in Drive A, press ⌜*f7*⌝ and then pick this document out with the File cursor – exactly as you did in the last session. When the File cursor is in the right position, press the 'E' letter key. (Remember E for Edit – or check the second Information line when you are unsure.)

LocoScript now puts one of its Selection menus on the screen, to give you the chance to confirm that you selected the right document. If necessary, either press ⌜CAN⌝ to abandon the menu and pick again or edit the details in the menu (see Session 4). Press ⌜ENTER⌝ to tell LocoScript to go ahead, once you've checked that the details are right. LocoScript then clears away the Disc Manager Screen and puts up the Editor Screen, with the document you have selected already in place. (If instead LocoScript

9108

displays a message, saying 'the document may not fit', what this is telling you is that the disc you are working on is almost full. For now, simply press ENTER to accept the option to 'send the result to Drive M', but in future you should free some space on your Examples disc – for example, by erasing the LOCOCHAR files. We describe how to erase files in Session 7.)

Your screen should look like this:

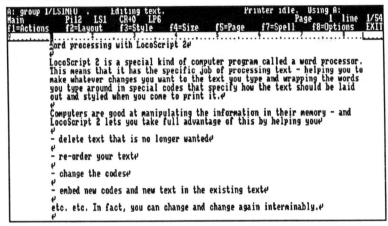

This is the first 28 lines of the document – 28 lines being the most that can be displayed on the screen at any one time. The Text cursor is right at the top of the document. Notice how LocoScript has laid out the document neatly between the margins marked on the ruler.

Moving around your document

As you will remember from Session 2, before you can change the text at a particular point in your document, you have to move the Text cursor there.

The Cursor keys

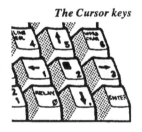

One way of moving the Text cursor, as we have seen, is to use the four Cursor keys, ←, →, ↑ and ↓. These keys are mainly used to move the cursor over the part of the document you can see at the moment. But keeping these keys pressed when the cursor reaches the edges of the screen makes the text of the document move – 'scroll' – so that you can see the next part of the document.

If you hold down SHIFT and/or ALT at the same time as pressing a Cursor key, you get a different type of movement. With SHIFT, the Text cursor moves in the direction you expect but in very much larger steps. (Remember how we said in connection with moving the Group cursor that holding the SHIFT key down made the cursor

9010

move in bigger steps?) With [ALT], the Text cursor doesn't move but the text on the screen does so that the Text cursor still finishes at a new place in your document.

Pressing the Cursor keys is not the only way of moving the Text cursor, nor is it always the best way. As you can imagine, holding down the [↓] key is a very slow way of moving from the first line of a long document to the last line. (Try it on this example document, if you like.) And there are some other movements that are not particularly easy with the cursor keys – for example, moving from the end of one line to the beginning of the next.

So LocoScript has some special, quick ways of moving from one place to another. One way is by using some special keys known as the Textual Movement keys. The other is by using a special menu option to move straight to a particular page.

Note: When you make a small move, the text of your document stays on the screen – perhaps scrolling a little to bring the part of the document you want to move to onto the screen. When you make a big move – for example, from the top to the bottom of the document, the screen is completely re-written when the new section of your document is displayed. You will also see a message summarising the move you are making.

The Textual Movement keys

The Textual Movement keys all have names that suggest the sort of movement pressing the key will produce. You have already used [PAGE] to move to the beginning of the next page. [DOC] moves to the end of the document; [WORD] moves to the beginning of the next word; [LINE] moves to the beginning of the next line; [PARA] moves it to the beginning of the next paragraph; etc. etc. The one which you might not readily understand is [EOL] – which moves the Text cursor to the End Of the Line.

(Note: To LocoScript, paragraphs are blocks of text that are separated from each other by a blank line or by extra spacing after the Carriage Return (see Session 10). Addresses, for example, are therefore just one paragraph.)

Most of these keys have two Textual Movements engraved on them – for example, there's a key with both DOC and PAGE on it. If you just press this key, you will get the 'PAGE' action. To get the 'DOC' action, you have to hold down the [SHIFT] key as you press the key. *(Hold down the [SHIFT] key as you press the key whenever you want the upper of two actions or characters marked on it. We will remind you to do this in the initial stages of this tutorial by putting ([SHIFT]+ . . .) after the key name.)*

Simply pressing a Textual Movement key (together with the [SHIFT] key if it is the upper action on the key that you want) moves the Text cursor forward through the

---

document. When you want to move backwards through the document, hold down ⌈ALT⌉ at the same time as pressing the key or the key combination. The Text cursor is then moved the corresponding distance back through the document.

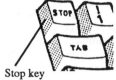

If pressing the key (or key combination) once doesn't move you far enough, press it again until the Text cursor is where you want it. To abandon a movement that you have started to make, press ⌈STOP⌉, wait for LocoScript to pause and then press ⌈STOP⌉ again.

Stop key

- Spend some time trying out these various key combinations and seeing their effects for yourself. In particular, see how easy it is to recover after you have accidentally moved the Text cursor the wrong way.

Moving to a particular page

You move the Text cursor to a particular page with the help of the Page menu, which is brought onto the screen by pressing ⌈f5⌉.

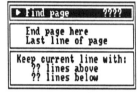

The Page menu is another of LocoScript's Command menus and the command you want is the one at the top of the menu – Find page ????. To use this option, you first check that the Menu cursor is on it and then you type the number of the page you want. So, for example, if you wanted to move to Page 2 of the example document, you would first press ⌈f5⌉ to bring the Page menu onto the screen (as you have done already). Then, as Find page ???? is pre-selected for you, just type 2 – making the menu option Find page 2.

When you have typed the number, press ⌈ENTER⌉. LocoScript then moves the Text cursor to the start of your chosen page (Page 2 in this case). While it does this, a message appears on your screen telling you about the move LocoScript is making.

Making small changes

Where the changes you want to make just involve deleting or inserting odd words and letters, the technique to use is the one we used in Sessions 2 and 3:

- move the Text cursor to the point in the document you want to change (Remember, the part of the cursor marking its true position is its lefthand edge)
- use ⌈←DEL⌉ and ⌈DEL→⌉ to rub out characters you don't want
- type in new characters

This is all very simple, especially as LocoScript always ensures that your document is correctly laid out **up to your current working position**. The text below your current working position isn't relaid until you move your working position further

---

down the document – or you press the [RELAY] key, whereupon the whole of the paragraph you are working on is relaid.

What we want to emphasise here is that it is always worth being very careful about positioning the Text cursor at the exact point in the document you want to make your changes: otherwise, you will probably have to make a further correction just to put this right. Remember, you need to position the Text cursor so that its lefthand edge is at the precise point in the document where you want to make your changes.

The only difficulty you might have in deciding on the 'right' place for the Text cursor is when you want to add something to a table of information. The problem with a table is that it contains a lot of 'blanks' which space out the items in the table and which look exactly like spaces you type – but which aren't really part of the document at all. The margins around your text are also full of 'blanks'. The trouble is that if you start typing when the Text cursor is on a group of these blanks, LocoScript may insert what you type into your document in a very different place to the one you expect.

Showing the difference between spaces and blanks

If you find this difficult to work with, then the answer is usually to show up the difference between these blanks and spaces that you have typed. To do this, press [f8]. LocoScript 2 then displays a menu similar to this:

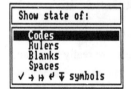

This is the Editor Options menu which you use to set how much extra information is displayed alongside the text while you are editing the document. Each option of the menu refers to a different piece of extra information you can display.

The Options menu is one of LocoScript's 'Settings' menus – like, for example, the Print menu you used in the last session. If the option has a tick beside it, it is said to be 'Set' and the information will be displayed; otherwise, the option is 'Cleared' and the information associated with this option won't be displayed. With all the options cleared, the screen shows only the characters that will be printed.

You can set as many of these options as you like. As you will remember:

- You set an option by moving the Menu cursor to the option you require and pressing the [+] key: this puts a tick beside the option.

- You clear an option that is set (ie. has a tick beside it) by moving the Menu cursor to the option and pressing the [-] key: this clears away the tick.

- You 'toggle' the setting of an option by moving the Menu cursor to the option and pressing the Space Bar.

The Menu cursor is moved in the usual way – either with the Cursor keys or by typing the relevant capital letters (see Session 3).

When you create a new document, the only one of these options that's set is the list of symbols. The symbol you will recognise is ↵ – the special Carriage Return character used to mark where you have pressed the [RETURN] key. The other symbols will be introduced later in the tutorial. LocoScript automatically sets this option so that you can see where you have pressed the [RETURN] key.

The options that let you see which blanks on the screen are really part of your document are 'Blanks' and 'Spaces'. (The other two options come into later sessions of this tutorial.)

If 'Spaces' is set, all the places you have typed a space will be marked by ʌ. You can then see all the space characters that you have put into your document. If 'Blanks' is set, all the unused parts of the screen are shown as dots. This includes the blanks immediately following a Tab.

Blanks as dots

```
......This means that it has the specific job of processing text - helping you to ..
......make whatever changes you want to the text you type and wrapping the words ...
......you type around in special codes that specify how the text should be laid ....
......out and styled when you come to print it.↵......................................
......↵.............................................................................
......Computers are good at manipulating the information in their memory - and .....
```

Spaces as blobs

```
This.means.that.it.has.the.specific.job.of.processing.text.-.helping.you.to.
make.whatever.changes.you.want.to.the.text.you.type.and.wrapping.the.words.
you.type.around.in.special.codes.that.specify.how.the.text.should.be.laid.
out.and.styled.when.you.come.to.print.it.↵
↵
Computers.are.good.at.manipulating.the.information.in.their.memory.-.and.
```

Either of these options will let you see which parts of the screen are really blank and which are spaces you have typed.

To demonstrate the effect of showing up the difference between blanks and spaces, we shall set both 'Blanks' and 'Spaces'. First type B to move the Menu cursor to Blanks. Then press the [⊞] key. The menu now has a tick beside Blanks. Now move the Menu cursor to the Spaces option (immediately below Blanks) and press the Space Bar. Now press it again a few times. The first time you press the Space Bar, a tick appears beside Spaces; the second time, the tick is cleared away; the third time, the tick re-appears; and so on. Finish with Spaces set.

Press [ENTER] to tell LocoScript to go ahead with this combination of extra information to be shown. LocoScript then rewrites the screen – taking account of the options you set. Notice the difference there now is between the blanks round the edges of the document and the spaces in the middle of it. The area in which you can expect LocoScript to move anything you type is the part of screen marked by dots.

For practice, press [f8] again – but this time use [⊞], [□] or the Space Bar to set the combination of Blanks and Spaces that you find most helpful. **Note:** If you save a document after setting any combination of the display options in this menu, this combination is also saved and re-appears the next time you edit the document.

Relaying after making changes

After you have made your changes, it is a good idea to press [RELAY] to relay the current paragraph so that you can see clearly the effects these changes have had.

At least, this is the case while you are a newcomer to word-processing with LocoScript. Once you are confident that the changes you make will have the right result, you can leave the relaying to LocoScript. As we mentioned earlier, LocoScript always ensures that your document is correctly laid out up to your current working position. It also checks, and if necessary corrects, all aspects of layout – the line breaks, the page breaks, etc. etc. – as it saves your document. This means you are guaranteed that, whatever state you leave your document in while you are editing it, it will always be neatly arranged on the page when you come to print it out or when you next edit it.

What this means in practice is:

- Each paragraph is checked and corrected as you move the Text cursor into the next paragraph.
- Everything is correctly laid out up to the last character you typed.
- The layout of your document is correct up to the point you have moved to by pressing one of the Textual Movement keys.

To get a suitable area of text to show this, move to the c of codes on the fourth line of the first proper paragraph and type word processing (followed by a space).

Move the Text cursor up and down between the line either side of the break. Use the [↑] and [↓] keys for this. LocoScript doesn't correct the layout while you do this so that you can cursor around the paragraph without the text moving.

Next move the Text cursor to the first letter of the text on the broken line and type all. Instantly, LocoScript relays the paragraph up to the word you have just typed – though the rest of the paragraph is now a bit ragged.

Now move the Text cursor down to the next paragraph. The moment you move the cursor onto the next paragraph, LocoScript relays the paragraph you have just left.

To see what happens to the layout of paragraphs when you move around the document by pressing [CHAR], [WORD], [PARA] etc., we need to put another break in the document. This time, move the Text cursor to the g of good on the first line of the next paragraph and type very. Now start moving the cursor forwards through the text by pressing [CHAR]. Watch carefully what happens to the characters on the screen.

As you see, LocoScript is relaying your document character by character as you press [CHAR]. Next swap to pressing [WORD] ([SHIFT]+[CHAR]). Again, you will see LocoScript relaying your document, only this time it is doing it word by word.

8809

```
LocoScript 2 is a special kind of computer program called a word processor.
This means that it has the specific job of processing text - helping you to
make whatever changes you want to the text you type and wrapping the words
you type around in special word processing codes that specify how all the
text should be laid out and styled when you come to print it.◄
◄
Computers are very good at manipulating▪
                        the information in their memory - and
LocoScript 2 lets you take full advantage of this by helping you◄
◄
- delete text that is no longer wanted◄
```

Moving the Text cursor with the Textual Movement keys always makes LocoScript tidy up your document, up to the current position of the Text cursor. This means that if you want to force LocoScript to relay your document right through to the end, all you have to do is press [DOC] ([SHIFT] + [PAGE]).

Throwing away unwanted changes

Finally, in this session, we shall see how to throw away all the changes that have been made since you started editing the document.

First, press [EXIT] to tell LocoScript that you want to finish work on this document (the current task). Then move the Menu cursor to Abandon edit and press [ENTER]. LocoScript clears away the document on the screen and returns you to the Disc Manager Screen. It doesn't save anything on disc.

To get the document back onto the screen, you have to edit it again – in the same way as we did at the beginning of this session. When the Editor screen appears, the document will be exactly as it was when you started editing it the last time.

Session summary

In this session, you have seen:
- How to select a document and open it for editing
- All the ways LocoScript has of moving the Text cursor from one position to another in a document
- What happens when you type in the 'blank' areas of your screen
- How to make it clear on the screen where you have typed spaces and where nothing has been typed
- When LocoScript adjusts the layout of paragraphs you have changed
- How to throw away all the changes you made

8809

Session 6

Changing a document – II: Large-scale changes

The changes we made to the example document in the last session were really very small. In this session, we shall make some quite drastic changes to a document – and really show the editing power of LocoScript. The sort of changes we shall make hardly bear thinking about when you're preparing text on a typewriter:

– duplicating sections of text
– moving sections of the text from one place in your document to another
– deleting a large block of text

The document we are going to edit in this session is a poem and it is stored in a document called POEM.EG in group 1 of your Examples disc. Display the Disc Manager Screen (see page 21) and if necessary, replace the disc in Drive A by your Examples disc, with Side 1 to the left. Remember to tell LocoScript that you have made this change by pressing [f7]. Now pick out POEM.EG with the File cursor and open it for editing, exactly as you opened LSINFO for editing at the beginning of the last session.

Note: It is possible, when using the editing techniques described here, to create very large documents very easily. On occasion, there may no longer be room on the disc to store the document you are editing – particularly if you are working on a disc that doesn't have a lot of free space on it. You may also run out of space on Drive M, the Memory drive. When either of these happen, you will see a message like this:

```
ERROR in: Drive M:
Disc is full
▶ Run disc manager
  Cancel operation
```

Turn to Appendix V (the Troubleshooting section) for instructions on what to do.

The common factor

All the operations we look at in this session – duplicating, moving and deleting sections of text – involve manipulating a block of text as a unit.

In each case, you mark out the section of text you are interested in and then you make a copy of this text in a special part of your computer's memory. This area of memory acts rather like a notebook: whenever you need the text again, you just make a copy of the relevant part of the notebook.

The different operations of duplicating, moving and deleting text come from the different actions you can take once you have marked out the block of text you are interested in.

The first choice is whether to retain the original text in the document. To retain it, you make a 'Copy' of this text – rather like you might make a copy in your notebook of a paragraph out of a book. Otherwise you 'Cut' it out – as you might take a Press cutting and stick it in your notebook.

The second choice is whether to 'Paste' a copy of the text in at some other point in the text.

- Duplicating is making a Copy and Pasting this back in
- Moving is Cutting out the original and Pasting a copy back in
- Deleting is Cutting out the original and not pasting it back in.

In each case, you start by marking out the block of text you are interested in and you store a copy of the text in one of LocoScript's 10 'Blocks' – Block 0, Block 1 ... up to Block 9. You can have as many of these 10 Blocks as you like in use at the same time, each storing a different piece of text – rather like a 10-page notebook.

When you come to paste the text back into this document, you paste in a copy of the text stored in the Block. This doesn't 'use up' the copy in the Block: indeed, you can paste in as many copies as you like. Think of this as copying from the notebook, leaving the notebook unchanged. LocoScript 2 continues to remember this text until you tell it to remember another piece of text as this Block – not just while you are working on this document but also for all other documents you work on before you switch off or reset your machine. (We will see in Session 14 how to use this to copy or move text between different documents.)

To demonstrate how these Block movements work, we shall Duplicate the first verse of the example poem, Move another verse and Delete a third verse. But, as marking out a section of text comes into all these actions, we shall start by marking out the first verse.

Note: If you ever forget which Blocks out of the 10 you are using and what you are using them for, press ⌐/↑⌐ to bring the Editor Actions menu onto the screen and   select the Show Blocks option:

The menu that appears lists the Block names that currently have something stored in them – ie. the ones you have used since you loaded LocoScript – together with the first few words of the text stored in each Block. Press ⌐ENTER⌐ when you have finished looking at the list to tell LocoScript you are ready to proceed.

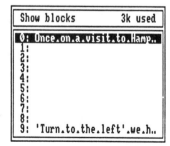

Marking out a section of text

The first step is to move the Text cursor to the beginning of your chosen section of text. Because we want to duplicate the first verse of the poem, move the cursor right to the top of the document (if it is not already there).

Remember, the true position of the Text cursor is after one character and before the next and it is marked by the lefthand edge of the cursor. So you need to place the Text cursor so that its lefthand edge marks the beginning of your chosen section.

Before going any further, check that the cursor is in the right place. *This is important because you can't change your mind part way through – except by pressing* [CAN] *and starting all over again.*

Now press [COPY]. A message then appears, both in the middle of the screen and on the third Information line, telling you to move the Text cursor to the end of your chosen section of text. As you move the cursor, the message in the middle of the screen disappears.

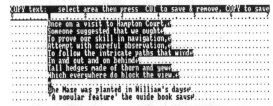

Copy key

Next move the Text cursor to the end of the chosen section of text. Again it is the lefthand edge of the cursor that must mark the end of the section of text, so the cursor oblong finishes over the first character beyond the section of text. Remember to go beyond the final space, blank line or carriage return if you want to include this.

In our example case, move the Text cursor to the beginning of the second verse, ie. leaving the cursor oblong over the first character of this verse.

As you move the cursor, you will see LocoScript highlighting the section you are marking out. (You will still be able to see the Text cursor because this blinks.)

Once again, position the cursor precisely where you want it – or accept that you may have some tidying up to do. You can just use the four Cursor keys to make these movements, but using the Textual Movement keys we introduced in the last session can make moving to precisely the point you want very much easier.

Don't worry if you overshoot: just move the cursor back again to the right position. (The highlighting will shrink back, too. It always just marks the section between the first character you marked and the current position of the Text cursor, wherever that is on the screen.)

When the Text cursor is in the right place, the section of text is marked out ready to be Duplicated, Moved or Deleted as described below.

Duplicating the marked text – Copy and Paste

With the chosen section of text marked out as described above, press [COPY] – to tell LocoScript that you want to keep the original text in the document.

LocoScript then puts up another of its messages in the middle of the screen and more permanently on the third Information line, asking you to type one of the numbers 0 . . . 9 or a letter. Like the message that appeared when you started marking out the block, the message disappears the moment you press a key (or if you wait too long) but, don't worry, the whole message is repeated on the third Information line at the top of the screen.

The numbers 0 . . . 9, you will remember, are the 'names' of LocoScript's 10 Blocks; the letters refer to LocoScript's Phrases feature which we cover in a later session (Session 14). All the operations we are looking at in this session – duplicating, moving and deleting – are Block operations, so you need to type a number – for example, 0. This tells LocoScript to remember the section of text we marked out as Block 0.

Now move the Text cursor to the place you want to put the copy. Again, remember the true position of the Text cursor is marked by the lefthand edge of the cursor. To duplicate the first verse of the example poem at the end of the poem, we need to move the cursor to the bottom of the page: move there by pressing [PAGE].

When the cursor is in position, press the [PASTE] key. Again, you get a message in the middle of the screen (and, more permanently, at the top of the screen) – this one, telling you to type the number of the block you want to insert. In this instance, type 0. LocoScript then 'pastes' in Block 0.

Paste key

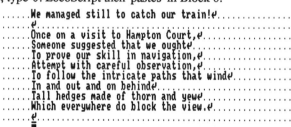

```
......We managed still to catch our train!↵..............
......↵..................................................
......Once on a visit to Hampton Court,↵.................
......Someone suggested that we ought↵...................
......To prove our skill in navigation,↵.................
......Attempt with careful observation,↵.................
......To follow the intricate paths that wind↵...........
......In and out and on behind↵..........................
......Tall hedges made of thorn and yew↵.................
......Which everywhere do block the view.↵...............
......↵..................................................
......▮..................................................
```

Remember, pasting the text in doesn't 'use up' the copy you made. LocoScript continues to remember this section of text as Block 0 until you tell it to remember something else as Block 0 (or switch your machine off) and so you can paste in as many copies as you like.

Moreover, there is no need to paste in the contents of a Block immediately – you can do any amount of editing before you paste a block back into your document.

Moving the marked text – Cut and Paste

To move a section of text, you mark this out, store it in a block and later paste a copy of the stored text in at a new position – in exactly the same way as you do when you want to duplicate a section of text. The only difference is that the original copy is deleted from the document – rather than left there.

To show the steps involved, we shall move Verse 2 to after Verse 3.

First, mark out Verse 2 as described above – moving the Text cursor first to the beginning of this verse, pressing COPY and then moving the Text cursor to the beginning of the third verse.

Cut key

So far everything has been exactly as if you wanted to duplicate this bit of text. But now, when the Text cursor is in the right place, press CUT – don't press COPY. Pressing CUT tells LocoScript both to store a copy of the text and to remove the original from the document.

LocoScript then asks you to type one of the numbers 0 . . . 9 or a letter – exactly as before. Again, you want to type a number – so, type 9 to tell LocoScript to remember this section of text as Block 9.

Now move the Text cursor to the place you want to move the text to. For our example, move to the beginning of the 4th verse. (Again, remember that the true position of the Text cursor is marked by its lefthand edge.) When the cursor is in position, paste Block 9 in by pressing the PASTE key and typing the number of the block – exactly as you did before.

Once again, you can paste in this text anywhere you like, as many times as you like. However, pasting in this way gives you multiple copies of the text – it doesn't keep on moving the same piece of text around the document.

Deleting the marked text – Cut

LocoScript has two ways of deleting a block of text.

The first – and the safer one – is to go through all the steps of moving a block of text from one place to another except for pasting in the block in the new position. In other words, you:

- press COPY
- mark out the section of text
- press CUT
- type the number of the Block this text is to be stored as, and
- never paste this block of text in again (unless you decide that you wanted this text after all!)

9108

The other method is similar but less safe because there is no way that you can restore the text if you change your mind. To see this method, we shall now use it to delete the first verse of our much-modified poem.

Mark out the section of text you want to delete as before except press ⌑CUT instead of ⌑COPY after putting the Text cursor at the beginning of the chosen section. So to delete the first verse, move the Text cursor to the top of the document (ALT+DOC), press ⌑CUT and then move the cursor to the beginning of the second verse. As with the 'Copy' techniques, LocoScript highlights the section of text you are marking out.

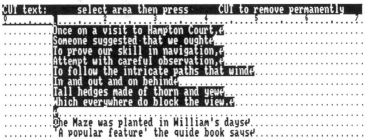

When the cursor is correctly positioned, press ⌑CUT again. LocoScript then removes the highlighted text from the screen.

The text you have just deleted has gone for good.

Finally...

That's looked at the major types of editing changes you can do with LocoScript. In later sessions, we look at more subtle changes you can make to your documents – by using different types of characters and by laying the text out in special ways on the page.

Finish this session by pressing EXIT and then selecting the Abandon Edit option as at the end of Session 5 – so that you can come back and work through this session later as if for the first time.

Session summary

In this session, you have seen:

- How to duplicate a section of your text once or many times
- How to move a section of text from one place in the document to another
- How to delete a block of text
- That starting with ⌑CUT is much less safe!

Session 7

Keeping your discs organised

It is very easy to create document after document with no clear scheme suggesting the disc you store them on, the groups you keep them in or the names you give your documents. The result is rather like stuffing sheets of paper into drawers. While you don't have many sheets of paper, it is quite possible to find the one you want, but the moment your drawers start to get full, it is a hopeless task finding anything.

The solution with the drawers is to tidy them up, grouping together some sheets of paper and moving others to a different drawer. Similarly, the solution to your problem with discs is also to tidy them up. You can work a lot more efficiently:

- if you use different discs for different types of documents, rather like you would use the different drawers of a filing cabinet
- if you use the different groups on a disc like you would use different folders within the filing cabinet
- if you give your discs, groups and documents names that help you remember what information they contain.

In this session, we shall show you:

- how to get new discs ready for use
- how to move documents to a different disc or a different group
- how to produce copies of documents
- how to get rid of documents you no longer need
- how to give discs, groups and documents names, and
- how to set up and inspect a short description of a document

These are the basic tools that enable you to keep your discs organised.

We shall also show you how to make back-up copies of your more important discs – to keep in case of accidents, like someone spilling coffee over the disc.

Every operation in this session is carried out on the Disc Manager Screen – that is, the screen on which the names of your documents are displayed. Display this screen now. (If you are not sure how to do this, turn to page 21.)

For most of the operations, we will be using the three Disc Manager menus called Disc, File and Group. The Disc menu for all the operations involving the whole disc; the Group menu for operations on a whole group; and the File menu for operations on individual documents. As always, the keys that you need to press to bring these menus onto the screen are displayed on the Information lines at the top of the screen.

8812

About discs

First, a brief note about the discs you use in your PCW.

Earlier in this tutorial, we happily created some new documents without worrying about how much room these would take up on the Examples disc and whether there was enough space on the disc for them. In fact, each disc you have can only hold so much information, specified by its capacity. The discs used in Drive A of 8000 series machines ('Normal-capacity' CF2 discs) can only hold up to 180k of information though not quite all can be used for documents. However, the discs used in Drive B of those machines ('High-capacity' CF2 or CF2DD discs) and the discs used in 9000 series machines can hold up to 720k of information. (1k of information is roughly equivalent to 1000 characters – or about 18 lines of text – so you can get about 90 pages of A4 on a 180k 'Normal-capacity' disc.)

When the Disc Manager Screen is displayed, you can gauge the capacity of your discs (and the Memory disc, Drive M:) at the top of each box summarising the contents of your drives. Also displayed here is the amount of storage space on the disc that is already being used to store files and documents and the amount of free space on the disc. If you look down at where the documents are listed you can see how big each document is, because each entry is followed by its size as some number of k. For example, the size of PCWINFO is given as 12k.

It's always important to be aware of how much free space there is on each disc you use. Otherwise you can waste a lot of time and go through a lot of unnecessary trauma trying to create a document or to store a copy of a document on a disc when there isn't enough room for it.

You also need to be aware of the amount of free space that is available on the disc when you edit a document. Although your edited document replaces the current one on disc, for safety, the new version is stored **before** the old version is deleted – so you have to have enough free space on the disc for the new version **before** you start editing the document.

Preparing a new blank disc

The first thing you need when you are re-organising your discs is a number of new discs ready to have documents stored on them.

Before anything can be stored on a new disc, it has to be 'Formatted': that is, the storage area on each side of the disc you want to use has to be marked out electronically. New discs are not marked out ready for use and so they have to be formatted before you can use them to store documents. If you have just bought a number of new discs, you might like to format all of these now – so that they will be ready for use as Data discs whenever you want.

The procedure is as follows. If you have a new blank disc available, then use the instructions to format this disc now.

Start by taking out the discs currently in the disc drive(s) and putting them to one side. The reason for doing this is one of safety. It is unfortunately very easy – even for experienced users – to format a disc that you didn't mean to, and the trouble with formatting a disc by accident is that it is wiped clean of all the data that was stored on it. Anything that was stored on a disc cannot be recovered after the disc has been formatted.

Now bring the Disc menu onto the screen by pressing  [f2] ([SHIFT]+[f1]). The Disc menu is a 'Commands' menu which, you will remember, means that the action that is carried out when you press [ENTER] is the one picked out by the arrow. The action LocoScript pre-selects for you is Copy disc whereas the option you want here is Format disc. So before you press [ENTER] you must move the Menu cursor (and hence the arrow) to Format disc. Then press [ENTER]: what happens next depends on whether you have one or two disc drives on your PCW.

Single-drive system

The first thing that happens is that you see a message on the screen checking that you want to go ahead – because if you format the wrong disc by accident, you lose all the information that you have stored on that disc. To continue with the format, press [+] to select the Format disc in Drive A option and then press [ENTER].

Next you see a message telling you to insert your new disc. Check that the Write-protect hole(s) in the top corner of the disc is closed and then insert the new disc into the disc drive. (On an 8000 series machine, you need to insert this disc with the side you want to format to the left.) Now press [ENTER] again. The PCW then marks out the storage area on the disc. A message on the screen tells you how this is progressing. This message counts the tracks on the disc as these are marked out. When it has finished, you will see the following message:

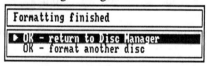

On a 9000 series machine, your disc is now fully formatted and you can simply press [ENTER] to 'Return to Disc Manager' at this point. But if you have a PCW8256, you need to move the Menu cursor to format another disc and press [ENTER] – because you now need to format Side 2. When the message telling you to insert the new disc appears, insert this disc with Side 2 to the left and press [ENTER].

This time when the message appears asking if you want to format another, leave the Menu cursor on return to Disc Manager and press [ENTER]. This returns you to the Disc Manager Screen. The new disc is now ready for use.

LocoScript 2 User Guide: Tutorial

Two-drive system

The first thing that happens is that you see a message on the screen checking that you really want to format the disc and, on an 8000 machine, asking you which type of disc you want to produce – a 180k disc for Drive A or a 720k disc for Drive B. What we shall do here is to format your new disc in Drive B, so move the Menu cursor to the Drive B option and press [ENTER]. You then see a message telling you to insert your new disc in Drive B. Check that the Write-protect hole(s) in the top corners of the disc are closed and then insert the new disc in Drive B. Now press [ENTER] again.

As the PCW marks out the storage area on both sides of the disc, you will see a message on the screen recording its progress. The message counts through each track as it is marked out. When it has finished, you will see a message asking whether you want to format another (illustrated on the previous page). When this message appears, leave the Menu cursor on Return to disc manager and press [ENTER]. This returns you to the Disc Manager Screen. The new disc is now ready for use.

Copying, moving and erasing documents

Much of the process of tidying up a disc involves making copies that you store on different disc or in a different group; moving documents from one place to another, either to a different disc or to a different group on the same disc; and erasing documents you no longer want.

Although these seem three very different actions, they are in fact very similar. In each case you pick out a document and tell LocoScript to make a copy of it and/or erase it. (Moving a document is making a copy and then erasing the original document.)

As a result, the steps involved in copying, moving and erasing documents are very similar. You start by using the File cursor to pick out the document you want to manipulate; then you press [f3] to bring the File menu onto the screen and select the action you want from this menu.

If the action you choose involves making a copy of the document, you then pick out the group you want to store the copy in (See 'Picking out a group' on page 42). Finally, LocoScript puts up a summary of the action you have picked out so that you can confirm everything is correct before it goes ahead.

To show you how this works, we shall now Copy, Move and Erase some documents on your Examples disc. If necessary, replace the disc in Drive A by your Examples disc. (Remember to press [f7] to tell LocoScript that you have changed the disc.)

9108

Note: If you have an 8000 series PCW with two disc drives, you need to be careful about which discs you use in which drive while manipulating documents:

- 'High-capacity' discs can only be used in Drive B (the high-capacity drive)
- 'Normal-capacity' discs can be **copied from** either drive but can only be **copied to** or **erased from** Drive A (the normal-capacity drive)

If you try using a disc in the wrong type of drive, you will see an Alert message telling you that this action isn't possible.

Copying a document

There are a number of reasons why you might want a second copy of a document:

- you might want a back-up copy as a safety precaution, or
- it might be more convenient to have a copy of a particular document on two different discs, or
- you might want a copy of one document as the starting point for a new document. It is often easier to edit the copy of an existing document than to start from scratch.

The first step is make sure that both the disc holding the document (the Source disc) and the disc on which you are going to store the copy (the Destination disc) are in your machine. This is not always possible on a single-drive machine: everything is fine when you want to make the copy on the same disc or on Drive M – but when you want to copy between discs, there is a special procedure to follow (see below).

What we are going to do here is make a second copy of DOCUMENT.000 (the document you created in Session 2) on the Examples disc. This makes the copy very straightforward because the same disc is both the Source disc and the Destination disc. Put this disc in Drive A. (Remember to press [f7] after changing discs.)

Now move the File cursor to the document you want to copy – ie. to DOCUMENT.000 on Drive A. (This document will be in group 0, if you followed our earlier instructions correctly.) When the File cursor is over the document name, press [f3] to bring the File menu onto the screen.

The File menu is another 'Commands' menu and the Copy file action is selected for you. Tell LocoScript this is the action you want by pressing [ENTER]. LocoScript then puts up a message, both in the middle of the screen and on the third Information line, telling you to pick out the group you want to store the copy in – the Destination group:

```
Pick destination:

select group and drive
then press ENTER
or CAN to abandon
```

Use [SHIFT] with the Cursor keys to move the Group cursor to this group. In our example case, you want to move the cursor to group 2 on Drive A. The message in the middle of the screen instantly disappears so that you can see what you are doing. When the Group cursor is over the right group, press [ENTER]. LocoScript then puts up a menu summarising the copying operation you have picked out.

Check the details on this menu carefully and, if necessary, correct them before pressing [ENTER] – or press [CAN] to abandon the copy. (Move the Menu cursor to the line of the menu you want to change and then edit the details on that line)

When you press [ENTER], LocoScript first checks whether there is already a file with this name in the Destination group. If there isn't, LocoScript goes ahead and copies the document but if there is, it puts up the following Alert message telling you this:

Replace with the new file is selected for you because, in most cases, this will be what you want. However, you should only select this option if you are sure you don't want this other version – because LocoScript has to delete the existing file before it can make the copy.

If you don't want to lose the old file, select Choose another name and press [ENTER]. You then get the chance to pick out the group and the name for the new file all over again. If you don't want to make the copy after all, select Cancel operation and press [ENTER]: LocoScript returns you to the Disc Manager Screen.

Copying between floppy discs on a single-drive machine

If you only have a single-drive machine and you want to store a copy of a document on a different disc, you have

– first to copy the document to one of the groups on Drive M, the Memory disc

– then replace the disc in the drive with your second disc and press [f7], and finally

– copy the document on Drive M to this second disc

There isn't any way of copying directly between two discs on a single-drive machine because direct copying needs both the Source disc and the Destination disc in the machine at the same time.

Moving a document

Moving documents from one place to another – either to a different disc or to a different group on the same disc – is a very powerful tool in re-organising your discs. To show the steps involved, we will now move SESSION.3, the document you created in Session 3, to the Memory disc (Drive M).

Again, you need to start by checking that both the Source disc and the Destination disc are in your machine. Here the Source disc is your Examples disc: this should be in Drive A. The Destination disc in this case is the Memory disc, which is automatically in Drive M. (Remember to press [f7] if you change discs.)

Now pick out the document you want to move (SESSION.3 in this case) with the

File cursor – exactly as you did above to copy a document. When the File cursor is over the document name, bring the File menu onto the screen by pressing ⬚f3⬚.

This time the option you want is Move file – so select this option with the Menu cursor and press ⬚ENTER⬚. LocoScript then puts up a message telling you to pick out the group you want to move the document to – again, exactly as it did when you were copying a document.

Move the Group cursor to this group (group 0 on Drive M in our example case). When the Group cursor is over the right group, press ⬚ENTER⬚ (again, exactly as for copy). LocoScript then puts up a menu summarising the move you want to make.

Check (and if necessary correct) the details on this menu and then press ⬚ENTER⬚ – or ⬚CAN⬚ to abandon the move. Because the first part of the operation is making the new copy, LocoScript first checks whether there is already a file with the same name in the Destination group. If there is such a file, you will see the Alert message we told you about earlier in the section on copying – offering you the choice of cancelling the operation or replacing the existing file with the new copy. If there isn't a file with the same name, LocoScript simply goes ahead and moves the document.

Note: To move a document between two floppy discs on a single-drive machine, you need to

– move the document to one of the groups on Drive M, the Memory disc – as described above

– replace the disc in the drive with your second disc and press ⬚f7⬚, and finally

– move or copy the document on Drive M to this second disc

After you have moved a document to Drive M, you should immediately copy it to another disc. If you don't, you risk losing this document altogether when you switch off or reset your PCW – or when there is a sudden power cut.

Erasing a document

Another important part of tidying up is to erase documents and files you no longer need – such as one of the copies of DOCUMENT.000.

Of course, you must be certain that you don't need a document or file before you decide to delete it. If you are at all unsure about whether you need a file, leave it alone – because the chances are that you will need it after all. This applies in particular to files on Drive M and on your Start-of-day disc: if you don't know about these files, don't delete them because they are probably important to LocoScript.

Once again, the steps are very like those of copying or moving a document:

First check that the disc holding the document you want to get rid of is in your machine; then pick out the document you want to delete (DOCUMENT.000) with the File cursor. Press ⬚f3⬚ to bring the File menu onto the screen and select the Erase file option.

This time when you press [ENTER], LocoScript puts up a menu giving details of the document you have picked out – to give you the chance to confirm that you picked out the right one. As always, check (and if necessary correct) the details on this menu before pressing [ENTER] – or press [CAN] to abandon the action.

LocoScript removes the document from the list of documents on your disc – but it doesn't actually erase it from the disc altogether. Instead, it puts the document into a state of 'Limbo' – as a 'Limbo file' – and it stays in Limbo until the space on the disc it is occupying is needed for another document.

Because moving a document is a combination of copying the document and deleting it, LocoScript also leaves in Limbo a copy of any document you move to a different disc.

LocoScript has this Limbo state for documents as a safety net for you – so that you have the chance of recovering a document that you throw away by accident or lose in the process of moving it (eg. because you moved it to Drive M but forgot to move it onto another disc). The previous version of any document you edit is also held in Limbo on the source disc.

Recovering a document from Limbo

When you realise that you have thrown away the wrong document, you need to recover it from Limbo as soon as possible. The longer you wait, the more likely it becomes that LocoScript has removed the document completely in order to make room for some other document. LocoScript never erases any document unless you ask it to, but it will remove files from Limbo – oldest first – if it needs to.

To recover the document, you should first get the Disc Manager Screen to display Limbo files. This is achieved through the Options menu. To bring this onto the screen, press [f8] ([SHIFT]+[f7]). This menu is a Settings menu and so works in the same way as the Options menu that's used to display extra information when you are editing a document (see Session 5). Both entries refer to extra information that can be displayed on the Disc Manager Screen and when there is a tick beside an entry, this information will be displayed.

You have already been introduced to what Limbo files are. LocoScript's Hidden files are files on your Start-of-day disc that hold the LocoScript 2 program and data that the program needs to run. You won't have any Hidden files on your Data discs. (You may also have some 'System' files on the Start-of-day disc and on Drive M: these files are also counted as Hidden files but their details are never displayed.)

You also 'set' and 'clear' the entries in the same way – pressing [+] to set an option, [-] to clear it, or the Space bar to 'toggle' between 'set' and 'clear'. (For details, see Session 4.) So to display Limbo files, put the Menu cursor on Show Limbo files and press [+] – and then press [ENTER] to tell LocoScript to go ahead. LocoScript then rewrites the screen, this time listing all Limbo files as well.

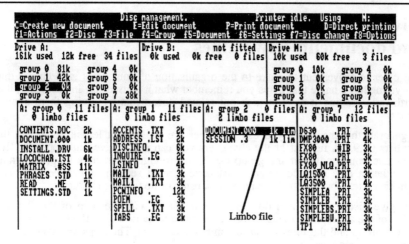

Move the File cursor to the document you want to recover. It will still have its original name. So to recover the document we have just thrown away, move the File cursor to the entry DOCUMENT.000 lim.

Now press ⬜ to bring the File menu onto the screen. Select Recover from Limbo and press ⬜. LocoScript now puts up a menu giving details of the Limbo file you have picked out and the name it will have when it is recovered. Normally, this will be the old name but if there is another document of this name in the group, LocoScript will leave the name blank for you to type in a new name.

Check the details in this menu are correct before pressing ⬜. LocoScript then brings your document back from Limbo.

Deleting a Limbo file

If a document contains confidential information, you might not want to leave it in Limbo after it has been erased – simply because it would be so easy for someone else to recover it. Instead, you will want to erase the document fully.

Suppose, you now wanted to get rid of DOCUMENT.000 completely. First delete the document in the normal way, as described above: this makes DOCUMENT.000 a Limbo file again. Then display Limbo files, point with the File cursor to the Limbo file you want to delete, and delete the Limbo file by using the Erase option of the File menu as before.

LocoScript then erases the document completely: it can't now be recovered.

Giving discs, groups and documents new names

The other improvement to make to the organisation of your discs is to ensure that everything has a name that helps you remember what it is used for. In particular, it is worthwhile making it easy to pick out related documents by giving them similar names.

In general, the characters you use in names are the capital letters A...Z and the numbers 0...9. (A full list of the characters you can use is given in Appendix III.) The name you choose for the group can be up to eight characters long; the name for either a disc or a document must have a main section of between one and eight characters, but it can also have an extension of up to three characters.

You give discs, groups and documents new names with the help of the Rename option of the appropriate menu (ie. the Disc menu to name a disc, the Group menu to name a group and the Files menu to name a document). The steps you take in each case are very similar:

- You start by picking out the item you want to name with the Group and File cursors. In the case of naming a disc, this means checking that the Group cursor is over one of the groups on this disc; for the group and the document, you have to point specifically at the one you want to name.
- When the cursor is in place, bring the appropriate menu onto the screen.
- Select the Rename option and press [ENTER]
- Type in the new name in the slot at the top of the Selection menu that appears; check the remaining details and press [ENTER]

The item you picked out is then given the new name.

To show this in operation, we shall now give your Examples disc the name TUTORIAL; then call the first group on this disc EXERCISE; and finally change the name of the remaining copy of DOCUMENT.000 to SESSION2.DOC

Note: In all cases, you need to have the disc you want to work on in its appropriate disc drive – ie. make sure you put a 'normal-capacity' disc in Drive A but a 'high-capacity' disc in Drive B.

Naming the disc

To name your Examples disc, insert this in Drive A (remember to press [f7] to tell LocoScript if you change the disc); then put the Group cursor on any one of the groups on this disc. Press [f2] ([SHIFT]+[f1]) to bring the Disc menu onto the screen.

Move the Menu cursor to the last option – Rename Disc. Press [ENTER]. LocoScript then displays a short menu containing a slot for the disc's new name. Type the new name for the disc – TUTORIAL in this case.

Don't worry about typing the name in capitals (LocoScript automatically converts any lower case letters you type into capitals) but do correct any mistakes before pressing [ENTER].

Pressing [ENTER] names the disc. Now, whenever this disc is put in the drive, you will be able to tell which disc it is just by looking beside the drive name at the top of the Disc Manager Screen. (It's a good idea to write this name on the disc label as well.)

Disc name —

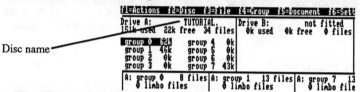

Naming a group

Move the Group cursor to group 0 on Drive A – the group that's going to be given a name. When the Group cursor is in position, press [f4] ([SHIFT]+[f3]) to bring the Group menu onto the screen. Select Rename and press [ENTER]. LocoScript then displays a short menu containing a slot for the group's new name.

With the Menu cursor on the name slot, type the new name for the group – EXERCISE in this case. Again, you don't have to worry about typing in capital letters. Check all the details and then press [ENTER]. This gives the group the new name – as you can see both where the contents of the disc are summarised and at the top of the column showing the names of the documents in this group.

Note: To clear a group name, move the Group cursor to this group, select Erase file in the f3 menu, type the name *group-name*.GRP in the Selection menu that appears and press [ENTER]

Group name —

Renaming a document

Move the File cursor over the remaining DOCUMENT.000 and press [f3] to bring the Files menu onto the screen. Select Rename file and press [ENTER]. LocoScript now puts up a menu containing a slot for the new name.

With the Menu cursor on the new name slot, type in SESSION2.DOC – the new name for the document. Once again, you don't need to worry about typing this in capitals. Check that the name you have typed and all the other details are right and then press [ENTER]. The document is now renamed.

LocoScript 2 User Guide: Tutorial   **85**

Short descriptions of documents

The name of a document should give you some idea of what it contains, but on many systems you can only find out more by editing the document and having a look at it that way. With LocoScript, you have another option – which is to set up a short description of the document – known as the Identity text – which you can 'Inspect' from the Disc Manager Screen. (You can also edit this text while you are working on the document itself, by selecting the Edit Identity option in the f1 Actions menu.)

Setting up the description

Suppose you wanted to set up a description of PCWINFO. To do this, you pick out the document with the File cursor and then press ⌈f5⌉ to bring a new menu – the Document menu – onto the screen.

This is another of LocoScript 2's 'Commands' menus and the option we want here is Inspect document. This should be pre-selected for you (with the arrow beside it), so all you need to do now is press ⌈ENTER⌉. You then get a further menu on the screen.

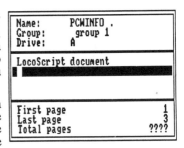

The job of this menu is to show you information about the document. The part of the menu we are interested in is the section in the middle – or, more specifically, the three blank lines. These are the lines on which you can set up your description.

Each line of the description can hold up to 30 characters and each line is set up separately. So you need to plan your description as three pieces of text, each up to 30 characters long. For example, as the description of PCWINFO, you might have:

        Fundamental information on

        using the AMSTRAD PCW

To set up this description, you move the Menu cursor first to the top of these three lines and type Fundamental information on; then press ⌈RETURN⌉ to move the Menu cursor to the second line and type using the AMSTRAD PCW. You have now set up the description: simply press ⌈ENTER⌉ to tell LocoScript to remember it. LocoScript clears away the menu and returns you to the Disc Manager Screen.

Note: Not all the characters that you can type using LocoScript 2 can be used in this description in particular, you cannot use any Cyrillic characters or many of the Mathematical symbols. A list of the characters you can use is given on page 274.

Inspecting the description

To look at the description you have just set up, you pick out the document (PCWINFO) with the File cursor and then press ⌐f5⌐ to bring the Document menu onto the screen as before. Again, the option we want is Inspect document, so all you should need to do now is press ⌐ENTER⌐. As before, you now see information about the document you picked out – but this time, you also see the description you set up.

Making back-up copies of discs

As well as keeping your discs organised, it is important to ensure you have a reserve – or 'back-up' – copy of every document you care about losing. This back-up copy should always be on a different disc in case the disc is damaged, eg. by someone scratching the disc.

The most straightforward way of making such back-ups is to make a copy of the whole disc on another disc – ie. a second disc with exactly the same information on it.

You have, in fact, already worked through all the steps involved in making a copy of a disc. During the preparatory session, you copied the supplied LocoScript 2 disc onto a new disc in order to make your Examples disc. So instead of giving full details here, we shall just give an outline of the steps you need to follow – because you can always turn back to pages 4 – 5 for a detailed explanation of what is going on.

1 Take out the discs currently in the disc drive(s) and put them to one side.

2 Check that the Write-protect holes on the disc you want to copy are **open** but the ones on the disc you want to make the copy on are **closed**.

3 Bring the Disc menu onto the screen by pressing ⌐f2⌐(⌐SHIFT⌐+⌐f1⌐).

4 Check that Copy disc is selected, then press ⌐ENTER⌐ to tell LocoScript to go ahead.

What happens next depends on whether you have a single-drive machine or a two-drive system – and, if you have an 8000 machine, on whether you want to copy a 'normal-capacity' disc or a 'high-capacity' disc.

Single-drive systems

On a single-drive system, you can only ever copy one type of disc and you only have one disc drive in which to copy it – so LocoScript doesn't have to ask you which type of disc you want to copy. It is also inevitable that the process of copying the disc will be carried out in a number of stages, each stage requiring you to first put in the disc you want to copy (the 'Source disc') and then replacing this disc by the disc you want to make the copy on (the 'Destination disc').

LocoScript first puts up a message checking that you want to go ahead and copy a disc. (This is a safety precaution against accidentally copying the wrong disc). Select the Copy disc option and press ⌐ENTER⌐. LocoScript then starts displaying messages prompting you to insert the 'Source disc' and then the 'Destination disc'.

All you have to do is insert the discs when prompted (with the correct side of the disc to the left if you have an 8000 machine) and then press [ENTER] when you are ready for LocoScript to go ahead. Messages on the screen keep you informed of how the copy is progressing, by telling you which track is being written or read at the moment. These messages also tell you which stage of the copy you are at. Finally, when all the stages have been completed, LocoScript puts up another message asking you whether you want to copy another.

If, for example, you are working on an 8000 series machine and you want to copy the second side of the disc, select Copy another and press [ENTER]. If you don't want to copy any more, select Return to Disc Manager and press [ENTER].

Two-drive systems

On a two-drive system, LocoScript starts by displaying a message checking that you want to go ahead and copy a disc, and asking you about the copy operation you want to carry out. The details of the steps you should take depend on the type of disc you want to copy and the type of machine you are working on.

Copying a 180k disc: Select Copy 180k disc and press [ENTER]; you then see a message prompting you to insert the 'Source disc' in Drive B and the 'Destination disc' in Drive A. Insert the discs as specified in the message, with the side of the disc you want to copy to the left. Then press [ENTER] when you are ready for LocoScript to go ahead. LocoScript then copies the entire side of the disc. When it has finished, you see a message asking you whether you want to copy another disc.

If you want to copy, for example, the second side of the disc, select Copy another and press [ENTER]: LocoScript then takes you through all the stages of copying another side of a disc. If you don't want to copy any more, select Return to Disc Manager and press [ENTER].

Copying a 720k disc on an 8000 series machine: Copying a 720k disc on an 8000 machine uses Drive B both to read the original disc and to write the new disc – and the copy is made in a number of stages, each stage requiring you first to put in the disc you want to copy (the 'Source disc') and then to replace this disc by the disc you want to make the copy on (the 'Destination disc'). Select Copy 720k disc and press [ENTER]. LocoScript then starts displaying messages telling you to insert the 'Source disc' and then the 'Destination disc'.

All you have to do is insert the discs in Drive B when prompted, always with Side 1 to the left, and then press [ENTER] when you are ready for LocoScript to go ahead. Messages on the screen keep you informed of how the copy is progressing, by telling you which track is being written or read at the moment (Track numbers 0...159). These messages also tell you which stage of the copy you are at.

In this case, LocoScript copies the whole disc. So when LocoScript puts up its message asking you whether you want to copy another, only select the Copy another option if you have another 720k disc you want to copy. Otherwise, select Return to Disc Manager and press [ENTER].

Copying a 720k disc on an 9000 series machine: Select the Copy disc option and press [ENTER]; you then see a message prompting you to insert the 'Source disc' in Drive B and the 'Destination disc' in Drive A. Insert the discs as specified in the message, then press [ENTER] when you are ready for LocoScript to go ahead. LocoScript then copies the entire disc.

When it has finished, you will see a message asking you whether you want to copy another disc. Only select Copy another if you have another disc that you want to copy. Otherwise, select Return to Disc Manager and press [ENTER].

Note: You never need to format a new blank disc before you make a copy of a disc onto it. The disc is automatically formatted as part of the process of copying the disc.

Using the Disc Manager
while editing a document

Occasionally, you will need access to the Disc Manager Screen while you are editing a document – so to finish this session, we shall show you how this is done.

Start by opening one of the Example documents for editing – say, LSINFO – using the same steps as you used at the beginning of Session 5. Now press [f1] to bring the Actions menu on the screen. (You can see that [f1] is the key to press by looking at the second Information line.)

We used this menu briefly in Session 6 to see what Blocks were set up. This time, we want to select Disc manager.

The menu is a 'Commands' menu – which, you will remember, means that the command LocoScript carries out when you press [ENTER] is the one picked out by the arrow. You move the arrow to the option you want by moving the Menu cursor, so move this to Disc manager and then press [ENTER]. Do this now.

LocoScript displays the Disc Manager Screen and gives you access to all the Disc Manager menus, as you can see by looking at the Information lines. But it hasn't abandoned work on the document you are editing – it has just put it on one side for the moment, as you can confirm from the top Information line which has the message A:group 1/LSINFO. Disc management whilst editing

You can now carry out most of the actions that you normally carry out from the Disc Manager Screen – such as the Copying, Moving, Deleting and Renaming actions that we have been looking at in this session of the tutorial. You can even start printing one of your other documents.

However, a number of actions won't be possible. In particular, you can't edit another

---

document and you can't do anything that directly affects the document you are currently editing. You can't, for example, copy it, move it, rename it or print it and you must not remove the disc holding this document from the drive and replace it by another. If you need to move documents off this disc onto another (for example, to make some more space on the disc) and you have a single-drive machine, you must move these initially to Drive M and only move them to your other disc once you have finished editing the document.

When you have finished using the Disc Manager, press [EXIT]. LocoScript then returns you to the document you were editing.

Session summary

In this session, you have seen how to do all the actions involved in keeping the documents on your discs organised and easy to find:

- How to get a new disc ready for use
- How to move a document from one disc or group to another
- How to generate a second copy of a document either on the same disc or on another disc
- How to get rid of unwanted documents
- How to get back a document you erased by accident
- How to give discs, groups and documents names that will help you remember what they are used to store
- How to make back-up copies of discs that contain valuable information
- How to use the Disc Manager without finishing work on the document you are editing

9108

Session 8

Indenting, centring and justifying

So far in this tutorial, we have seen how to put text into a document and how to change the text once it is there – and we have seen how LocoScript always ensures that your documents are perfectly laid out.

But changing the words in a document and tidying up the result, impressive though that is, is only one of the ways in which a word processor like LocoScript can process your text for you. In this session, we shall look at the way LocoScript can give your work an even more professional look through

- indenting lines and paragraphs
- positioning headings and other single lines centrally or over to the right
- justifying text – that is, giving it a straight righthand edge as well as a straight lefthand edge

The document we are going to edit in this session is stored as TABS.EG in group 1 of your Examples disc. So the first thing to do is to pick out this document with the File cursor and then open it for editing. (Turn to Session 5 if you are not sure how to do this.)

Indenting lines and paragraphs

There are three effects that you can produce through indenting – ie. through moving the lefthand edge of a line or paragraph away from the left margin of your page:

- paragraphs with the first line indented
- paragraphs in which all the lines are indented from the left margin
- 'labelled' paragraphs – for example, paragraphs numbered 1), 2), 3)

Indenting the first line

This is the simplest possible way of indenting a paragraph.

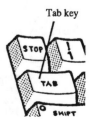

Tab key

The first step is to move the Text cursor to the beginning of the paragraph you want to indent. For example, move the Text cursor to the beginning of the first paragraph of our example document. Then press TAB.

8809

Immediately, a → symbol appears at the start of a new line, inserted above the current line. Then when you press [RELAY], the paragraph is relaid with all the characters on the first line shifted to the right.

The special character you have inserted is called a Simple tab – and its effect is exactly the same as that of a tab on a typewriter. Like ↵, it is one of the special symbols that are never printed but you can choose to display on the screen through the Options menu ([f8] – see Session 5).

If you look at the Ruler line at the top of the screen, you will see that the beginning of the line is now immediately below the first → symbol on this line. This symbol marks the first tab position.

```
                      Advantages of a Word Processor↵
                      ↵
                   →     Where are lots of other jobs that you will want your word-processor to
                   help you with. If you are a Secretary of a club, then you will want your
                   word-processor to help you circulate details of forthcoming events or
                   copies of the club newsletter to members. Or if you are preparing a report
                   on something, then you will probably have one or more tables to prepare. Or
```

Now press [TAB] again. Another Simple tab is inserted in the document and, this time when you relay the paragraph, the first line of the paragraph becomes indented to the second position marked by a → symbol – ie. to the second tab position.

No other line of the paragraph or of any other paragraph is affected – as you can see if you press [PAGE] (which, you will remember, forces LocoScript to relay down to the bottom of the page).

Indenting the whole paragraph

When you want to indent a whole paragraph, you again start by moving the Text cursor to the beginning of the paragraph and again you want to press [TAB] – but this time you need to hold down the [ALT] key as you press [TAB].

To see how this works, move the Text cursor to the beginning of the second paragraph, hold down the [ALT] key and press [TAB]. Immediately, another of the special characters – the → symbol – appears at the start of the line. Now press [PAGE] to see what effect inserting this character has had.

Again, all the characters on the first line of this paragraph have shifted to the right, and again this is the only paragraph to be affected. But now the beginning of every line of this paragraph is at the first tab position.

```
                   you might have some sales literature to prepare, which you want to lay out
                   and style really nicely. ↵
                   ↵
                 →     With LocoScript 2, there's essentially endless scope for revising and
                   styling your text - so much so that you might get so carried away with
                   producing the perfect document that you never actually get around to
                   printing it! ↵
                   ↵
                   Moreover, because you can save your work on disc any time you like:↵
```

The special character you have inserted is known as an 'Indent Tab' and whichever tab position it 'points' to is used as the lefthand margin for the rest of the paragraph. This means that you can pick out any of your current set of tab positions as the temporary lefthand margin. The last Tab you type to take the start of the paragraph to your chosen tab position must be an Indent tab but the rest can be either Indent tabs or Simple tabs.

To see this, move the Text cursor to the first letter of the first paragraph (ie. after the Simple tabs) and hold down [ALT] and press [TAB] again to insert an Indent tab. Press [RELAY]. Each line of the paragraph now begins at the third tab position.

'Labelled' paragraphs

This looks the most complex type of indenting but, in fact, it is no more complicated than indenting the whole paragraph. We shall demonstrate this using the fourth paragraph, which you see has already been numbered.

Move the Text cursor to the beginning of the text that follows the 'label' – ie. the 1). Insert an Indent tab by holding down [ALT] and pressing [TAB]. Now press [RELAY]: the rest of the paragraph is then indented to this tab position.

> Moreover, because you can save your work on disc any time you like:↵
>
> 1)ₕ You can start and stop work on a document at will; you don't have to finish somewhere that is easy to carry on from – like the bottom of a page – as on a typewriter.↵
>
> 2)↳ You can make copies of the document stored on disc – making it very

Once again, what you are doing is using the tab position the Indent tab points to as the lefthand margin for the rest of the paragraph.

• All these actions have used tab positions already set into our example document. You will see how to set and adjust tab positions in Session 11.

Positioning single lines

Lines are normally positioned so that they start at the left side of your page. This is only one of the places you might want to put a line; you might, for example, want to centre a heading or to right align the lines of the address at the top of a letter.

With LocoScript, you can:

- centre the line between the margins
- right align the line, ie. put the righthand end of the line on the right margin (instead of the lefthand end on the left margin)
- combine all three on the same line, ie. a section over to the left, a section in the middle and a section over to the right

9108

You position lines in these different ways by using a couple of the options in the Layout menu (or by using some special keystrokes that we will come to in the next session).

Centring a line

To centre a line, you move the Text cursor to the beginning of the line and then tell LocoScript to centre it.

For example, the very first line of the example document is a heading. To centre this heading between the margins, move the Text cursor to the start of the heading – ie. to the A of Advantages of a Word Processor. Now press ⌐f2¬ to bring the Layout menu onto the screen.

Move the Menu cursor to Centre and press ⌐ENTER¬. Instantly, the whole line moves right until it is neatly positioned midway between the margins.

```
⌐⌐⌐⌐.....?....?....?....?.█........'........'........'..........⁄.........'...⌐⌐
                         Advantages of a Word Processorↄ
   ↲
   → There are lots of other jobs that you will want your word-processor to
help you with. If you are a Secretary of a club, then you will want your
word-processor to help you circulate details of forthcoming events or
copies of the club newsletter to members. Or if you are preparing a report
```

The Centre option is only for use on single lines. To see what happens when you use the Centre option at the beginning of a paragraph, move the Text cursor to the last paragraph and tell LocoScript to centre this. (Press ⌐f2¬ and then ⌐ENTER¬ as before). Now press ⌐RELAY¬ to relay the paragraph. As you see, only the first line is centred.

Moving a line over to the right

Moving a line over to the right is very like centring it: you move the Text cursor to the beginning of the line and then tell LocoScript to 'right align' it.

At the end of the example document is a name. To show you how to move lines over to the right, we shall 'right align' this name.

To start, move the Text cursor to the beginning of the name Fred Smith. Now press ⌐f2¬ to bring the Layout menu onto the screen again. This time the option you want is Right align. When you press ⌐ENTER¬ this time, the name jumps to the righthand side of the screen. Notice how the h of Smith now touches the right margin.

The Right Align option, like the Centre option, is only for use on single lines.

Positioning different parts of the same line

As well as centring and right aligning whole lines, you can centre and right align sections of a line, giving you effects like:

```
Author              Title                Cost
```

All you have to do to achieve such results is move the Text cursor to the beginning of the section of the line you want in the middle of the page and tell LocoScript to Centre everything to the right of this position – exactly as you did before. Then you move the Text cursor to the beginning of the part of the line you want over to the right and tell LocoScript to Right align the end section of the line – again, exactly as before.

You can similarly split lines into a section over to the left and a section over to the right – or a section over to the left and a centred section. What won't give sensible results is telling LocoScript to move a section of a line over to the right and then telling it to centre part of that section because this is meaningless.

Note: Once you have told LocoScript to centre or to align some text or, for that matter, to indent a paragraph, it remembers this – whatever changes you make to the line (correcting a spelling mistake, for example). This is by no means true of all the word-processors you might meet.

Justifying text

The final enhancement we look at in this session is 'Justification' – that is, giving your text both a straight righthand edge and a straight lefthand edge, by expanding all the spaces between the words. Justifying text instantly makes it look very professional – not least because it is impossible to do on a typewriter. The majority of the text in this user guide is justified.

Justified text

Justified text has both a straight righthand edge and a straight lefthand edge. It gets this by expanding all the spaces between the words. Justifying text instantly makes it look very professional – not least because it is impossible to do on a typewriter.

Unjustified text

Unjustified text is text with a ragged righthand edge. At the moment, all the text in the example document has a ragged righthand edge.

At the moment, all the text in the example document has a ragged righthand edge. In other words, it is unjustified. Suppose, for example, that this was exactly what you wanted for the first paragraph and the last – but between these you wanted the text to be justified. To arrange this, you again use the Layout menu – but this time you need the Justification option. You probably noticed an option called Set justification earlier when you were using the menu to centre and to right align lines.

Start by moving the Text cursor to the beginning of the text you want to justify – in this case, that means moving it to the beginning of the second paragraph. Then press ⌐f2⌐ to bring the Layout menu onto the screen.

Move the Menu cursor (and the arrow) to Set justification and press ⌐ENTER⌐ to tell LocoScript to do this. Now move the Text cursor down the document and you will see that it now justifies every line, giving you a nice straight edge. Stop when you get to the beginning of the last paragraph and press ⌐f2⌐. This time the Layout menu appears with a difference – Clear justification instead of Set justification.

Move the Menu cursor to Clear justification and press ⌐ENTER⌐ to tell LocoScript to do this. Then press ⌐PAGE⌐ to force LocoScript to re-lay the text down to the bottom of the page. As you see, the last paragraph is unjustified.

• To finish this session, press ⌐EXIT⌐ and then select the Abandon edit option – so that you can come back and work on this session again, as if for the first time. Abandon edit, you will remember, throws away all the changes you have made.

Session summary

In this session, you have seen:
- How to indent the first line of a paragraph
- How to indent a whole paragraph
- How to produce 'labelled' paragraphs
- How to centre a line between the margins or move it over to the right of the page
- One way in which you can make your text justified

Session 9

Stressing words and phrases

In this session, we see how to enhance text by picking out words and phrases and changing their appearance when they come to be printed – making them bold (thickened) or italic (slanted) or underlining them – or perhaps doing all three.

The document we are going to edit in this session is stored as PCWINFO in group 1 of your Examples disc. So pick out this document with the File cursor and then open it for editing. (Turn back to Session 5 if you are not sure how to do this.)

Using the Style menu

The first thing we shall look at is how to change the appearance of words and phrases through using one of the LocoScript menus – the Style menu. To bring this menu onto the screen, press ⌐f3¬. (If you look at the Information lines at the top of the screen, you will see f3=Style to remind you that this is the key to press.)

Press ⌐f3¬ now. The following menu appears on the screen:

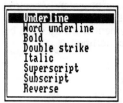

As you see, this menu contains options like Bold, Italic and Underline – exactly the tools we want to emphasise individual words and phrases. It also contains a couple of options you are unlikely to be familiar with – Double strike and Reverse. Double strike tells LocoScript to tell the printer to type each character twice: the result is rather like telling LocoScript to make the characters bold, and indeed on some printers there is no difference. Reverse is a special way of making characters stand out on the screen by writing them as black characters on a bright background, rather than the usual bright characters on a black background. It doesn't affect how the characters are printed.

Press ⌐CAN¬ when you have finished looking at this menu. (As you will remember, pressing ⌐CAN¬ abandons any menu you bring onto the screen.)

We shall now use the Style menu to underline the heading.

To start, put the Text cursor immediately in front of the T of The – the first character we want to give the special style. (Remember that the true position of the Text cursor is marked by the lefthand edge of the cursor blob.) When the cursor is in position, and not before, press ⌐f3¬.

As you can see from the menu, there are two possible types of underlining. The standard type underlines both words and the spaces between words; the other option

---

`Word Underline` – just underlines words. For the heading, we want both words and spaces underlined, so the option we want is `Underline`.

The Style menu is a 'Settings' menu like the Options menu we used in Session 5 to choose what extra information to display on the screen. The options that are set at the moment have ticks beside them and you set or clear options by pointing to them with the Menu cursor and then pressing ⊞ to set or ⊟ to clear or the Space bar to 'toggle' between 'set' and 'clear' – exactly as you did in Session 5.

So to set `Underline`, check the Menu cursor is on `Underline` and press ⊞. (If necessary, move the Menu cursor to `Underline` either with the Cursor keys or by typing U.) LocoScript puts a tick beside `Underline`, just like the ticks you saw in Session 5 next to the options in the Options menu.

You could now go on and select another option – say, `Italic`. But beware: some of the options in this menu are mutually exclusive – ie. you can either have one or the other, not both. In particular, you cannot set both `Underline` and `Word Underline` at the same time – so setting `Word Underline` automatically clears `Underline` and setting `Underline` automatically clears `Word Underline`.

Underlining is all we want here, so just press ENTER to tell LocoScript to go ahead. The menu is cleared away and you are returned to the document.

You don't get instant underlining in the same way that LocoScript instantly centred or right aligned the line – because LocoScript waits until it relays the text before showing the change of character style. Step through the document word by word by pressing the WORD key and then you will see your text being underlined.

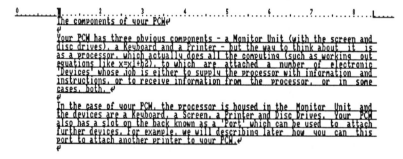

Move the Text cursor down a couple of paragraphs, and you will see that more of the document has been underlined than we originally intended. Indeed if you move the Text cursor to the end of the document (eg. by pressing DOC) the whole document will be underlined. Why should this be?

The answer is that we have told LocoScript where to 'turn on' underlining but we haven't told it where to turn it off. To put this right, move the Text cursor immediately after the last letter of the heading.

Now press ⌈⁷³⌉ again. The Style menu appears on the screen again – but note how it still has the tick next to Underline. This is to show you that Underline is currently 'turned on'.

To turn underlining off here, we simply clear the Underline option. Point to Underline with the Menu cursor as before but, this time, press ⌈·⌉ or the Space Bar. LocoScript takes away the tick beside Underline to show that underlining has been turned off.

Press ⌈ENTER⌉ to tell LocoScript that everything is now set as you want and to return to working on the document.

To see what effect this has had, press ⌈PAGE⌉ – to force LocoScript to relay down to the bottom of the page. Now only the first line is underlined – as we wanted.

To see something else about the workings of the Style menu, move the Text cursor back up to the heading you have underlined – anywhere on the line will do – and bring the Style menu onto the screen again. Notice how Underline is shown as being turned on – because the menu shows you the character style at the Text cursor. (Similarly, the Size menu – introduced in the next session – will always show you the size of characters at the Text cursor.)

What goes into the document

What we have actually done by using the Style menu is to put some special codes into your document – one where we wanted underlining to be turned on and another different one where we wanted underlining to be turned off again.

These special codes (and others like them) are called word-processing codes and they are really the key to LocoScript's power. Each code tells LocoScript that the following text should be styled or laid out in a particular way, and as you choose which codes to put in, they give you a lot of control over how your finished document looks.

Word-processing codes don't normally appear on the screen and they are never printed. They just affect the way the text of your document appears – both on the screen and when it is printed. However, you can display the codes on the screen through one of the options in the Options menu, the same menu we used in Session 5 to display spaces and blanks on the screen.

Press ⌈⁷⁸⌉ to bring the Options menu onto the screen. The option you need to display the word-processing codes is Codes. Set this option by pointing to it with the Menu cursor and pressing ⌈·⌉. When you press ⌈ENTER⌉, the screen changes to:

```
└────┃...........╵..........┊.........╵.........╵..........╵........╷.........╵....└────
     ┃(*UL)The components of your PCW(÷UL)↵
     ↓
     Your PCW has three obvious components ⊢ a Monitor Unit (with the screen and
     disc drives), a Keyboard and a Printer ⊢ but the way to think about  it  is
     as a processor, which actually does all the computing (such as working  out
```

The codes we added with the Style menu are now clearly visible as (+UL) and (-UL) – the (+UL) appearing where we turned on underlining, the (-UL) appearing where we turned underlining off. Also notice how displaying these codes has apparently pushed the text towards the righthand margin. However, this is just an effect you see on the screen: the codes don't push the text towards the right margin when you come to print the document.

Note: (+UL) and (-UL) are just ways of representing the codes on the screen. You can't put these codes in simply by typing the characters (+UL) or (-UL) – though there is a way of putting them in by just pressing keys, as we shall see shortly. These codes are just one character to LocoScript: in particular, it only takes one stroke of a Delete key to remove the whole code from your document – whether they are displayed on the screen or not.

- Before you go on, use the Style menu to turn on and turn off the other effects – Bold, Double, Italic and Reverse:
  - Move the Text cursor to the start of the word or phrase you want to affect.
  - Press ⌈f3⌉.
  - Move the Menu cursor to an option you want to set (turn on) or clear (turn off).
  - Press ⌈+⌉ to set the option; press ⌈−⌉ to clear it; press the Space Bar to toggle the setting of an option, ie. set one that's clear or clear one that's set.
  - When all the options are set or cleared as you want, press ⌈ENTER⌉.

Look at the codes LocoScript puts in each time you press ⌈ENTER⌉. Notice how there is a separate (+...) code for each option you turned on (ie. changed from cleared to set) in the menu and a (-...) code for each option you turned off (changed from set to cleared).

Now clear the Codes setting in the ⌈f8⌉ Options menu. (Turn back to Session 5 if you are not sure how to do this.) All the word processing codes you have put in are now hidden. Notice how you can still see where underlining and reverse are turned on, but you can't see just by looking at the text what you have marked as bold, double or italic. These effects cannot be shown on the screen. However, there is a simple way of telling what styles are set at the Text cursor: just look at the Information lines at the top of the screen. If Bold, Double and/or Italic are set at the Text cursor, this is displayed.

It is usually a good idea to work with the Codes displayed when you put word-processing codes into your documents. Then you can see very readily which parts of your document have been given special styles.

Note: All of these styles (except Reverse, which is a screen style – not a printer style) can be reproduced on a dot-matrix printer such as the one supplied with the PCW8256, 8512 and 9256 machines. However, on a daisy-wheel printer, you can't print italic characters if there are no italic characters on the printwheel you are using.

Using the Set and Clear menus

An alternative way of putting in these word-processing codes is to use a couple of special menus – the Set menu and the Clear menu. You use the Clear menu to put in any code that starts with a –, such as (-UL) or (-Bold). You use the Set menu to put in both codes that start with a +, such as (+UL) and others that don't have either a + or a –.

To show how these menus are used, we shall underline the Section 1 heading – ie. put a (+UL) code at the start of this heading and a (-UL) code at the end.

Move the Text cursor to the S of Section. Press the [⊞] (or 'Set') key and then wait. In a little while, the Set menu appears on the screen.

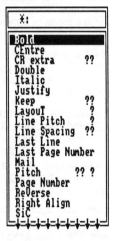

This menu is too long to display on the screen: hence the arrows at the bottom of the menu. To see the remaining options, keep pressing [↑]. The menu entries will then scroll to show you the other options until all the remaining options have been displayed. To see the options at the top of the menu again, move the Menu cursor to the top of the menu and then keep pressing [↑]. Try this out.

To select UnderLine, either move the Menu cursor to this option or type UL – ie. the letters written in capitals in the option you want. As you type, the Set menu shrinks down – initially just to the options starting with a U, then to just UnderLine when you type the L. When the Menu cursor is on UnderLine, press [ENTER]: the menu is cleared away and the (+UL) code is inserted in your document.

Now move the Text cursor to the ↵ after the s of Devices. Press the [□] (or 'Clear') key and then wait. This time it is the Clear menu that appears on the screen.

This menu works exactly like the Set menu. So to select the UnderLine option, type UL (as before, the menu shrinks as you do this); then press [ENTER]. The menu is cleared away and a (-UL) code is inserted in the document. The words between the two codes are now underlined.

• Try using these menus to put in other word processing codes. For the moment, just use the Bold, Centre, Double, Italic, Justify, ReVerse, Right Align, UnderLine and Word underline options. Notice, in particular, how the codes for centring and right aligning are (CEntre) and (RAlign). You don't have codes like (+CEntre) or (-CEntre); (+RAlign) or (-RAlign), because these instructions only apply to one line and so don't need to be turned off.

8809

Using keystrokes

The final way you can put in word processing codes is by typing special sequences of keystrokes: no menus are involved. The keystrokes have to be learnt, but once you know what these are, this becomes easily the quickest way of putting in the codes.

The keystrokes are essentially the same ones as you use when you put in the same codes using either the Set or the Clear menu as appropriate – because, in fact, the Set and Clear menus are just representations of the keystrokes that are used to enter the codes. The main difference is that you just type the keystrokes – you don't wait for the menu to appear. Also, because no menu appears on the screen, you don't have to press [ENTER] to finish the keystroking.

So if you want to insert a (+...) code through a sequence of keystrokes, you press [⊞] and then you type the same letters as you would type to move the Menu cursor directly to the option you want in the Set menu – ie. the letters written in capitals in the menu.

To see how this works, move the Text cursor to the start of the current line, press [⊞] and then type RA. This puts in a (RAlign) code and right aligns the line (ie. moves the line over to the right). The Right Align option in the Set menu has a capital R and a capital A. (You will see LocoScript extend the Text cursor into a 'patch' while it waits for you to complete the code.) Similarly, press [⊞] and type B to put in a (+Bold) code; or press [□] and type I to put in a (-Italic) code.

Now, turn back to the previous page where the Set and Clear menus are displayed and try using this technique to put in other codes. If you get confused, press the [⌗] key (the 'Help' key) or wait a moment. The relevant part of the Set or Clear menu will then appear and you should be able to see from this what you need to type to get the right result. However, then you will have to press [ENTER] to clear the menu away again.

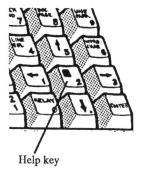

Help key

Note: If you accidentally type the wrong letter while keystroking a code, what to do depends on what happens:

– If your PCW bleeps, just type the letter you meant to type.

– If the wrong code is inserted, press [←DEL] and start again.

– If neither of these happen, press [←DEL] and type the letter you meant to type.

8809

Superscripts and subscripts

We finish this session by looking at a couple of the options in the Style menu that we ignored earlier – Superscripts and Subscripts. These are characters written above and below the normal line of the text, either as footnote markers [1] etc. or in mathematical or chemical formulae like H_2O.

In the middle of the second paragraph, there is a fragment of mathematics, currently written as x=x1+b2. This should be $x=x_1+b^2$ – ie. we should have the 1 as a subscript, written below the general line of the text, and the 2 as a superscript, written above the general line of the text.

To put this right, you need:

- a (+SuB) code before the 1 to make this a subscript
- a (-SuB) code before the + so that the + is on the line
- a (+SupeR) code before the 2 to make this a superscript; and
- a (-SupeR) code after the 2 so that the rest of the text is on the line.

You can put these codes in either:

- by using the Style menu
- or by using the Set menu for the (+...) codes and the Clear menu for the (-...) codes
- or by using keystrokes.

For practice, we shall put in these codes by using keystrokes. But first, check that you are displaying word-processing codes – so that you can 'see' what you are doing.

Move the Text cursor to the 1. The code to insert in front of the 1 is (+SuB); so press ⊞ and then type SB (either in capitals or in small letters: it doesn't matter). If you look at the screen as you type, you will see LocoScript spread the Text cursor into a patch as you type and then snap in (+SuB)

Now move the Text cursor just after the 1. The code you need here is (-SuB); so this time press ⊟ and then type SB. (Again, you will see the patch on the screen until LocoScript recognises which code you want.)

The codes around the 2 are put in similarly. The (+SupeR) code is inserted by pressing ⊞ and typing SR; the (-SupeR) code is inserted by pressing ⊟ and then typing SR.

When you have finished, you should have:

x (+SuB) 1 (-SuB) +b (+SupeR) 2 (-SupeR)

This has, in fact, made the equation $x=x_1+b^2$ – but the only confirmation you get of this on the screen are the codes you have put in. The true effect cannot be shown on the screen but you will see it when you print the document out.

8809

Finally...

Finish work on this document in the usual way by pressing [EXIT]. This time, we recommend that you select the Save and Print option so that you can see the effect of the word-processing codes you have inserted.

Session summary

In this session, we have seen:

- How to change the appearance of words or phrases by using the Style menu
- How to put Superscripts and Subscripts in your documents
- How to display the word-processing codes you insert
- How to put in word-processing codes using the Set and Clear menus
- How to put in word-processing codes using keystrokes

Session 10

Using character sizes and line spacings

So far we have been working exclusively with the Elite style of characters (12 characters per inch), 6 lines per inch down the page and a line spacing of 1 (ie. printing on every line). In this session, we are going to show you how you can use different sizes of characters and line spacings for individual words and phrases.

Before we start, a word of warning. These are very powerful features of LocoScript, but not ones to be used overmuch. Constantly changing the size and spacing of your text will give you a poor-looking result, particularly on a daisy-wheel printer where changing the character size only means that the characters are spaced more closely or more widely as appropriate.

The document we are going to edit in this session is called ACCENTS.TXT and it is stored in group 1 of your Examples disc. So the first thing to do is to pick out this document with the File cursor and then open it for editing. (Turn to Session 5 if you are not sure how to do this.)

Note: Not all the different character sizes can be reproduced on every printer. Whenever you ask for a character size that can't be reproduced on your particular printer, LocoScript will use a suitable substitute. However, it is always best to set a character size that suits your printer. For further details, see your printer's own manual.

Making local changes

The word-processing instructions we will look at in this session are the ones that:

- change the character size used for a particular word or phrase so that it stands out
- change the line spacing for individual lines to achieve special results, for example, in tables – or to prepare mathematical equations with simultaneous superscripts and subscripts (see below).

The common factor: Using the Size menu

The common factor in making local changes of character size or line spacing is the Size menu. If you look at the Information lines at the top of the screen, you will see that this is brought onto the screen by pressing ⬚f4⬚. Press ⬚f4⬚ (⬚SHIFT⬚+⬚f3⬚) now. The following menu appears on the screen:

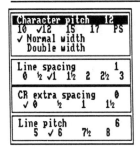

This menu is divided into four parts – each one dealing with a different aspect of character size and line spacing.

Character Pitch describes the size of the characters in terms of the number of characters that can be fitted into each inch across the page. For example Character Pitch 10 tells you that there will be 10 characters per inch across the page; Character Pitch 17 means 17 characters per inch.

A large part of preparing a document is the tedious job of checking it for typing errors.

Pitch 10

A large part of preparing a document is the tedious job of checking it for typing errors.

Pitch 17

Normal width and Double width add an extra dimension to character size by giving you the choice of the standard number of characters per inch (Normal width) or half that number of Double width characters. On a dot-matrix printer, the characters will be literally twice as wide; on a daisy-wheel printer, the characters are spaced more widely.

You thus always have two parts of the character size to select: the basic pitch and whether you want Normal or Double-width characters.

Line Spacing gives the number of standard lines the printer advances between printing one line and the next. Thus a Line Spacing of 1 gives you a 'single-spaced' document with text printed on every line, while a Line Spacing of 2 gives you a 'double-spaced' document with text printed on every other line.

Line Spacing 1	*Line Spacing 2*
A Line Spacing of 1 gives you text on every line. This is the Line Spacing to use for finished documents.	*Use Line Spacing 2 for draft copies –* *to give you room to mark changes.*

CR Extra Spacing gives the number of standard lines the printer advances in addition to the Line Spacing after printing a line that ends in a Carriage Return (say, the last line of a paragraph) and the next line. For example, a CR Extra Spacing of a ½ automatically gives you an extra half-line space between paragraphs:

CR Extra Spacing 0	*CR Extra Spacing 1/2*
This is text with a Line Spacing of 1 and a CR Extra Spacing of 0. *As you see, the paragraphs follow on without any extra break.*	*This is text with a Line Spacing of 1 and a CR Extra Spacing of 1/2.* *This time you do see a break between the paragraphs.*

8906

Line Pitch gives the standard number of lines per inch down the page, in the same way that the Character Pitch gives the number of characters per inch across the page. A Line Pitch of 6 therefore gives you six lines per inch, ie. lines ⅙th of an inch apart.

The current settings are given on the top line of each part of the menu. Written underneath are all the possible setting options. The Size menu is another of LocoScript's 'Settings' menus (like the Options menu and the Style menu), so to set any of these sizes and spacings, you point to the option you want with the Menu cursor and press the [⊞] key. The previous setting is automatically cleared.

To show this in action, we shall now go through the steps involved in changing the character size and the line spacing at various points in our example document. As with other menus, it is important to position the Text cursor before bringing the Size menu onto the screen; so before you go any further, clear the menu off the screen by pressing [CAN].

Changing the character size

Suppose, for effect, you wanted to make 'amalgamates' in the first paragraph stand out by putting this in 15 Pitch 'Double-width' characters.

Move the Text cursor to the beginning of 'amalgamates' (ie. to the point in the document where you want to change over to using 15 Pitch characters) and press [f4] to bring the Size menu onto the screen.

The first line of the menu tells you that the current character size is 12 characters per inch. The possible settings are listed underneath. The options 10, 12, 15 and 17 are very straightforward, being simply the number of characters per inch. These are the 'Fixed' character pitches. PS needs some more explanation.

PS stands for Proportional Spacing. Using PS gives a very professional look to your documents because the space occupied by each character isn't fixed, as it is for the other character pitches, but depends on the width of the character itself. Thus, narrow characters such as i and l occupy very much less space than wide characters such as M and W. (**Note:** If you want to produce proportionally spaced text on a daisy-wheel printer, you really need a PS printwheel to give you the best results.)

The overall result is about 12 characters per inch.

At the moment, there are ticks beside 12 and Normal width to show that these are the current settings. What we want is 15 Pitch Double width, so the first job is to set 15 Pitch instead of 12 Pitch; then we will set Double width instead of Normal width.

When you move the Menu cursor down to the line of options, the Menu cursor initially goes to 12. Use the Cursor keys ([←] and [→]) to move it to 15 and press [⊞] to select this option. (You could have pressed the Space bar here instead of [⊞]. As you will remember, pressing the Space Bar 'toggles' between set and clear – see Session 4.)

To set Double width instead of Normal width, you have a choice of setting Double (say, with the ⌷⊞⌷ key) or clearing Normal (either with the ⌷⊡⌷ key or by pressing the Space Bar) – because you can only have either Normal width or Double width. (Remember how this was also true when you were choosing between High Quality and Draft Quality for printing in Session 4?) So, say, move the Menu cursor to Double width and press ⌷⊞⌷

As with any 'Settings' menu, you could now go on and set other parts of this menu but for the moment, just press ⌷ENTER⌷ to tell LocoScript to go ahead. If you now show word-processing codes (by using the Options menu: see Session 9), you will see that you have inserted a (+Pitch15D) code in the document.

The (+Pitch15D) code 'turns on' using this size of character and, just as you needed a second code to 'turn off' bold after a (+Bold) code (Session 9), you now need another code at the end of 'amalgamates' so that you go back to using 12 Pitch Normal-width characters there.

Again you can put in this code through the Size menu. Move the Text cursor to the end of 'amalgamates' (as always, remember that the true position of the Text cursor is marked by the lefthand edge of the cursor oblong) and press ⌷f4⌷ to bring the Size menu onto the screen. This time, the current setting is 15D – ie. 15 and Double width are ticked. Use the same steps as before to set first the Pitch you want and then Normal or Double width, this time selecting 12 Pitch and Normal width.

Again, the code you have inserted is one that tells LocoScript to 'turn on' using a particular size of characters (12 Pitch). It doesn't tell LocoScript to 'turn off' the pitch you last set.

Note: You may well have expected 'amalgamates' to look different now it is a different character size. It doesn't for the simple reason that characters on the screen are always the same size and spaced in the same way. However, the fact that you changed the character size will change the number of characters that can be fitted on the line and this may well mean a change in where LocoScript decides to break the line. This can be particularly obvious when you use smaller characters because the lines may now appear to run into the righthand margin.

Changing the spacing

When you want to make a local change to the distance between one line and the next, there are three aspects to the line spacing to consider:

- the **Line Pitch** – the standard number of lines per inch down the page
- the **Line Spacing** – the number of standard lines the printer advances between printing one line and printing the next
- and, if the lines you want to affect are ended by ↵s, the **CR Extra Spacing** – that is, the number of standard lines moved in addition to the Line Spacing after a line ending in a carriage return.

What you have to work out is the combination of these three that will give you the result you require.

Selecting the Line Pitch

Start by considering the Line Pitch. There are four choices of Line Pitch but in general, you only use two of these – 6 lines per inch and 8 lines per inch. Five lines per inch and 7½ lines per inch are only included to support continental and other special printers. Six lines per inch is the standard setting for most printers. So we advise you to keep to a Line Pitch of 6, unless you really need 8 lines per inch.

Selecting the Line Spacing

Setting the Line Spacing in a LocoScript document is like setting the Line Spacing lever on a typewriter. It sets the number of lines of the Line Pitch that the printer moves between printing one line of a paragraph, say, and printing the next line.

LocoScript offers a range of possible Line Spacings – 0, ½, 1, 1½, 2, 2½ and 3. There is nothing to stop you choosing any of these, but as on a typewriter, the usual choice is between Single-spacing (a Line Spacing of 1) and Double-spacing (a Line Spacing of 2) – and your choice will depend on the type of document you are working on. If you are working on a letter, for example, you will probably want this to be single-spaced: but if you are working on the draft of an article, you will probably want it double-spaced so that you have plenty of room for corrections.

Selecting the CR Extra Spacing

LocoScript gives you the option of setting a CR Extra Spacing to let you have a more subtle spacing between paragraphs than just a single blank line. By setting the CR Extra Spacing to ½, for example, you can give yourself half-line spaces between your paragraphs – an altogether more 'classy' effect.

An example

Suppose, for example, that you want to double-space the paragraphs at the top of the example document and put half-line spaces between the lines in the table of accents and keystrokes.

The first step, as always, is to move the Text cursor to the place you want the different style to start from. In the case of a different line spacing, this place is anywhere on the first line that you want to have the new line spacing.

When the Text cursor is in position (on the first line of the first paragraph), bring the Size menu onto the screen as before by pressing ⌐f4⌐.

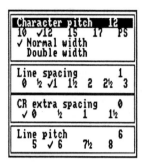

Looking at the menu, you can see that the Line Pitch is 6, the Line Spacing is currently 1 and the CR Extra Spacing is 0. To set the Line Spacing to 2, move the Menu cursor down to the list of possible Line Spacings and then across to 2. Press ⊞ to set a Line Spacing of 2 and then tell LocoScript to go ahead by pressing ENTER in the usual way. If you are displaying codes you will see LocoScript put in a (+LSpace2) code which tells it to 'turn on' a Line Spacing of 2.

Now move down to the line above the table. This is the line after which you want LocoScript to return to the 'old' line spacing and to set a CR Extra Spacing of ½. As you move to this line, you might well expect the lines to space out on the screen as LocoScript relays your document. This doesn't happen because all the screen shows is your lines of text, each on a separate line of the screen. However, the position of the End-of-page line(s) and the Line number for the Text cursor recorded on the second Information line will have changed.

When the Text cursor is in position, press ⌐4⌐ to bring the Size menu back onto the screen and then move the Menu cursor to the Line Spacing options and set a Line Spacing of 1. Then move it down to the CR Extra Spacing options and set a CR Extra Spacing of ½. Each time, position the Menu cursor on the option you want and then press ⊞

Tell LocoScript to go ahead with this new Line Spacing and CR Extra Spacing by pressing ENTER. If you are displaying codes, you will see that this puts (+LSpace1) (+CR½) into your document – which tells LocoScript to 'turn on' a Line Spacing of 1 and a CR Extra Spacing of ½.

Using keystrokes

Just as you don't have to use the Style menu to put in the codes to pick out particular words in italic or bold, you don't have to use the Size menu to put in the word processing codes needed to change character size, line spacing and line pitch. You can put in these codes by pressing the appropriate sequence of keys – or by calling up the associated Set and Clear menus (see Session 9).

To illustrate this, we shall show you how to type a fairly typical mathematical formula in a LocoScript document:

$$y^2 = x_a{}^2 + x_b{}^2$$

We shall concentrate here on the keystroking that you would use to type this equation in 15 Pitch characters. Initially, the keystrokes to use may not be that easy to recall – but all you really need to know is whether the code you want starts with a + or a – or neither. As you will remember from the last session, if it starts with a –,

8809

the first key to press is ⌷; if it starts with a + or neither, the first key to press is ⊞. If you don't know how to continue after that, all you have to do is either wait for the appropriate menu to appear or press the ▣ 'Help' key to bring the menu onto the screen immediately.

The problem with typing an equation like the one above is that, as a rule, you can't have a superscript and a subscript at the same point on a line. But with LocoScript, that's no problem. All you do is type the xs, ys and superscripts on one line; type the subscripts on the next line; and adjust the line spacing between them so that the second line is printed on top of the first. The only restriction is that you have got to be using one of the 'Fixed' character pitches: this operation doesn't work if you are using Proportionally-spaced characters.

Suppose you wanted to insert this equation at the end of the example document. Once the Text cursor is at the place you want to put the equation, you start by typing:

⊞P15 ⟨ENTER⟩

to put in the code that 'turns on' 15 Pitch characters. Note that the last step in putting in this code is to press ⟨ENTER⟩ – when to put in a code like (+Bold), you just type ⊞B. The difference is that the code we are putting in here incorporates a number. *Whenever there's a number in the code, the last part of the keystroking is to press* ⟨ENTER⟩

The next thing to type is the xs, ys and superscripts, ie.:

y⊞SR2⌷SR=x⊞SR2⌷SR+x⊞SR2⌷SR

            Set superscript   Clear superscript

Finally on this line, you want the codes that tell the printer not to advance between printing this line and the one on which you type the subscripts. These are:

    (+LSpace0)   – which sets a Line Spacing of 0; and

    (+CR0)   – which sets a CR Extra Spacing of 0

so the keystrokes you need are:

⊞LS0 ⟨ENTER⟩ ⊞CR0 ⟨ENTER⟩

Again, as both codes involve numbers, you have to finish each code by pressing ⟨ENTER⟩. Start the next line by pressing ⟨RETURN⟩ and then type 'the subscripts':

(four spaces)⊞SBa⌷SB*(two spaces)*⊞SBb⌷SB

                                    Clear subscript

To line up with
the previous line   Set subscript

8809

Before you finish this line, you need the codes that tell LocoScript to go back to using the 'old' Line Spacing, CR Extra Spacing and Character Pitch. You could do this through codes like (+LSpace1) which tells LocoScript to 'turn on' a Line Spacing of 1. However, although the only codes you can insert through the Size menu are (+...) codes, you can use keystroking to insert codes that tell LocoScript to 'turn off' the special settings you are using. LocoScript then resets the size or spacing to its initial value. (We will explain what these initial values are in the next session.)

The codes you can use here are:

(-Pitch) – which returns the character pitch to its initial value of 12

(-LSpace) – which returns the Line Spacing to its initial value of 1; and

(-CR)   – which returns the CR Extra Spacing to its initial value of 0

and the keystrokes to put these codes in are:

⌈⊡⌉P ⌈⊡⌉LS ⌈⊡⌉CR

(No numbers this time, so no need to press ⌈ENTER⌉)

Session summary

In this session, you have seen:

- How to write individual words and phrases in different character sizes
- How to type simultaneous superscripts and subscripts
- How to make temporary changes to the line spacing and how this can be used to good effect
- What effect these changes have on the document you see on the screen
- How all these changes are put to good use in typing mathematical formulae
- What using different character sizes means when it comes to printing the document

The steps we have used in this session have only changed the size of characters and the line spacing for individual words and phrases. At times, you will want to change the character size used for whole sections of a document – even for a whole document. The techniques involved in doing that are closely linked with the techniques used for setting margins and tabs covered in the next session of this tutorial.

Session 11

Margins, tabs and tables

So far in this tutorial, you have worked with margins and tab positions that have been set up for you. For much of what you do, the margins LocoScript automatically gives you when you create a document will be fine: they are, after all, a very sensible ¾" from either edge of a sheet of A4.

What LocoScript doesn't automatically give you is any tabs. The only tabs you have used so far have been in the Example documents. One way you could get some tab settings in a new document would be to copy one of the Example documents and delete all the text. However, making do in this way isn't necessary. In this session, we show you how easy it is to set the margins and tab positions yourself, whether this be for the whole document, special paragraphs or really quite complicated tables.

The margins and tabs for a document can be set up – and changed – at any time while you are editing the document. The document we are going to edit to show how this is done is stored in the document called INQUIRE.EG in group 1 of your Examples disc. So the first step is to pick out this document with the File cursor and open it for editing. (Turn back to Session 5 if you are not sure how to do this.)

Note for LocoScript '1' users: LocoScript 2 Layouts work in a very different way from the Layouts you are used to. Try as far as possible to forget everything you have learnt about using Layouts in the past as you study this session.

The key concept – Layouts

Associated with every part of a document is a 'Layout' which tells LocoScript how the text should be laid out. In particular, it defines:

- the position of the left and right margins
- the position and the type of any tabs
- whether paragraphs are justified (spaced out so that both the left and the right edges of the paragraph are straight) or unjustified (with a ragged right edge)

The Layout also specifies whether the text should all be italic and defines a character pitch, line pitch, line spacing and CR extra spacing. These are the initial values for the character size, etc. As we saw in the last session, you can change to a different character size or whatever, whenever you like. The codes we put in then to 'turn off' the special setting – for example, a (-Pitch) or a (-LSpace) code – tell LocoScript to go back to using the value set in the Layout. (Some other details are also defined in a Layout but these are a little esoteric and so need not concern us here.)

All the documents you have created so far have started with the standard Layout that LocoScript uses when no other Layout has been specified. This is LocoScript's 'Default' Layout which gives you 12 Pitch characters, single-spaced, unjustified text and a suitable margin either side on A4 paper.

The first thing we are going to see is how to give your document overall the margins, tabs etc. that you want.

Changing the Layout

The menu that helps you change the Layout you are using is the Layout menu. This is the same menu that we used in Session 8, for example, to centre lines. So the first step is to press ⌷f2⌷ to bring this menu onto the screen.

The option you want here is Change layout. The menu is a Commands menu, so move the Menu cursor to select the Change layout option: then press ⌷ENTER⌷ to tell LocoScript to go ahead.

The screen now changes – giving you a new set of Information lines, because you are now working with LocoScript's Layout Editor. In particular, you now have new menus to work with – to help you set up the Layout you want. The Ruler line will also feature in setting up your Layout: we will be seeing how you can use the Cursor keys to point to positions on this Ruler line.

(The rest of the screen still shows your document – but you can't change any of the text while you are using the Layout Editor.)

Details of the Layout   Ruler line for the Layout

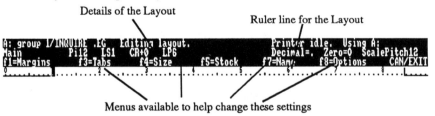

Menus available to help change these settings

The second Information line gives you very much the same information about the Layout as you see on the second Information line while you are editing the document – the character size (Pitch), the Line Spacing, the Line Pitch, etc. However, the group of details towards the end of the line are new:

- Decimal records whether a full stop or a comma is used as a decimal point (the significance of this will become clear later in this session when we describe the different types of tab you can set)

---

114   LocoScript 2 User Guide: Tutorial

- Zero records if the number 0 is written with or without a slash through it
- ScalePitch records size of the characters used to mark out the Ruler Line. For example, ScalePitch12 means that each mark on the line represents one 12-Pitch character or ½" (12 Pitch means 12 characters to the inch.)

The settings that are displayed to start with are the details of the Layout that is currently in use – the Default Layout in this case. We shall now see how to change these settings.

Setting the margins

Suppose, for example, that you wanted to set the lefthand margin 1¼" from the side of the paper. As the Scale Pitch is 12, 1¼" corresponds to character position 15 on the Ruler line.

The first step in changing either of the margins is to move the Ruler cursor (that's the cursor on the Ruler line) to the new position for the margin. So press the ◁ and ▷ keys until the Ruler cursor is at character position 15.

When the Ruler cursor is in place, bring the Margins menu onto the screen. If you look at the third Information line, you will see that the key to press is ∏.

The Margins menu is another of LocoScript 2's 'Commands' menus – with an arrow beside one of the options to show that this option is currently selected.

Check that Set Left Margin is selected (it should have been pre-selected for you); then press ENTER. The lefthand margin then instantly leaps to the new position.

To set the right margin to character position 80, say (ie. 6⅔" from the lefthand side), you go through very much the same steps – positioning the Ruler cursor and then pressing ∏ to bring the Margins menu onto the screen. However, this time the option to select is Set Right Margin. The righthand margin moves to its new position when you press ENTER.

Setting and clearing tabs

Tabs are markers that tell LocoScript where you want pieces of text directly under one another, for example in a table. They provide a very much better way of aligning text than typing spaces – particularly if you use proportionally spaced characters, because then what appears aligned on the screen won't necessarily be aligned when you come to print your document.

There are a number of different types of tab – Simple tabs, Right tabs, Centre tabs and Decimal tabs, each with their own way of aligning text.

For the most part, you will just want 'Simple' tabs. A Simple tab is the sort of tab you get on a typewriter – ie. one that sets the position of the first letter you type after pressing ⌜TAB⌟. It is also the type of tab you need for such things as indenting the first line of a paragraph or indenting the whole of a paragraph.

The other types of tab are mainly for use in tables, as we shall see later in this session.

The steps involved in setting and clearing tab positions are like those you have just used to set the margins – but using the Tabs menu instead of the Margins menu. If you look at the Information lines, you will see that the key to press to bring the Tabs menu onto the screen is ⌜f3⌟.

For example, to set a tab position at character position 20, move the Ruler cursor to position 20 and then press ⌜f3⌟.

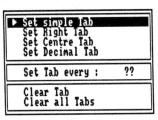

As you see, this menu gives you a choice of different tabs to set.

The Tabs menu is another of LocoScript 2's 'Commands' menus – so all you have to do to put in the tab is select the option that gives you the right sort of tab and press ⌜ENTER⌟. Thus to put a Simple tab at character position 20, you select Set simple Tab and press ⌜ENTER⌟. A Simple tab marker then appears on the Ruler line at character position 20.

For practice, now go through the same steps again – this time, putting a Simple tab at character position 25.

To get rid of a tab you put in the wrong place or you no longer need (say, the tab you have just put at character position 25), move the Ruler cursor to the tab position and then either press ⌜⊡⌟ or call up the Tabs menu again. This time you want the bottom section of the menu.

In general, you will want the Clear Tab option – which clears the tab picked out by the Ruler cursor. However, if what you really want to do is to get rid of all the tabs on the Ruler line, the option to use is Clear all Tabs.

Select Clear Tab now. LocoScript 2 clears away the tab when you press ⌜ENTER⌟.

To move a tab, you combine these actions – inserting a new tab at the new position and removing the tab at the old position. So, for example, to move the tab you have just inserted at position 20 to position 25, move the Ruler cursor to position 20 and either use the Clear Tab option or press ⌜⊡⌟ to remove this tab; then move the Ruler cursor to position 25 and use the Set simple Tab option to insert a fresh tab there.

If you want to set up a number of these simple tabs at regular intervals across the page, you don't have to set these up individually. Instead, you use another of the Tab menu options – Set Tab every: ??.

Suppose, for example, that you wanted tabs at every 8th position all the way across the page. To do this, move the Ruler cursor to the Left Margin and then press [f3] to bring the Tabs menu onto the screen. When the menu appears, move the Menu cursor down to Set Tab every: ?? and type 8 – the spacing you want for these tabs: then press [ENTER]. LocoScript then puts in Simple tabs at every 8th position across the page starting at Character position 23 (8 after the position of the Ruler cursor, which we have just positioned at character position 15).

Note: The initial Layout of a document can handle up to 15 tabs. If you need more than this, you need to set up one of the 'alternative' Layouts described below.

Setting other aspects of the layout

Other aspects of the layout are set by using the other two menus, Size and Options.

The Size menu is exactly the same as the Size menu you used in the last session to tell LocoScript 2 to 'turn on' a different Character Pitch, Line Spacing, CR Extra Spacing or Line Pitch. And it works in the same way: you use the Menu cursor to pick out the settings you want and press the [⊞] key to set these.

The only difference appears when you press the [ENTER] key to tell LocoScript 2 to go ahead with these settings. Instead of inserting word-processing codes, the details on the second Information line change to the settings you have picked out.

So, for example, to change the Character Pitch to 10 and to set a CR Extra Spacing to ½, press [f4] ([SHIFT]+[f3]) to bring the Size menu onto the screen and then set 10 Pitch and a CR Extra Spacing of ½ exactly as you would to put the necessary codes into your document. When you press [ENTER], look at the Information lines and see how the details displayed there change.

When you want to set whether the text will be justified or unjustified, the menu to use is the Options menu. This is brought onto the screen by pressing [f8] ([SHIFT]+[f7]).

The Options menu is another of LocoScript 2's 'Settings' menus, so you change the current settings by pointing to options with the Menu cursor and pressing [⊞] to set the option, [⊟] to clear it or the Space Bar to 'toggle' between set and clear – exactly as in all other 'Settings' menus.

Justify is the option you are likely to use most often. When this option is set, both the right and the left edges of the paragraph will be straight. Otherwise, the right side will be ragged.

```
 ▐ Justify ▌
   Italic

 √ Decimal marker is .
   Decimal marker is ,

 √ Zero character is O
   Zero character is 0

 Scale pitch        12
 10  √12   15   17   PS
```

The Scale pitch option allows you to set the size of characters represented by the markers on the Ruler line.

The Default Layout makes the document unjustified, giving it a ragged right edge. To make your text justified, press [f8] to bring the Options menu on the screen,

8809

select the Justify option and press [⊞]. When you press [ENTER] the second Information line changes to show that this option has been set.

Note: By all means, experiment with setting and clearing the Justify and Italic options of the Options menu but you are advised not to change the other three settings at this stage. In particular, we would advise you not to change the Scale Pitch, especially where you use different layouts in the same document, because any change you make will affect the text alignment when you print. Before going on, leave Justify cleared.

Returning to the document

When you are happy with the Layout you have, press [EXIT]. You arc then returned to the document. (There may be a slight pause as LocoScript relays your document up to the Text cursor. As you remember, it is a rule in LocoScript that your document is correctly laid out up to your current working position.)

Before you do anything else, scroll down the document to see what effect changing the Layout has had. (Keep pressing either the [↓] key or the [PARA] key to do this.)

Notice how none of the lines now reach the righthand margin. The reason for this is that the Ruler line is marked out to show the number of 12 pitch characters you can get across the page but the new Layout uses 10 pitch characters. As we pointed out before, the screen can only show one size of characters, so lines of 10 pitch characters are apparently shorter simply because you get fewer characters on a line.

You may find this mismatch disconcerting but you should never need to worry: just trust LocoScript. It will always get where the next line should start right, whatever size of characters you use.

Another thing to do is to move the Text cursor up and down the document and notice how the line number given at the top of the screen changes. This number no longer steps up smoothly in ones because the new Layout has a CR Extra Spacing of ½. The screen doesn't show this CR Extra Spacing but it is included in the line number which records the number of standard lines down the page you are working. Once again, don't worry – just trust LocoScript: it will get the page breaks right.

Alternative Layouts

So far, we have just been concerned with setting up a Layout for the whole of your document. In general, this will give you all the margins, tabs etc. that you need.

However, you may well need different margins and tabs, for example, for tables or for paragraphs that you want to indent from both the left and the right margins. With LocoScript 2, all you have to do is to:

- tell LocoScript where you want to start using this different Layout, and
- set up the details of this Layout

What you do is insert a special code into the document which records all the details of the new Layout and tells LocoScript to use this new Layout for the text that follows the code. This code is displayed on the screen as (LayouT). (We'll see how you do this shortly.)

When you want to finish using this Layout and use a different Layout, you just insert another (LayouT) code, only this time the code contains different details – the details of the Layout to be used from here on.

Once you have told LocoScript the details of the Layout you want to use, it remembers these – whatever changes you make to the text itself. The only way it can lose this information is if you delete the Layout code itself.

However, this doesn't mean that you are stuck with this Layout until you delete the current Layout code and put in another. Whenever you want, you can change some or all of the details recorded in the Layout code, giving a new definition of how the text should be laid out. These changes affect the Layout in the area you are working – but nothing more. (We'll see how to change the Layout later in this session.)

Important: Every time you change to using a different Layout, LocoScript starts afresh on all its special settings. The character size becomes the one set in the Layout, the Line Spacing becomes the one set in the Layout etc. etc. LocoScript also clears all the character emphases like Bold, Italic and Underline – so if you want these to continue into the new Layout, you must follow the (LayouT) code with the appropriate 'turn on' codes for the print effects you want.

Setting up a New Layout – for a table

Suppose you wanted to set up this table at the end of the document:

Description	Part No	Unit price	Number	
Wall Unit	WU321	@ £24.80	3	74.40
Mounting brackets	MB326	@ £6	4	24
Attachments	AT328A	@ £0.99	1 set	.99
Total				£99.39

The first step is to position the Text cursor where you want to start using the special Layout. In our example case, this means moving the cursor to the end of the document (for example, by pressing [DOC]).

Then press [f2] to bring the Layout menu onto the screen. The option you want this time is New layout: select this option and press [ENTER] now.

The details that are displayed to start with are the details of the Layout that is currently in use at the Text cursor. LocoScript assumes that you will probably only want to change one or two aspects of the new layout. In this case, for example, you only want to set the position of some tabs.

The new layout is set up exactly as you set up the 'main' Layout – by positioning the Ruler cursor (if necessary) and then using the appropriate menu option. What we are going to look at here is the special case of setting up tabs for a table. (You can set up to 30 tabs in this new Layout if you so want.)

Tabs for tables

The columns of this table need to be lined up in different ways:

- In the first and second column, the lefthand ends of each entry are to be aligned
- In the third column, the righthand ends of the entries are to be aligned
- In the fourth column, each entry should be centred
- In the last column, the decimal points in the numbers are to be lined up

LocoScript has a different type of tab for each of these cases.

- To align the lefthand ends, use a Simple tab – the type of tab used already
- To line up the righthand ends, use a Right tab
- To centre the entries over each other, use a Centre tab
- To line up the decimal points, use a Decimal tab

So the Layout for this table needs a Simple tab at position 30, a Right tab at position 50, a Centre tab at position 60 and a Decimal tab at position 75. (You don't need a Simple tab for the first column because this column starts at the left margin and so will automatically be aligned along its lefthand edge.)

Start by clearing away the tabs you don't want. To do this, bring the Tabs menu onto the screen and select Clear all tabs.

Then insert new tabs as follows:

- To insert the Simple tab, move the Ruler cursor to position 30, bring the Tabs menu onto the screen and select Set simple Tab
- To insert the Right tab, move the Ruler cursor to position 50, bring the Tabs menu onto the screen and select Set Right Tab
- To insert the Centre tab, move the Ruler cursor to position 60, bring the Tabs menu onto the screen and select Set Centre Tab
- To insert the Decimal tab, move the Ruler cursor to position 75, bring the Tabs menu onto the screen and select Set Decimal Tab

Giving the Layout a Name

The final aspect of the Layout to set is its Name. Setting a Name isn't essential, but it's very helpful: the name of the Layout you are currently working with is displayed on the second Information line as you edit the document.

Layout names are up to twelve characters long and, as with document names, it is a good idea to pick a name that reminds you what the Layout does. However, you are nothing like as restricted in your choice of a Layout name as you are in choosing a

---

document name. Not every character you can type can be used – for example, you can't use symbols or Cyrillic characters – but you can include (among others) both capital and lower case letters, spaces, hyphens, Greek letters and even some accented characters. (A full list of the characters you can use is given in Appendix III.)

Suppose you chose the name `Table` for the Layout you have just set up. To give it this name, press ⌈77⌉ to bring the Name 'menu' onto the screen.

To start with, this shows the name of the Layout you based your new Layout on (ie. the Layout that was in use before you started to set up the new Layout).

To set the new name, you can either edit the old name exactly as you would normal text (there is a small cursor within the band of highlighting that you can position with the Cursor keys) or you can press ⌈□⌉ to clear away the old name and type the new name afresh. *Pressing* ⌈□⌉ *clears away everything to the right of the small cursor: this is true for any slot for information in a LocoScript menu.*

So, to set the name of this Layout, press ⌈□⌉ to clear away the old name and then type `Table`. Finally, press ⌈ENTER⌉ to tell LocoScript to go ahead with this name.

Returning to the document

When you have set the Layout you require, press ⌈EXIT⌉. You are then returned to the document.

LocoScript 2 has inserted two things in your document associated with your new Layout:

- a (LayouT) code
- a ↵

As you can see, we have wall units in a full range of colours and finishes.
I feel confident that you will find precisely the style of kitchen wall
units that you were looking for and you will find our prices particularly
competitive.↵
(LayouT)↵

The (LayouT) code is the special code that holds all the information about the Layout. (You can see this code if you use the Options menu (⌈76⌉) to display word-processing codes.) The ↵ has been inserted so that you can make use of all the features of the Layout straight away. Most aspects of the layout take effect immediately in any case, but the new margins only come into play on the line following the code. This often means in practice that you get an extra blank line in your document: if you don't want this extra line, rub out either this or the preceding ↵ with the Delete keys.

8809

Using the special types of tab

To show you how these tabs work in practice, we shall now type in the table we described above:

Description	Part No	Unit price	Number	
Wall Unit	WU321	@ £24.80	3	74.40
Mounting brackets	MB326	@ £6	4	24
Attachments	AT328A	@ £0.99	1 set	.99
Total				£99.39

Now that you have the Layout code for this table in the Document, all you have to do is simply type in this table as follows:

Description⟨TAB⟩ Part No⟨TAB⟩ Unit price⟨TAB⟩Number⟨RETURN⟩
Wall Unit⟨TAB⟩ WU321 ⟨TAB⟩ @ £24.80⟨TAB⟩3⟨TAB⟩74.40⟨RETURN⟩
etc.

In other words, type each piece of text in the table quite normally but when you want to move from one column to the next, simply press ⟨TAB⟩ and then carry on typing the next bit of text. You don't need to do anything difficult like typing the right number of spaces as you might well have to do on a typewriter!

Watch what happens as you type each of the entries so that you see the effects the different types of tab have.

As you type Unit price (and all the entries in that column), notice how the letters are pushed to the left by each new character you type. The reason for this is that you are working here with a Right Tab – which, you remember, tells LocoScript that you want the righthand edge of all the entries in the column to be aligned. LocoScript shuffles the characters in this way to ensure that all the entries end in the same place.

As you type Number (and the other entries in this column), you will see a similar but different action as LocoScript responds to the Centre Tab. In order for all the entries in this column to be centred about the tab position, LocoScript does some shuffling to the left but not as much as for the Right tab.

As you type the final column of numbers (74.40, 24 etc.), you will see LocoScript shuffling characters to the left again – but only until you type the decimal point. Any characters you type after this character are positioned normally. This is how LocoScript ensures that the decimal points in the entries are aligned.

Note: Layouts are normally set up for decimal numbers like 35.20 where the character to align in a column of decimal numbers is full stop. If you want to align decimal numbers written in the Continental style (for example, 35,20), you must use the Options menu in the Layout Editor to set comma as the character that marks the decimal point.

8809

Changing the Layout

As well as creating new Layouts to use, you can also change the Layout you are working with at present. Suppose, for example, that you want to change the Layout for the table because the gap you have left for the Description is five characters too small.

As always, the first thing to think about is the position of the Text cursor. In this case, all you need to ensure is that the cursor is in the part of the document that uses this Layout. In this case, you just need to make sure that the Text cursor is on some part of the table.

When the cursor is in place, press [f2] to bring the Layout menu onto the screen and select the Change layout option. When you press [ENTER], LocoScript puts you into the Layout Editor.

You can now change any of the details of this Layout – including its name – exactly as if you were setting the Layout up for the first time. So to reset the Tab positions, you position the Ruler cursor, press [f3] to bring the Tabs menu onto the screen and use the options of this menu to set and clear tabs – exactly as we showed you earlier in this session.

When you are ready, press [EXIT]. This returns you to the document but there is then a slight pause as LocoScript relays the table up to the Text cursor. As you remember, it is a rule in LocoScript that all the document must be correctly laid out up to the current working position. If you then move the cursor down to the bottom of the document, you will see the rest of the table being relaid as well.

Using the same Layout elsewhere in the document

As we said earlier, all the information about the Layout is held in the (LayouT) code – so whenever you want to use the same Layout again, somewhere else in the document, you simply need to make a copy of the (LayouT) code and the Carriage Return, and paste these in just above the text you want laid out in the same way.

For example, if you wanted to insert a similar table between the first and second paragraphs of the example document, you could save yourself the trouble of setting up all those tabs again by storing a copy of the (LayouT) code already in your document in a Block (see Session 6) and then pasting it in at the new position – exactly as if the code were a piece of text.

Copying the Layout code into a Block, say, is best done with the word-processing codes displayed on the screen. So if necessary, start by using the Options menu ([f8]) to display these codes. With the Layout code displayed on the screen, position the Text cursor immediately in front of the code and press [COPY]; then place it immediately after the code and press [COPY] again. Now store the code in a free Block – by typing, say, 0 to store it in Block 0.

8809

To paste a copy of this code between the first and second paragraphs, put the Text cursor at the beginning of the blank line between these paragraphs, press [PASTE] and type 0. You have now inserted an exact copy of the Layout you used at the bottom of the document – and all the text that follows this code now has the Table Layout.

Note: Pasting in this Layout code has changed the Layout of all the text between the newly-inserted code and the next Layout code down the document. Sometimes, this change doesn't obviously affect the text – but as a rule, you will now need another (LayouT) code that restores the 'old' Layout.

Stock Layouts

In a well-designed document, you will use a small number of different Layouts for particular types of text. For example, you may well have one Layout for the text itself, another for the Introduction and a third for Notes.

Setting up these three Layouts and then copying them to different parts of the document via the Blocks is not an ideal way of working – so LocoScript 2 has a better solution. This is a set of 'Stock' Layouts which you can use as **patterns** for new Layouts – ie. what you get in the Layout code is a copy of all the settings in the Stock Layout. Note, though, that you can only set 15 tabs in a Stock Layout, rather than the 30 that you can set in a Layout code.

A LocoScript 2 document can have up to ten of these Stock Layouts – ready set up (along with other information) in the 'Document Set-up'. (We will show you how to set up Stock Layouts in Session 17, when we describe how to change the Document Set-up.) What is more, these Stock Layouts can be automatically set up in new documents you create, as we shall see in Session 21 – making it particularly easy to apply a 'House Style' to a series of documents.

Stock Layouts have names and numbers. The names are used to describe the types of paragraph the Layouts are meant to be used for. For example, this Example document has a Stock Layout called Intro, which you could use for the first paragraph. The numbers are always 0...9. We shall see later how both names and numbers are used to tell LocoScript that you want a copy of a particular Stock Layout.

All the Stock Layouts define a pair of margin positions, a character size, a line spacing, tab positions, etc. However, Stock Layouts 0 and 1 are special in that Stock Layout 0 is the one used for Headers and Footers (see Session 16) and Stock Layout 1 is the layout that is automatically used at the beginning of the document.

Using a Stock Layout

Using a Stock Layout is just like setting up and using an alternative Layout – except that, instead of setting the margins, etc. individually, you tell LocoScript to set up a Layout with the same settings as the Stock Layout.

To show how this is done, we shall now put in the instructions to use a layout that we have set up for you – the Intro Layout – for the first paragraph.

The first step is to position the Text cursor. In this case, put the cursor on the line above the first paragraph. When the cursor is in position, press `f2` to bring the Layout menu onto the screen.

The option you want here is again New layout. Check the Menu cursor is on this option: then press `ENTER` to tell LocoScript to go ahead. When the Layout Editor menus appear, press `f5`. LocoScript then puts another menu on the screen:

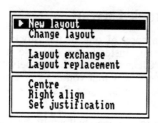
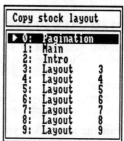

This menu lists all the Stock Layouts that have been set up – giving both their names and their numbers. It is a Commands menu, so you just point with the Menu cursor to the Stock Layout you want (in this case, the Stock Layout you want is the one called Intro) and press `ENTER`. Then press `EXIT` to return to the document.

When you press `ENTER`, LocoScript inserts a (LayouT) code into the document and starts a new line just as before. The only difference is that this time the code holds the details of the 'Intro' Stock Layout. As before, the new line is inserted so that you start using this layout immediately: rub out the extra ⏎ if you don't need it – but be careful not to delete the new Layout code at the same time.

The Layout code tells LocoScript to use this Layout until told otherwise, so you now need to insert another Layout code at the end of the paragraph to tell LocoScript to go back to using the original Layout – Stock Layout 1 (the 'Main' layout) – for the next paragraph. Use similar steps to the ones given above to insert a Layout code that holds the details of Stock Layout 1.

Important: Layouts that you set up by copying a Stock Layout can be changed in exactly the same way as other Layouts. And, once again, the changes only affect the details stored in the Layout code that applies to the part of the document you are working on: in particular, they don't affect the Stock Layout you copied when you were creating the new Layout. (This is a major difference between LocoScript 2 and the earlier LocoScript '1' where changing a Layout was tied in with changing all the other uses of the same Layout.)

However, there is one important exception to this rule. If you change the layout of the text before the first (LayouT) code in the document, you automatically change

Stock Layout 1 as well. This is the effect that we used at the beginning of this session to set up the margins, etc. we wanted for the whole of the example document.

It's also important to remember that the details held in the Layout code are a copy of the details set for the Stock Layout **when you put the Layout code into the document**. If, later, you change the Stock Layout, you don't automatically change the copies of the Layout in the document. (We will be seeing the procedure that you can take to 'update' Layouts throughout a document in Session 17.)

Using keystrokes to use a Stock Layout

When the Layout you want is simply a copy of one of the Stock Layouts, then there's no need to use the Layout menu. Instead you can use a sequence of keystrokes (or the corresponding Set or Clear menu) to change between using one Layout and another – in very much the same way that you use keystrokes to turn on and turn off changes of style like bold or italic (see Session 9) or changes of character pitch or line spacing (see Session 10).

To demonstrate the keystrokes you need to use, we shall apply the Intro Layout to the third paragraph. As before, the first step is to position the Text cursor, immediately above the first line you want laid out with this layout. So move the Text cursor in front of the ↵ on the previous line.

The code we want to put in is (LayouT). This has neither a + or a – at the start of the code, so the first keystroke is to press [⊞]. Then type LT2: LT because you want to insert a (LayouT) code and 2 because this is the **number** of the Intro Layout you want to use. Then, because you typed a number, press [ENTER]. As we pointed out in the last session, whenever the keystroking includes a number, the last key of the keystroking is always [ENTER].

These keystrokes insert a (LayouT) code that holds all the same details as the Intro Layout. LocoScript doesn't automatically give you a new line this time – instead it leaves it up to you to decide whether you need to insert an extra Carriage Return. (Remember, the margins and tabs of a new layout aren't used until the line after the code.) Here, you don't need another new line because we have carefully put the Layout code on the end of the line before the paragraph we want to affect.

Now move the Text cursor to the start of the blank line below this paragraph. This time, press [⊞] and type LT1 [ENTER]. The code this inserts tells LocoScript to go back to using Layout 1 – the Layout that's being used for the majority of the text.

(If you didn't want to go back to Layout 1 but to use, say, Layout 3 next, you would press [⊞], type LT3 and press [ENTER] to put in a (LayouT) code – in exactly the same way as we put in the (LayouT) code containing the same details as the Intro Layout above. You don't have to go back to Layout 1 before you go on to using Layout 3.)

8809

That's all there is to it – except to check that there is a Carriage Return between the Layout code and the text you want it to apply to.

Displaying the different layouts

When your document uses a number of layouts, each with different margins and tab positions, you can always get a rough idea of what these margins and tab positions are by looking at the way the text you type is laid out. LocoScript gives as faithful a representation as possible on the screen.

Sometimes, for example when you are adding entries to a table, you will need to know where the margins and tabs are in more detail. LocoScript gives you two ways of seeing this.

Firstly, you can use the Ruler line. This displays the margins and tabs at the current position of the Text cursor. So by looking at the Ruler line, you can always see what margins and tabs are in force where you are working.

The alternative is to use another of the options in the ⌈f8⌉ Options menu – the Rulers option.

With the Rulers option set, you see a Ruler line above each paragraph where there has been a change of layout – whether to one of the extra layouts or back to Layout 1. These extra Ruler lines let you see the pattern of margins and tabs anywhere in the document – not just at the place you are working.

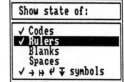

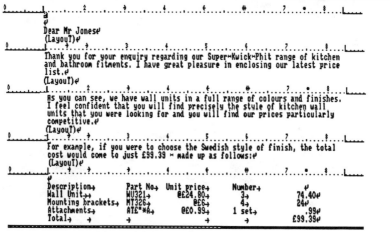

Note: These extra Ruler lines are for display only. You can't edit them.

• Finally in this session, press [EXIT] and select Save and Print. Now you will really see the results of your efforts.

Session summary

In this session, you have seen:

- What Layouts are and, in particular, what Stock Layouts are
- How to set up the margins, tabs etc. you want for the whole document
- How to make use of the Stock Layouts
- How to set special margins, tab settings etc. for particular paragraphs
- How to go about setting up a table

Session 12

Direct printing

When you have a pre-printed form to fill in, you don't have to go back to using the typewriter you parked under the stairs. Instead, you can use your PCW as if it were a typewriter – but with the added advantage that you can still use all the facilities of LocoScript to perfect and style the text before it goes onto the form. What you do is use LocoScript in its Direct Printing mode.

You use the Direct Printing mode from the Disc Manager Screen, so the first step is to display this screen. (Turn back to page 21 if you are not sure how to do this.)

When the Disc Manager Screen is displayed, press the 'D' letter key and then press [ENTER] to confirm that you want to go ahead. (D for Direct Printing should be easy to remember but, as usual, it is written on the second Information line in case you need to check.) LocoScript then displays a screen very like the screen you see when you start work on a new document.

You could now start typing the text you want to put onto this form – but before you do this, it is best to get the printer ready to print on the part of the page you want.

Getting the right print position

Load a piece of paper into the printer – if you have a form to hand that you could fill in, use this – but don't press [EXIT] yet. You have some printer adjustments to make first to ensure that the printer prints in the right position on the paper. These adjustments can only be made while LocoScript is in its Printer Control State. (Remember: loading the paper into the built-in printer automatically puts LocoScript into its Printer Control State.)

To get the right position down the page, turn the Paper Feed Knob on the side of the printer until the line of the paper you want to print on is lined up with the print head.

Once the position down the page is right, you then set the position across the page. This is known as 'setting the Left offset'. The Left offset is the distance the print start position is shifted to the right of its normal start position. The menu that helps you do this is the Left offset menu. By looking at the Information lines, you will see that this menu is brought onto the screen by pressing [f6] ([SHIFT]+[f5]).

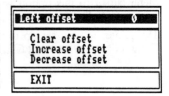

8809

The top line of this menu gives you the current setting of the Left offset; the rest forms a menu of commands that you can use to change the Left offset. The current setting is simply whatever Left offset you used last (either directly or indirectly as a consequence of the Paper Type you have been using – see Session 19).

If you know where you need printing to start, as so many tenths of an inch from the printer's natural start position, then you can type this in directly. Leave the Menu cursor on the Left offset line at the top of the menu and type in the Left offset you need in tenths of an inch. For example, if you know you want a Left offset of at least 1.5", type 15. Then press ⌷ENTER⌷ to confirm this is the Left offset you want and then press ⌷ENTER⌷ again to clear away the menu.

In general, you won't know this distance – so, instead, you move the Menu cursor to Increase offset (if you want to move the print position over to the right) or Decrease offset (if you want to move the print position to the left). If the offset is currently zero, the only sensible option to select is, of course, Increase offset.

Notice how the option you select with the Menu cursor becomes marked with a diamond. This diamond shows that the options in this menu are a special kind of Command option – one in which LocoScript carries out the command that's selected when you press ⌷ENTER⌷ and **then returns to the current menu**. In a way, a diamond works like a pair of arrows back to back – going off to carry out your command and then coming back to the menu. This action makes it easy for you either to select another command from the menu or to repeat the same command, as we shall do here. In this instance, the result is almost as if you are moving the print head directly by pressing ⌷ENTER⌷.

Note: The print head is only guaranteed to move in this way on the built-in printer. Other printers may not show you the Offset you are setting by moving the print head.

Press ⌷ENTER⌷ repeatedly until the print head is over where you want the first letter you type to be printed. As you move the head, you will see the Left offset in the menu change. When the print head is in the right place, you move the Menu cursor down to the EXIT option at the bottom of the menu and press ⌷ENTER⌷. You can move the Menu cursor to this option with the Cursor keys in the usual way, but the quick way to get to this option is simply to press ⌷EXIT⌷.

The printer is now set up to print in the right position, so you can leave Printer Control State (by pressing ⌷EXIT⌷) and go back to preparing the text you want to print.

Preparing the text

Type something – anything will do – but for the moment, don't press RETURN . If you make any mistakes, correct these exactly as if you were preparing a document.

If you want to insert an existing Block of text or one of your Phrases (see Session 14), then you can just Paste these in. Although it is important that you shouldn't press RETURN at this stage, it doesn't matter if the text you paste in includes ↵s. Indeed, a neat way of ensuring that you have the same address on an envelope as you have in a letter is to copy the address in the letter to a Block (see Session 6), and then paste this Block in when you use Direct Printing to prepare the envelope.

When you have set up the text you want, you then need to consider:

– whether you need to change the position of the righthand margin so that LocoScript won't print off the edge of the page

– what Character Pitch, Line Spacing etc. you want to use and whether you want to apply any special styling (Bold, Italic, etc.)

You make these changes in exactly the same way as you do while you are working on one of your documents. You can change any feature of the Layout – margins, character pitch etc. – with the aid of the Layout menu (f2), just as we did in the last session. Similarly, you can add styling to the text either by using the Style and Size menus or by using keystrokes to put in the relevant word-processing codes – exactly as described in Sessions 9 and 10.

Inserting the text

When you have set up the text you want, between the correct margins and embellished in the way you want, press PAGE to move the Text cursor immediately after the last letter of your text and then press RETURN . LocoScript immediately clears the screen and prints what you typed, starting each line at the left offset position you set. When it has finished you can prepare another line or paragraph.

Each time, before you press RETURN , check that the print head is over the point at which you want printing to start. Turn the Paper Feed Knob so that printing will start on the right line; press PTR and then use the Left offset menu as described above if you want printing to start at a different place on the line.

Note: If you simply want to leave one or more blank lines, just press RETURN the appropriate number of times. However, the blank lines won't be printed immediately: instead they are 'saved up' for printing with the next section of text.

Finishing

To finish using LocoScript's Direct Printing mode, press ⌈EXIT⌉. The Exit menu that appears has two options. Either option will return you to the Disc Manager Screen. The difference between them is that the first option, Finish Direct Printing, will print any text you still have on the screen before returning you to the Disc Manager, whereas Abandon Direct Printing will throw this text away. Select the option you want and press ⌈ENTER⌉. You are then returned to the Disc Manager Screen. Nothing of what you have done is recorded on disc.

Session summary

In this session, you have seen:

- How to use a Commands menu in which options are picked out by diamonds rather than arrows
- How to print something directly onto a piece of paper, and still use all the facilities for styling provided by LocoScript.

Session 13

Finding and Exchanging

In this session we look at another advantage of a word-processor such as LocoScript over a typewriter – the word-processor's ability to find particular words and to exchange one word or phrase for another throughout the document.

Why might you want this facility? Well, you might need to produce a document describing a new product before the name for the product has been finalised. Because LocoScript has Find and Exchange facilities, you can prepare the initial versions using the development name for the product, confident that you can replace this name with the final name throughout the document even at the very last moment.

The document we are going to edit in this session is called DISCINFO and it is stored in group 1 of your Examples disc. So the first thing to do is to pick out this document with the File cursor and then open it for editing. (Turn back to Session 5 if you are not sure how to do this.)

Finding a particular word

Finding a word or phrase is essentially a way of moving the Text cursor.

The Textual Movement keys we introduced in Session 5 move the Text cursor about your document very efficiently when you know at least the page and probably the paragraph on the page you want to move to, and how far away that is from the page and paragraph you are currently working on. Finding a word or a phrase is the efficient way of moving the Text cursor when you don't have any clear idea where the word or phrase you want to move to is.

What you do when you want to 'Find' something is give LocoScript the word or phrase to look for and tell it whether you are only interested in whole words or whether you want to know about words that have the same spelling but a different combination of capital and small letters. It then searches forwards through the text for this, starting at your current working position. How it works is as follows.

To start with, you must check that the Text cursor is positioned higher up the document (ie. nearer to the beginning) than the word or phrase you want to find – because the search is always carried out forwards through the text. If you are really unsure where the word you want is to be found, move the cursor to the start of your document (where the cursor probably is now).

Press [FIND]. Do this now. LocoScript 2 then puts up a special menu.

Find key

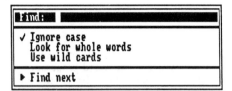

The slot at the top of the menu is reserved for the word, part of a word or phrase you want LocoScript to find. This 'Find text' can be up to 30 characters long, and can include carriage returns (↵) and tabs (→).

Below this is a list of the additional features you can give LocoScript 2's search:

- Ignore case tells LocoScript to pick out places where the same spelling is used but not necessarily the same combination of capital and small letters. For example, ignoring the case when searching for cat will pick out CAT, Cat and cat. If you don't tell LocoScript 2 to ignore case, it will only pick out cat.

- Look for whole words tells LocoScript to reject places where your Find text forms part of a longer word. For example, looking for whole words when searching for cat will make LocoScript 2 reject words like catalogue and scatter that have cat in the middle of them.

- Use wild cards tells LocoScript that the Find text you have given it is a pattern for a number of possible pieces of text. (See below)

The first job is to type in the text you want LocoScript to find.

The part of the Menu reserved for the Find text is highlighted. This highlighting is a standard LocoScript Menu cursor, marking the part of the menu that is currently active. Type in the word 'information'.

If you make any mistakes in typing this, edit it exactly as you would normal text. As in other menus where you can change the information, there is a small cursor within the Menu cursor that you can position with the Cursor keys. You can also press [→|] to clear away everything to the right of this cursor.

Once the text is ready, the next job is to set the options for the search. We describe these options below. For the moment, we will ensure that all these options are cleared (by pointing to the ones with ticks beside them and pressing [→|]) – so that we see what LocoScript will pick out for you if you don't select any of the extra search features.

The bottom entry of the menu is a 'Commands' menu with just one option – Find next. This is automatically selected for you – as you can see from the arrow beside it.

So when you are ready, just press ⬚ENTER⬚ to tell LocoScript to start 'Finding the next' example of your Find Text. LocoScript then searches forwards through the document, trying to match the Find text against the document. When it finds a section of the document that matches the Find text, LocoScript puts the Text cursor on the first character of the section. If LocoScript doesn't find a bit of the document that matches the Find text, it leaves the Text cursor at the end of the document.

Cursor positioned on
the i of information

```
↵
- if you use different disks for different types of documents, rather like
you would use the different drawers of a filing cabinet↵
↵
- if you use the different groups on a disk like you would use different
folders within the filing cabinet↵
↵
- if you give your disks, groups and documents names that help you remember
what information they contain.↵
↵
In this session, we shall discuss:↵
↵
```

Press ⬚FIND⬚ again. Up on the screen comes the same 'menu' again – but with a subtle difference. This time the top part of the menu already contains the Find text you typed in last time. This is so that you can readily repeat the search.

You can now search for something else – by changing the existing Find text to this new text – or you can choose different additional search features. But if you simply want LocoScript to look for this again (because, say, the section of the document LocoScript found isn't the one you wanted to move to), you just press ⬚ENTER⬚ to tell LocoScript to go ahead.

So to find the next place information is in the example document, all you have to do is press ⬚ENTER⬚. LocoScript then searches forward again, matching the Find text against the document. It succeeds so the phrase is once again picked out, but this time you are looking at a different part of the document.

Now go back to the start of the document and press ⬚FIND⬚ again, but this time give LocoScript a different Find text to search for – disc. Press ⬚◁⬚ to clear away the old text before typing the new text you would like LocoScript to search for. When the new Find text is ready, press ⬚ENTER⬚.

When LocoScript stops this time, press ⬚FIND⬚ and then immediately ⬚ENTER⬚ so that it finds the next example of disc. Then do this a few times more, just to see which examples of disc LocoScript picks out.

Using the search options

Having searched for disc with none of the search options selected, it's now worth seeing how the search changes when you tell LocoScript to ignore case and to look only for whole words, and how to give it a pattern to look for – rather than a real word.

Ignoring case

Move the Text cursor back to the top of the document (for example, by using [ALT]+[DOC]); then bring the Find menu onto the screen again. This time, leave the Find text alone but select the Ignore case option (ie. point to Ignore case with the Menu cursor and press [+] or the Space Bar to set this option).

Now press [ENTER] to tell LocoScript to carry out its search. Then use [FIND] again some more times – without altering either the Find text or the options – to see what LocoScript finds now you have told it to ignore case. Notice how it is picking out all the same instances that it did before, but it is also picking out some new ones – Disc and Discretion, for example. Telling LocoScript to ignore case has extended the search to a number of other instances of the letters disc.

Whole words only

Once again, move the Text cursor back to the top of the document and bring the Find menu onto the screen again. This time, select Look for whole words (again, by pointing at this option and pressing [+] or the Space Bar).

Press [ENTER] to start LocoScript searching and then use [FIND] some more times – without altering either the Find text or the options – to see what LocoScript finds this time. Notice how now it is only picking out disc and Disc: in particular, how it is not picking out words like discs which have the search word as their root. When you ask for Whole Words, LocoScript takes you literally and just gives you precisely what you asked for.

Using wild cards

The other search option – Use wild cards – allows you to give LocoScript the 'pattern' of a word or a few words to look for rather than the exact words. For example, if you wanted LocoScript to search for either disc or disk, then you could tell LocoScript that you want words that match the pattern dis*(some letter)*.

The key to creating this pattern is the 'Wild card' character ? which LocoScript understands as standing for any character. So, for example, the pattern that can be used to pick out both disc and disk would be dis?.

To see this in action, move the Text cursor back up to the top of the document and press [FIND] again. Clear away the old Find text (by pressing [⊡]) and replace it by dis?; then make sure that all three of the search options are selected (ticked). It

---

is particularly important to check that the Use wild cards option has been selected – otherwise LocoScript will just look for dis?

Press [ENTER] to start LocoScript on its search and then use [FIND] some more times – again, without altering either the Find text or the search options. You should see it pick out both disk and disc.

• That's all there is to Finding words or phrases in even very long documents.

Exchanging one word for another

Exchanging a word or phrase for another is the quick and reliable way of changing all references to one product, say, into references to another product.

You might, for example, have a sales brochure for an old product on disc that you want to use as the basis for the brochure for your latest product. As a first step, you could use LocoScript's 'Exchange' facility to replace the old product name by the new one throughout the document.

Exchange is essentially the Find facility we introduced above with added features so that it doesn't just search for a phrase, it also replaces that phrase with new text. You should notice a number of similarities between Find and Exchange.

To demonstrate using Exchange, we shall use it to replace first all the instances of disk by disc, and then some of the instances of document by file.

Like Find, Exchange always works forwards through the document from your current working position so you must start with the Text cursor higher up the document than the first word you want to change. In our case, this means moving it to the very beginning of the document (for example, by holding down [ALT] while pressing [DOC]).

When the Text cursor is in place, press the [EXCH] key. Do this now. (EXCH is the upper option on the [FIND] key, so to press [EXCH], you hold down the [SHIFT] key while you press [FIND].)

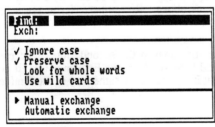

8809

The top slot of the Exchange menu is once again reserved for the Find text – the word, part of word or phrase you want it to replace. The similar slot below this is for the Exchange text, ie. what you want LocoScript to put in instead. Both phrases can be up to 30 characters long, and can include ←s and →s – exactly as for Find.

Below this are the different options that LocoScript 2 offers for the exchange. Three of these will be familiar to you – because they are the three search options you used when you were Finding words, earlier in this session. These options are again used to refine the search side of the operation.

The other option – Preserve case – tells LocoScript to copy (as far as possible) the current use of capital and small letters in making the replacement. For example, if the current word is Cat and the exchange text is dog, LocoScript 2 will insert dog if case isn't preserved but Dog if case is preserved. We will see this in practice shortly.

The bottom section of the menu is a 'Commands' menu, offering you the choice of 'Manual' exchange or 'Automatic' exchange. We will see what these options offer below.

Filling in the Exchange menu

When the Exchange menu appears on the screen, both slots at the top of the menu could be empty or both could have some text already in them or just the top one could be filled in – depending on what you have done so far in this editing session.

The top slot will be filled in if you have already searched for a particular word or phrase – either by using this Exchange feature or by using Find. This text is the last Find text you used. The second slot will be filled in if you have already used Exchange.

The menu is filled in like this so that you can readily repeat the same Exchange that you did earlier. Again, LocoScript is making it as easy as possible to continue with the current task.

The Menu cursor is initially on the Find text, so start by editing this to the new Find text. Use the same steps as above. (Remember: if you press [⬚], this will clear away everything to the right of the small cursor within the Menu cursor.) The Find text of our first exchange is disk.

Now move the Menu cursor down to the second slot, (if necessary, press [⬚] to clear any existing text) and type in disc, the Exchange text. If you make a mistake in typing this, you can edit it in exactly the same way as the Find text.

Making use of the Exchange options

When both texts are ready, move the Menu cursor down to the options part of the menu – to select the different features you want for the search.

```
√ Ignore case
√ Preserve case
  Look for whole words
  Use wild cards
```

Three of these options are exactly the same options as you had when you were Finding words – so we shall simply concentrate on the other option Preserve case. This tells LocoScript 2 that you want the word it inserts to copy the word it is replacing as far as possible in its use of lower case and capital letters. In practice this means:

– if the old word is all in lower case letters, then the replacement word should be as well

– if the old word is entirely in capitals, then the replacement word should be in capitals as well, and

– if the old word starts with a capital letter, then so should the replacement word

The options part of the menu is a 'Settings' menu, so you use [⊞], [⊟] and Space Bar in the usual way to set and clear options as necessary. (Details in Session 4, if you need them.) For the moment, just select Preserve case so that you can see this in action.

Note: You can only specify wildcards in the text you give LocoScript to find. Any ?s in the Exchange text will simply be put into your document.

Manual or Automatic?

Now move the Menu cursor down to the bottom part of the menu.

```
▶ Manual exchange
  Automatic exchange
```

This section of the menu gives you a choice of the two types of exchange you can have, Manual and Automatic. In a Manual exchange, LocoScript stops each time it finds the Find text and waits for you to say whether you want it to replace this one with the Exchange text or carry on to the next. In an Automatic exchange, LocoScript replaces each instance of the Find text it finds.

Which option to select depends on whether:

– you want to confirm each exchange before this is made, or

– you want LocoScript to go ahead and change every example it finds

Manual exchange has an arrow beside it to show that this is already selected for you – just as one of the actions in other 'Commands' menus you have used has been. Again, LocoScript has pre-selected your most likely choice of action.

8809

Automatic exchanges

For our first exchange, we want LocoScript to go ahead and make the changes – so the option to select is Automatic exchange. Move the Menu cursor to this option and press [ENTER].

LocoScript now goes ahead and exchanges every disk it finds by disc without further reference to you – all the way down to the bottom of the document. You can see it making each exchange as it goes.

However, making exchanges all the way down to the bottom of the document will often be a little more 'enthusiastic' than you really want. You may well only want to exchange your search word down as far as a particular point in the document.

One way of doing this is to watch carefully where LocoScript has got to in the document and, when it has gone far enough, press [STOP]. This, you will remember, makes LocoScript pause and you can get it to abandon doing any more exchanges by pressing [STOP] again.

A more controlled way of going about this is to tell LocoScript from the start how far you want to go. To see how this works, move the Text cursor back up to the top of the document then press [EXCH] again. (Remember: All exchanges are carried out **forward** from the current position of the Text cursor.)

Now change the Find text to document and the Exchange text to file. (Starting each edit by pressing [+] to clear away the old text and then typing in the new text is probably the easiest way of doing this.)

Leave the exchange options as they are and, once again, move the Menu cursor down to Automatic exchange so that this option is selected. But now press [PARA] instead of [ENTER].

Again, LocoScript goes ahead and replaces examples of the Find text by the Exchange text but, this time, it stops when it gets to the end of the first paragraph. Pressing [PARA] told LocoScript that you only wanted it to exchange document for file up to the end of the current paragraph. (Remember, paragraphs in LocoScript 2 are blocks of text separated by lines of white – so for example, a whole address can be one paragraph.)

Now press [EXCH] again. This time, move the Menu cursor to Automatic exchange and press [PAGE] instead of either [ENTER] or [PARA].

Again, LocoScript goes ahead and exchanges document for file but, this time, it stops when it gets to the end of the first page. Pressing [PAGE] told LocoScript that you only wanted it to do this exchange up to the end of the current page.

Manual exchanges

Now press ⌈EXCH⌉ again. This time, we want to confirm each exchange before it is made – the option that is automatically selected for you. So you just have to press ⌈ENTER⌉ to tell LocoScript to go ahead.

LocoScript stops at the first instance it finds of the Find text and displays a message both in the middle of the screen and in the Information lines, prompting you to press either the ⌈⊞⌉ key, the ⌈□⌉ key or ⌈CAN⌉. And it does this over and over again to the end of the document.

```
Match found:

press X to exchange and continue
: to simply continue
or CAN to abandon
```

If the message in the middle of the screen is covering the part of the screen you need to see in order to decide which key to press, either wait a moment or press ⌈#⌉. This message is then cleared away, leaving just the copy at the top of the screen. You can now see the piece of text LocoScript has picked out for exchange.

Press ⌈⊞⌉ to make the exchange and carry on to the next example; press ⌈□⌉ to simply carry on to the next example; or press ⌈CAN⌉ to abandon the exchange. Try out both pressing ⌈⊞⌉ and pressing ⌈□⌉. When you have seen this enough, press ⌈CAN⌉.

- And that's all there is to exchanging one word or phrase for another.

Finally...

Finish this session by Abandoning the edit (ie. by pressing ⌈EXIT⌉ and selecting Abandon edit) – so that later you can work through this session as if for the first time.

Session summary

In this session you have seen:

- How to move the Text cursor to a particular word or phrase, neither knowing which page it is on nor which paragraph it is in
- How to exchange one word or phrase for another in a particular paragraph, on a particular page or throughout your whole document.

Session 14

Moving text around

Early on in this tutorial, we showed you how to mark out a block of text within your document and then either move it to another point in the same document or put in one or more copies at other places in the document.

This kind of text movement saves you a lot of typing effort – but it only saves you from re-typing text that you have already typed in this document. How about when you want to 'poach' text from another document you've prepared or from someone else's document or documents prepared on a different word processor?

In this session, we shall show you how to:

– move blocks of text from one document to another
– insert whole documents into other documents
– set up a series of standard phrases that take just two keystrokes to insert into any document
– insert documents that have been prepared on other word-processing systems
– process LocoScript documents so that they can be used on a different word-processing system

In short, we shall show you how to move text around from any document to any other document to really minimise the amount of re-typing you will have to do.

The document we are going to edit in this session is DISCINFO, which you will remember is stored in group 1 of your Examples disc. So, the first step is to open this document for editing. (Turn back to Session 5 if you are not sure how to do this.)

Moving text to another document

Moving or copying a section of text between one document and another uses the LocoScript system of Blocks, in exactly the same way as they are used to move or duplicate a section of text within a single document.

The feature of the Blocks system this makes use of is the way LocoScript remembers the text stored in any of its 10 Blocks after you have finished editing the current document and started editing another. As you will recall, LocoScript remembers the text you copy to a Block until you either store something else in this Block or you switch off or reset your machine.

So whenever you simply want to take some text in one document (the 'Source' document) and make a copy of this text in another document (the 'Destination'

---

document), all you have to do is edit the 'Source' document and copy the section of text into a Block; then edit the 'Destination' document and paste the Block in – exactly as if you were still working on the same document.

To show how this works, suppose you wanted to use the second and third paragraphs of the example document in a new document. The first step is to mark this section of text out as a Block, exactly as you marked out sections of text in Session 6. Store a copy of this text, for example, as Block 0.

Now abandon editing this document and create a new document. (As we will be suggesting you throw this new document away, don't worry about setting up a special name for it – just accept the name LocoScript suggests.) When the new document is open on the screen, paste Block 0 into this document by pressing [PASTE] and then typing 0 – exactly as if you were pasting it in at a new position in the 'Source' document.

That's how to move or copy text between documents through the Blocks.

Important: Moving blocks of text containing word-processing codes, whether from one point to another in the same document, or from one document to another, can produce some unexpected effects both at the place you took the text from and at the place you have inserted the text.

For example, if the text you move contains a (+UL) code but no (-UL) code, the text immediately following the place you removed the block from will no longer be underlined but the text following the block in its new position will now be underlined. However, this looks more of a disaster than it is – because to repair each piece of text you just need to insert a (+UL) in the place you removed the text from and a (-UL) immediately after the text you have just inserted.

Please note that it is (+UL)very important(-UL) to ensure that the motor is turned off before making any adjustments.⏎

(-UL) at end of underlined text

(+UL) at start of underlined text

Please note that it is (+UL)very important(-UL) to ensure that the motor is turned off before making any adjustments.⏎

Section of text to be removed is highlighted. It includes the (-UL) code

Please note that it is (+UL)very before making any adjustments.⏎

Text now underlined, because the (-UL) code has been removed

A similar problem happens when you insert a block of text containing Layout codes, because the code brings with it all the information about how the text that follows it is laid out – up to the next Layout code.

Looking at the Blocks

You will usually be able to remember what you have stored in a Block and which Block you stored it in – but if you are ever unsure, you can jog your memory by looking at the first few words of each Block.

The menu that helps you do this is the Actions menu of either the LocoScript Editor (which you are using now) or the Disc Manager Screen. In either case, the Actions menu is brought onto the screen by pressing ⌐f1¬: so press ⌐f1¬ now.

The Actions menu is another of LocoScript's 'Commands' menus – ie. the option that will be carried out when you press ⌐ENTER¬ is the one currently picked out by the arrow. The option you want here is Show blocks. Select this option and then press ⌐ENTER¬ to tell LocoScript to carry out this action. What you now see on the screen will be a 'menu' like this:

Down the lefthand edge of this menu are the names of the Blocks (0...9) and, beside each name, is the beginning of the text stored as this Block. If there isn't anything written beside a name, then nothing is stored in that Block.

If the menu shows you have Blocks that you no longer need, you can clear these out while this menu is on the screen – by moving the cursor to the Block and pressing ⌐□¬. This has the added advantage of freeing some space on Drive M.

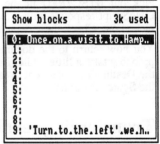

When you have found out the names of the Block(s) you want, press ⌐ENTER¬ to tell LocoScript to carry on.

Inserting a whole document

The extreme example of moving text between one document and another is to insert the whole of the first document in the second. While you could do this by copying the whole of the Source document into a Block and pasting this in, this involves you in taking much more trouble than is necessary. You can insert a whole document directly – through the Actions menu.

Suppose you wanted to insert the whole of this session's example document (DISCINFO) at the beginning of the new document you have just created.

The first step, as you might expect, is to position the Text cursor where you want to insert the document. In this case, move the Text cursor to the top of the document.

When the Text cursor is in position, bring the Actions menu onto the screen. If you can't remember which key you press to bring this menu onto the screen, look at the Information lines and you will see that the key to press is [f1]. Press [f1] now: the following menu should appear:

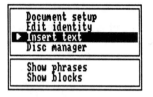

Now move the Menu cursor to Insert text and press [ENTER]. LocoScript 2 then displays the Disc Manager Screen so that you can pick out the document you want to insert. (The message on the screen reminds you to do this.)

Pick out DISCINFO in the usual way with the File cursor; then press [ENTER]. LocoScript responds with a Selection menu giving the details of the document you picked out. Check these details are right and then press [ENTER] (or [CAN] to abandon).

You now return to the document and LocoScript 2 inserts the document. This will probably take a little while: LocoScript can have quite a lot of work to do adjusting the Destination document to take account of the word-processor codes embedded in the Source document.

Transferring text through standard phrases

Another way of making text available in a number of documents is through LocoScript's system of Phrases. This option is especially useful if there are a number of quite short phrases that you use in a lot of the documents you prepare. If you store these as Phrases, all you have to do to type each of them is press two keys.

In many respects, Phrases are very similar to Blocks: text is copied into both Phrases and Blocks in essentially the same way and, once stored, the text can be 'pasted' in anywhere you like by pressing the [PASTE] key followed by a character key. In both cases, the character key pressed is the name of the Block or Phrase to be inserted. With Blocks, this is one of the numbers 0...9: with Phrases, it is one of the letters A...Z.

However, there are also some important differences. In particular, any Blocks you set up are forgotten the moment you switch off or reset your machine. Phrases, on the other hand, can be saved together in a file on disc and so you can readily 'reload' a set of Phrases you have used before. You can even have one set of Phrases that is loaded automatically as part of the process of loading the LocoScript 2 program. For this reason, the chances are that you always have some Phrases available.

Another important difference is that you can only store a limited amount of text – about 1000 characters – in any set of Phrases. Each Phrase is meant to be just a few words, whereas you typically store one or more paragraphs in a Block. You can also use Phrases to store special combinations of word-processing codes – for example, a particular combination of Character Pitch, Line Spacing and Character Styling (Bold, etc.) that you use for Subheadings, say. However, you are not advised to store Layout codes as Phrases because these tend to fill up the space you have available for Phrases.

Setting up a group of Phrases

1. Looking at the current set of Phrases

The first step is to find out/remind yourself which phrases are available so far. The menu that helps you do this is the Actions menu of either the LocoScript Editor (which you are using now) or the Disc Manager Screen. In either case, the Actions menu is brought onto the screen by pressing ⌷f1⌷: so press ⌷f1⌷ now.

The option you want here is Show phrases. Select this option and then press ⌷ENTER⌷ to tell LocoScript to carry out this action. What you now see on the screen will be a 'menu' like this:

Down the lefthand edge of this menu are the names of the Phrases and, beside each name, at least the beginning of the text stored as this Phrase – just like the display when you select the Show Blocks option. But unlike the Show Blocks menu, this Show Phrases menu only lists the Phrases that are currently being used. If a Phrase isn't shown, then nothing is stored in that Phrase, but if an apparently empty Phrase is shown, then it is being used to store word-processing codes.

Initially, only the first 12 Phrases you have stored are displayed. To see further down the list, move the Menu cursor down the menu and then keep pressing ⌷↓⌷. The list will then scroll to show you the other Phrases. To scroll back up through the list, move the Menu cursor up the menu and then keep pressing ⌷↑⌷. Alternatively, if you want to see a particular Phrase, type the name of the Phrase. LocoScript 2 will then move the Menu cursor directly to this Phrase, adjusting the section of the list that's displayed as necessary. For example, you can readily display Phrase Z by typing z.

---

2. Clearing out Phrases you no longer need

The Show Phrases menu can also be used to clear out Phrases that you don't need.

For example, suppose that you don't want to keep Phrase Z. All you need to do to clear away this Phrase is to move the Menu cursor to Phrase Z (for example, by typing Z) and then press [⊡]. Pressing [⊡] clears the text next to the Phrase name – just as it cleared the slots in the Find and Exchange menus (see Session 13).

Press [ENTER] when you have cleared the Phrases you want, to clear away the menu.

3. Adding new Phrases

To add phrases to your current set, you have to be working on a document that contains examples of the phrases that you want to add to your set. (You can, if you like, just type these phrases in temporarily and get rid of them when you have finished copying them into Phrases.)

Picking out each Phrase is just like marking out a section of text for storage in a Block. You move the Text cursor to the beginning of your chosen phrase and press [COPY]; then move the Text cursor to the end of the phrase and press [COPY] or [CUT] as appropriate. The only difference is that you now type a letter as the name of the Phrase you want to store the phrase in.

So, for example, to pick out 'High-Capacity''Double-track' discs as a Phrase, you would mark this phrase out exactly as if you were going to store it as a Block, but finishing by typing (say) H when you were asked to type a number or a letter.

Choosing which letter to type is the hardest part of the operation. To help you remember later which phrase you want, you should choose a letter that is appropriate to the phrase you are saving – for example the first letter of the phrase. But, at the same time, you must remember which letters you have already used. You don't want to choose a letter that is already being used for another Phrase (unless you no longer want this Phrase).

The new phrase is now added to this set of Phrases – at least until you switch off or reset your machine. To make the phrase a permanent member of the set of Phrases, you have to save the whole set – as we shall describe below.

Note: You can have up to 26 Phrases (Phrase A...Phrase Z) but their total length is limited to about 1000 characters. When you use up all the available space, you will see a message on the screen telling you that you have over-run your phrase store.

When this message appears, you will lose some of the phrase you were setting up. It is a simple enough task to set up the phrase again, but first you must make some space by getting rid of some phrases you no longer want to use.

To get rid of a Phrase (say, Phrase Q), you can either use the Show Phrases menu as before or you can mark out a phrase of nothing by not moving the Text cursor between the two times you press COPY and then store this as the new Phrase Q.

Using Phrases

To insert a phrase in the document you are working on, all you have to do is position the Text cursor, press PASTE and then type the letter that's the name of the Phrase you want – exactly as if you were inserting a Block (see Session 6). The text stored in the Phrase you name is then inserted into the document at the cursor position. Of course, if you specify a Phrase that's empty, nothing will be inserted.

So, for example, to insert Phrase H ('High-Capacity' 'Double-track' discs) at the beginning of the second paragraph of the example document, position the Text cursor at the start of this paragraph, press PASTE and then type H. Phrase H is then inserted:

```
solution to your problem with discs is also to tidy them up. You can work a
lot more efficiently:↵
↵
▪ if you use different discs for different types of documents, rather like
you would use the different drawers of a filing cabinet↵
```

                            PASTE H

```
solution to your problem with discs is also to tidy them up. You can work a
lot more efficiently:↵
↵
'High capacity' 'Double track' discs ▪
▪ if you use different discs for different types of documents, rather like
you would use the different drawers of a filing cabinet↵
```

Obviously, it is important to know which Phrase holds the text you want. If you (or the person who set up the Phrases) chose the letters well, you may well be able to remember pretty much what is stored in each Phrase. However, you can always check by 'looking up' the Phrase in the Show Phrases menu (as above).

• The Phrases available to you remain the same (barring further additions and/or deletions) until either you switch off or reset your machine or you load a different set of Phrases. If you want to use a particular set of Phrases again, you have to save these – as described below. Otherwise, the next time you load LocoScript you will only have your 'old' set of Phrases available.

Saving the current set of Phrases

Once you have finished making your changes to your current Phrases, it is a good idea to save these as a set of Phrases – particularly, if you expect to use this set again.

Saving the current set of Phrases is one of the tasks carried out when the Disc Manager Screen is displayed. This makes it, ideally, a job to do when you are returned to the Disc Manager Screen between editing one document and working on

---

LocoScript 2 User Guide: Tutorial   **149**

another. So the next thing to do if you are following the Tutorial is to press [EXIT] to finish work on the current document, and then select Abandon edit and press [ENTER] – to throw this document away.

Before you go any further you must decide where you want to store the Phrases, because you need to arrange that the disc you want to store them on is available. This disc must be in the drive before you start saving the set of Phrases because you cannot change the disc in the drive in the middle of the process of saving Phrases.

LocoScript 2 was supplied with a single set of Phrases – stored in a file called PHRASES.STD in the SYSTEM group of the Start-of-day disc. The name and location (disc and group) for this file are important because these ensure that the Phrases stored in this file are automatically made available as part of the process of loading LocoScript 2. If you want your current set of Phrases to be the ones automatically made available, you must replace the current PHRASES.STD file on your Start-of-day disc with your new set.

If you just want the set of Phrases to be the ones available while you are working on certain types of documents, then you should save the Phrases in a file certainly on the same disc and preferably in the same group as the documents you want to use it with. In this case, you can either replace an existing file (if you want to update a particular set of Phrases) or store the Phrases in a new file.

Note: You can also save your Phrases by calling up the Disc Manager Screen from within a document. However, when you do this, you won't be able to remove the disc holding the document you are editing from the drive – so you won't necessarily be able to put the disc on which you want to store the Phrases into your machine at the moment. You may have to save your Phrases temporarily on Drive M instead and then copy the file to the right disc later.

The first step is to pick out the group in which you want to store your Phrases. If you are replacing an existing file of Phrases, move the File cursor to this file. Otherwise, move the Group cursor to the group you want to store the Phrases in.

So, for example, to save the current set of Phrases as a new file in group 1 of your Examples disc, simply move the Group cursor to this group.

The menu on the Disc Manager Screen that helps you save your current set of Phrases is the Actions menu, which you bring onto the screen by pressing [f1]. The option you want is Save phrases.

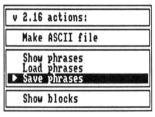

Select this option and press ⟨ENTER⟩ in the usual way. When you press ⟨ENTER⟩, LocoScript puts up one of its Selection menus, giving details of the place you have chosen to store your set of Phrases. The Name part of the menu will always show PHRASES.STD – LocoScript's standard name for a Phrases file.

You can give your new Phrases file any name you want – providing, of course, that it is a valid name and that it is not already the name of one of the documents in the same group. However, it is probably a good idea to keep the name PHRASES as the first part of its name – to make it easier for you to remember what is stored in this file. For example, you might call the example set of Phrases PHRASES.EG.

When you've checked the details in the Selection menu, press ⟨ENTER⟩ to tell LocoScript to go ahead. When you store the Phrases in a new file, LocoScript simply creates the new file and then returns you to whatever you were doing before. But when you choose to replace an existing file, LocoScript first puts up one of its Alert messages – to warn you that you are about to overwrite an existing file. You confirm that this is what you want to do by pressing ⟨ENTER⟩.

Loading a set of Phrases

As we said earlier, LocoScript automatically loads the Phrases stored in the PHRASES.STD file in the SYSTEM group of your Start-of-day disc as part of the process of loading the LocoScript 2 software. LocoScript makes these Phrases available for you: you don't have to do anything.

When you want to use a different set of Phrases that you have stored on disc, you have to go through a special procedure to load these. Again, this is something that you do from the Disc Manager Screen.

Of course, you can only load a Phrases file that is currently in one of your drives – so it is important to organise this **before** you try to load your set of Phrases.

To see the loading of Phrases in action, reset your machine (which, you will remember, you do by inserting the Start-of-day disc in Drive A and holding down the ⟨SHIFT⟩ and ⟨EXTRA⟩ keys as you press ⟨EXIT⟩). This reloads the LocoScript 2 program and the Phrases in the PHRASES.STD file in the SYSTEM group on the Start-of-day disc. You can readily check this from the Disc Manager Screen by using the Show phrases option in the Actions menu – exactly as we did earlier (except that then we were using the Show phrases option of the Editor Screen's Actions menu).

Now load the Phrases you have just stored in the PHRASES.EG file on your Examples disc as follows:

The first step is to make PHRASES.EG available – so put your Examples disc in a drive and press ⌈f7⌉ to tell LocoScript that you have changed a disc. When the disc you want is in the drive, select the Phrases file – by moving the File cursor until it is over this file.

Now press ⌈f1⌉ to bring the Actions menu onto the screen. The option you want this time is Load phrases. Select this option and press ⌈ENTER⌉ in the usual way.

Again, LocoScript responds with one of its Selection menus. Check that the details given in the menu are right: then press ⌈ENTER⌉ to tell LocoScript to go ahead (or ⌈CAN⌉ to abandon).

LocoScript then 'forgets' the previous set of Phrases and replaces them by your chosen set of Phrases (PHRASES.EG in this case) – as you can readily confirm by inspecting the current set of Phrases with the help of the Show phrases option, just as you did before.

Exchanging text with other programs and word processors

I: Preparing a LocoScript document for use by another program

LocoScript documents contain a number of special codes that specify how the text appears on the screen and how it is printed. These codes are special to LocoScript and can't be used by other programs. A number of the codes used to represent characters are also special to LocoScript.

So before you use a LocoScript document with another program, you have to make a copy of the document that has been cleared of all the special layout codes and with standard codes for the characters. This is called 'Making an ASCII file' (ASCII is a standard system for representing text characters).

There are two types of ASCII file you can make.

One is called a 'Simple text file'. This has none of the detailed layout information, though it does record where you pressed ⌈TAB⌉ and ⌈RETURN⌉. A Simple text file is the type of ASCII file you need to make when you simply want to pass information between LocoScript and another program.

The other type of ASCII file is a 'Page image file'. Here, all the spacing, line breaks, page breaks, etc. are preserved by putting in extra spaces, extra carriage returns and special characters called Form Feeds. This is the type of ASCII file to make when you want to preserve the way LocoScript has laid out the document – for example, because you want to 'paste' your LocoScript document into a document prepared on another word processor.

ASCII files are made from the Disc Manager Screen – so you start by displaying this screen. The next step is to ensure that you have the disc(s) you need in the drive(s). You need to have access to both the LocoScript document and to the disc you are going to store the ASCII version on. In our example case, you just want the Examples disc in a disc drive. (Press [f7] if you change the disc.)

When you have the discs etc. set up, pick out the LocoScript document you want to make an ASCII version of with the File cursor in the usual way. For example, pick out DISCINFO. Then press [f1] to bring the Actions menu onto the screen.

The option you want here is Make ASCII file. This is the top option in the menu and is pre-selected for you, so typically all you have to do is check that Make ASCII file is selected and press [ENTER].

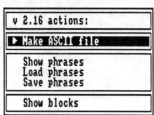

Now move the Group cursor to the group you want to store the ASCII version in. (LocoScript displays its usual message telling you to do this.) Always choose the first group on the disc to make it easier for other programs to access the file. If this disc isn't in the drive at the moment, move the Group cursor to one of the groups on Drive M – for temporary storage. Press [ENTER].

A menu then appears giving details of the LocoScript document you picked out and of the ASCII file you propose to make. Down the bottom of the menu is a mini 'Commands' menu with the two options – one for each type of ASCII file.

Check the details of the LocoScript document given in the menu and type a name in the slot provided for the ASCII file – ASCII.EG in this case. That done, select the type of ASCII file you want and then press [ENTER] to tell LocoScript to go ahead or press [CAN] to abandon. Simple text file is automatically selected for you (as you can see from the arrow beside it), so all you have to do to make the file is press [ENTER].

LocoScript then creates the ASCII version and stores it in the file you specified. Before you use this file, move it to one of the discs you use with your other program – for example, by using LocoScript's own moving and copying facilities ([f3] – see Session 7). Your LocoScript discs are best used only for LocoScript documents.

Important: Not all of LocoScript's characters can be represented in ASCII. As a result, the text in the ASCII file may be 'damaged' – ie. some of the characters may be replaced by different characters. In some cases, you can avoid this problem by running the ASCII file through a special conversion program before using it in your program. You may need a 'tame expert' to put together such a program for you – but start by asking your dealer if such a program is already available.

8809

II: Inserting text prepared on a different system

Suppose you use an accounts package, for example, and you want to transfer some of the information this has generated to the document DISCINFO.

First, you must use the accounts package to produce a file containing the information you want to transfer. This file must contain just standard text characters: it must not contain any special codes that tell the accounts package how to lay out this information. In other words, what you want – once again – is a simple ASCII file. If it is possible to set up such a file from within your program (and it usually is), you will find details of how this is done in the program's own user guide.

This file must be stored on a disc that you can use in your PCW. On an 8000 series machine, this means a 3" compact floppy disc formatted for use under CP/M; on a PcW9256, this means a 3½" floppy disc formatted for use under CP/M. (Don't worry if this doesn't mean a lot to you: it will make sense to your dealer or to an experienced computer user.)

If you run your accounts package on your PCW, then you won't have any problems. The file will automatically be stored on the right kind of disc. If the accounts package runs on a different computer, you will have to find a way of making a copy of the ASCII file on a PCW disc – preferably on the disc that also holds the document you want to add this information to. You may need the help of an 'expert' here – your dealer, perhaps.

Once you have the file ready, display LocoScript's Disc Manager Screen. Insert the disc holding the ASCII file and and, if possible, the disc holding the document. (Remember to press [f7] to tell LocoScript about the disc change.) In our example case, both the document and the ASCII file are on the Examples disc so you just need to insert this disc.

If the document and the file are on different discs and you have a machine with a single disc drive, insert the disc holding the ASCII file, press [f7] (to tell LocoScript you have changed discs) and then make a copy of this file on Drive M (see Session 7). Then replace the disc with the one holding your document and again press [f7].

Now edit the document in which you want to insert this text (DISCINFO in this case). Once the document is on the screen, move the Text cursor to the place you want to insert the new text – the end of the document, for example.

The menu option you want here is Insert text – just as it was when you wanted to insert a whole LocoScript document into another. This, you will remember, is one of the options in the Actions menu – so after you have positioned the Text cursor, press [f1] to bring the Actions menu onto the screen.

Move the Menu cursor to Insert text and press [ENTER]. LocoScript 2 then displays the Disc Manager Screen so that you can pick out the file you want to insert.

Pick out the ASCII file you want with the File cursor in the usual way and press [ENTER]. (The message on the screen reminds you to do this.) In this case, the file to pick out is ASCII.EG – the ASCII file we have just made. LocoScript then puts up a Selection menu giving the details of the file you picked out. Check these details are right and then press [ENTER].

You now return to the document and LocoScript 2 inserts the ASCII file. This can take a little while, depending on the length of the file you are inserting.

When all the file has been inserted, notice how this text has been cleared of all the codes that were in the original LocoScript document. You can go now through putting in word-processor codes to lay it out nicely, exactly as if you had just typed the text in.

Session summary

In this session, you have seen all the ways in which text can be shared between LocoScript documents and between LocoScript documents and other computer programs. In particular, you have seen:

- How to save a block of text from one LocoScript document and insert this in another LocoScript document
- How to insert a whole LocoScript document in another
- What side-effects you can get when you move text containing word processing codes from one place to another and how to cure these
- How to set of a series of short phrases that you can insert in any document just by pressing a couple of keys and how to make these available for use
- How to process a LocoScript document so that it can be used by another program
- How to insert text that has been prepared by some other program, eg. another word processor

Session 15

The Professional touch –
I: Niceties of Layout

So far, everything we have done has been geared towards simply producing text printed on a page. The results we have produced have been pretty impressive – involving different styles and sizes of characters, tables, properly justified text, etc. – but really professional text production features:

- total control over Line Breaks – ie. over where one line ends and another begins
- total control over Page Breaks – ie. over where one page ends and another begins
- special pieces of text at the top and/or the bottom of each page (known as Headers and Footers)
- and numbered pages

LocoScript 2 has all these features, and in this session and the next we show you how to use them.

In this session, we show how you can control Line Breaks and Page Breaks. The document we are going to edit is called SPELL.TXT and it is stored in group 1 of your Examples disc. So, the first step is to open this document for editing.

Controlling Line Breaks

LocoScript normally fits as many words as it can on each line before moving onto the next line. Where it breaks the line is at the last possible space or hyphen.

This gives good results most of the time but not all of the time.

- If you are using very short lines (or very large characters) or relatively long words, you can have lines where the space at the end of the line or the spacing between the words is so large that it looks ugly.
- Exactly the same problem arises where you have a list of options – like French/German/Spanish – with no spaces in it, so that it looks like one long word to LocoScript.
- Where you have someone's name, you could have their initials on one line and their surname on another, or even the initials split across the break between two lines.
- You won't want a line break to happen at every hyphen – for example, you won't necessarily want one at the hyphen in add-on when you are describing, say, add-on programs for LocoScript such as LocoSpell and LocoMail.

8809

It's possible to cure most of these problems simply by putting in extra hyphens and spaces. For example, a simple way of filling up a gap at the end of one line is to put a hyphen at a suitable point in the next word (the first word on the next line) because then LocoScript will move onto the next line at this hyphen, rather than at the start of the word.

But there is a problem with this simple solution: the moment you make even a small change to the paragraph, these extra characters will probably be in the wrong places and you will have to rub them out again.

LocoScript has some very much better solutions.

'Soft' hyphens and spaces

LocoScript's Soft hyphens and spaces solve the problem of short lines or lines that are too widely spaced – without giving you any extra hyphens or spaces to get rid of later when other changes are made.

The special feature of Soft hyphens and spaces is that they only become visible when LocoScript breaks the line at the soft character. The rest of the time, you wouldn't know they were there!

When the reason for the problem is that the next word is relatively long, the solution is to put a Soft hyphen at a point in the word where you would be happy to see the word divided.

There is a good example of this in the first paragraph of the example document, where the automatic layout has left a large gap at the end of the fourth line because there isn't enough room for the word `encyclopaedia`. The paragraph would look very much better with `encyclo-` at the end of the fourth line and `paedia` at the beginning of the fifth. So what you need is a Soft hyphen after the `o`.

Where the item you want to divide is a list of options like `French/German/Spanish`, the sort of split you want is `French/` on the end of one line and `German/Spanish` at the beginning of the next line. (This actual example appears in the second paragraph.) In this case, you don't want a hyphen at the end of the line, so the special character to put in after the slash is a Soft space.

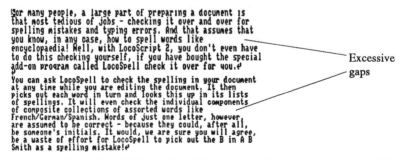

For many people, a large part of preparing a document is that most tedious of jobs - checking it over and over for spelling mistakes and typing errors. And that assumes that you know, in any case, how to spell words like encyclopaedia! Well, with LocoScript 2, you don't even have to do this checking yourself, if you have bought the special add-on program called LocoSpell check it over for you.

You can ask LocoSpell to check the spelling in your document at any time while you are editing the document. It then picks out each word in turn and looks this up in its lists of spellings. It will even check the individual components of composite collections of assorted words like French/German/Spanish. Words of just one letter, however, are assumed to be correct - because they could, after all, be someone's initials. It would, we are sure you will agree, be a waste of effort for LocoSpell to pick out the B in A B Smith as a spelling mistake!

Excessive gaps

Inserting Soft hyphens and spaces

Soft spaces and hyphens are inserted into a document through sequences of keystrokes very like the ones we have used already to put in word-processing codes like (-Bold) and (-UL). The keystroking for a soft space is to press ⊡ followed by the Space bar; the keystroking for a soft hyphen is to press ⊡ and then type a hyphen.

So to let LocoScript split encyclopaedia between the o and the p, position the Text cursor and then press ⊡ and type a hyphen. The moment you type the hyphen, LocoScript not only puts in the character but relays the paragraph up to where you are working to take account of the Soft hyphen you have inserted.

```
For many people, a large part of preparing a document is
that most tedious of jobs - checking it over and over for
spelling mistakes and typing errors. And that assumes that
you know, in any case, how to spell words like encyclo■
         paedia! Well, with LocoScript 2, you don't even have
to do this checking yourself, if you have bought the special
add-on program called LocoSpell check it over for you.◄
```

and then after relaying:

```
For many people, a large part of preparing a document is
that most tedious of jobs - checking it over and over for
spelling mistakes and typing errors. And that assumes that
you know, in any case, how to spell words like encyclo-
■aedia! Well, with LocoScript 2, you don't even have to do
this checking yourself, if you have bought the special add-
on program called LocoSpell check it over for you.◄
```

Similarly, to split French/German/Spanish after the first slash, position the Text cursor and then press ⊡ followed by the Space Bar. Once again, you will see LocoScript relay the text to take account of this change.

```
You can ask LocoSpell to check the spelling in your document
at any time while you are editing the document. It then
picks out each word in turn and looks this up in its lists
of spellings. It will even check the individual components
of composite collections of assorted words like French/■
         German/Spanish. Words of just one letter, however,
are assumed to be correct - because they could, after all,
be someone's initials. It would, we are sure you will agree,
be a waste of effort for LocoSpell to pick out the B in A B
Smith as a spelling mistake!◄
```

To see that these characters really do disappear when they are not needed, move the Text cursor to the beginning of the word 'words' in the first paragraph and type longer ; then press [RELAY]. When the paragraph is relaid, there is no longer any need to split the word encyclopaedia and, sure enough, the hyphen disappears.

But if you use the Options menu ([f8]) to display word-processing codes, you will see that the hyphen is still there – shown now as (-). The Soft space you inserted is now shown as (⌣). If the text is changed in the future, LocoScript could use the Soft characters again: you won't need to type these characters in at the same places again.

'Hard' hyphens and spaces

LocoScript's Hard hyphens and spaces solve the problem of line breaks in the middle of someone's initials or at a place you don't like in hyphenated words.

The special feature of Hard hyphens and spaces is that LocoScript will never break the line at the Hard character. So to ensure that someone's name (initials and surname) isn't split between two lines, replace the spaces in the name by Hard spaces. Similarly, you stop a line breaking at a particular hyphen by replacing the hyphen by a Hard hyphen.

If you look at the first couple paragraphs of the example document, you will see two places where these Hard characters should be used. The name A B Smith is split after the B and add-on is split at the hyphen.

Inserting Hard hyphens and spaces

Hard spaces and hyphens are also inserted into a document through sequences of keystrokes – and the keystroking is very similar to that used for the soft characters. The only difference is that the keystroking starts with [⊞] rather than [⊟].

So to re-unite Mr Smith's initials with his surname, delete the space after the B of his initials and replace it by a hard space by pressing [⊞] followed by the Space Bar.

    be a waste of effort for LocoSpell to pick out the B in A B
    Smith as a spelling mistake!↵

The moment you press the Space Bar, LocoScript relays the paragraph up to where you are working to take account of the Hard character you have inserted.

Unfortunately, just putting a Hard space between the B and the Smith hasn't fully solved the problem – because now the line break is after the A.

    be a waste of effort for LocoSpell to pick out the B in A
    B Smith as a spelling mistake!↵

You also need another Hard space between the A and the B.

    be a waste of effort for LocoSpell to pick out the B in
    A B Smith as a spelling mistake!↵

The problem with the word add-on is solved in a similar way. You just have to delete the standard hyphen and then replace it with a hard hyphen by pressing [⊞] and typing a hyphen. Immediately LocoScript relays the paragraph up to where you are working to take account of this change.

• As we pointed out above, the keystroking for these special characters is essentially the same as that for word-processing codes. So you can call up the corresponding Set or Clear menu when you can't remember the keystroking for one of these characters – just as you can when you can't remember the keystroking for a particular code. (See Session 9.)

Controlling Page Breaks

The simplest way LocoScript works out where one page should end and the next begin is by doing a simple line count: once you have a certain number of lines of text on a page, it is time to move onto the next one.

But such a simple way of working out where the page breaks should be means you can find yourself with:

- one line of a paragraph on a different page from the rest of the paragraph – the so-called widows and orphans that professional typesetters will go to great lengths to avoid
- page breaks in the middle of paragraphs – when many people prefer page breaks to be between paragraphs
- part of a table on one page and the rest on the next, when it is much better to have a complete table on one page

You can 'cure' most of these problems by putting in strategic blank lines – but this cure suffers from the same sort of problems as putting in extra spaces and hyphens to cure your problems with line breaks. When you come to make a change, these extra lines will be in the wrong place and you will have to rub them out and start all over again.

Another time that you will need to control where a new page starts is when you want to leave space for a picture at the top of a page. You can't do this simply by typing lots of blank lines – because LocoScript will simply treat these lines as spare blank lines from the bottom of the previous page and promptly 'swallows' them. LocoScript always swallows any spare blank lines at the bottom of a page to ensure you have text on the first line of the next page – because, most of the time, this is what you want.

LocoScript has better solutions to these problems as well.

Keeping lines together

The problems of paragraphs and tables being split across a page break are solved by telling LocoScript to keep the lines of the paragraph or the table together.

Furthermore, LocoScript has some special ways of preventing page breaks in the middle of paragraphs which we describe in Session 17. (In fact, all the documents you have been working with so far have been set up to prevent Widows and Orphans – the single line of a paragraph on a different page – so you don't have to do anything to guard against this particular problem.)

What we look at here is how to pick out a group of lines, such as the lines of a table, and tell LocoScript to keep these together. This keeps any group of lines together, whether these are within a paragraph, span a couple of paragraphs or cover a number of paragraphs.

The key to keeping lines together are some special word-processing codes known as Keep codes which tell LocoScript to Keep a certain number of lines together. Once again, LocoScript gives you a choice of ways of putting these codes into a document – through the Page menu or by keystroking. We shall now show you how to use both of these methods.

(i) Using the Page menu

Suppose you want to ensure that the third and fourth paragraphs of the example document are always on the same page.

As you might expect, the first job is to position the Text cursor. It is a good idea to position the Text cursor either on the first line of the group or on the last line – so move it to the first line of the third paragraph. When the Text cursor is in position, bring the Page menu onto the screen. If you look at the Information lines at the top of the screen, you will see that the key to press is ⌊f5⌋. Do this now.

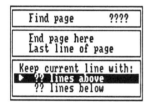

The part of this menu you need here is the bottom section, which asks you to specify the number of lines to be kept together with the current line (ie. the line with the Text cursor on it). When the Text cursor is on the first line of your chosen group, you need to tell LocoScript how many lines below the current line to keep with this line; when the Text cursor is on the last line of the group, you need to tell LocoScript how many lines above the current line to keep with the current line.

Both options work like, say, the Find page ?? option in the Page menu. You select the option you want with the Menu cursor (it's a Commands menu, so the arrow automatically moves as well), type in the number you want and press ⌊ENTER⌋ to go ahead.

The number you want is the total number of lines you want to keep above or below the current line – including the current line itself. In this case, that number is 11.

```
be a waste of effort for LocoSpell to pick out the B in
A B Smith as a spelling mistake!↵
↵
Where are a number of different checks you can do. You can
check the whole document, or just a section of the document
'forward' or you can check the spelling of a single word.↵
↵
↨
```

```
All these options are available through the Spell menu,
which you bring onto the screen by pressing [f7] (As always,
you can see that this is the key to press by looking at the
Information lines at the top of the screen.) If you aren't
using LocoSpell, then the menu just displays a message
telling you that there wasn't a copy of LocoSpell on your
Start-of-day disc↵
```

⎫
⎬ 11 Lines
⎭

8809

As the Text cursor is on the first line of the group, the option to select is ?? lines below. Move the Menu cursor to this option, type the number of lines you want to keep together – 11 in this case – and press ⌈ENTER⌉. This sets the number of lines you want to keep together into the menu and inserts the relevant Keep code (+Keep11) into the document. The position of the page break immediately changes to take account of this code.

```
be a waste of effort for LocoSpell to pick out the B in
A B Smith as a spelling mistake!ꞌ
  ꞌ
..................................................................
(+Keep11)There are a number of different checks you can do. You can
check the whole document, or just a section of the document
'forward' or you can check the spelling of a single word.ꞌ
  ꞌ
All these options are available through the Spell menu,
which you bring onto the screen by pressing [f7] (As always,
you can see that this is the key to press by looking at the
Information lines at the top of the screen.) If you aren't
using LocoSpell, then the menu just displays a message
telling you that there wasn't a copy of LocoSpell on your
Start-of-day discꞌ
```

11 Lines

• If you positioned the Text cursor on the last line of the group, the code you need is (-Keep11) and the option you will want is ?? lines above – but otherwise the steps are exactly the same, including the total number of lines to keep together.

Note: It's a good idea to put Keep codes on both the first and the last lines of any table you expect to be adding to. Providing you don't more than double the number of lines in the table, these codes will ensure that the whole table is kept on one page – without you having to change the codes.

(ii) Using keystrokes

To demonstrate the keystroking needed to put in the Keep codes, we shall now go through a similar exercise to tell LocoScript to keep the second and third paragraphs together.

As usual with keystroking, the first key to press depends on whether the code you want to insert starts with a + or a –. When you want to tell LocoScript to keep the current line with the lines below it, the code you need is (+Keep*n*) and so the first key to press is ⌈⊞⌉. If you want to keep the current line with lines above it, the code you want is (-Keep*n*) and the first key to press is ⌈⊟⌉. After that, type K followed by the total number of lines and press ⌈ENTER⌉ (because of the number) – or press ⌈⊞⌉ or wait until the corresponding Set or Clear menu appears on the screen.

As before, the first step is to position the Text cursor – say, on the top line of the paragraph.

This time you want to keep 13 lines together, making the code you want (+Keep13) – so press ⌈⊞⌉, type K13 and finally press ⌈ENTER⌉. LocoScript immediately relays the document and changes the Page Break to take account of this code.

That's all there is to it. What is more, inserting a (-Keep*n*) code takes very much the same steps – except that you start by pressing ▣. For practice, try using these keystrokes to insert a (-Keep3) code on the top line of the second page so that this line is kept together with the last two lines on the previous page.

Putting in page breaks of your own

The key to leaving a gap for a picture at the top of a page (or at the bottom) is to tell LocoScript precisely where you want it to move from one page to the next by inserting some special codes. These special codes tell LocoScript to 'end the page here' or that a particular line is the 'last line of the page'. Blank lines following one of these codes are not 'swallowed' and so can be used to leave the space you need for the picture.

Once again, LocoScript gives you two possible ways of putting in these special codes – through a menu (the Page menu) or by keystroking. The codes override any Keep codes that you have put in, so you don't need to change your 'old' Keep codes to match.

(i) Using the Page menu

Suppose you wanted to leave a gap after the second paragraph of the current document and start the third paragraph on a new page.

One way of achieving this is to mark the last line of the second paragraph as the last line of a page. To do this, move the Text cursor to the last line of this paragraph – any position on this line will do – and then press [f5] to bring the Page menu onto the screen. This time the option you want is Last line of page.

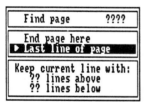

Select this option and press [ENTER] in the usual way. (The Page menu is a 'Commands' menu – with the selected option picked out by the arrow.) LocoScript then inserts a (LastLine) code, telling LocoScript that this must be the last line on the page. It also puts the End-of-page line immediately below the line you have marked as the last line of the page.

be a waste of effort for LocoSpell to pick out the B in
A B Smith (LastLine)⸮s a spelling mistake!⸘
‥‥

⸘
(⸸Keep11)There are a number of different checks you can do. You can

You will also see that the next page now starts with the blank line that separated the second paragraph from the third. This time LocoScript hasn't thrown away the 'spare' blank line. You will normally want to get rid of this line.

The other way of leaving a gap after the second paragraph is to tell LocoScript to end the page immediately at the end of the paragraph. That is done by a special character rather like the ↵ character that tells LocoScript where to end one line and go onto the next. The character is known as a Form Feed and it is represented on the screen by ↧. Like ↵, ↧ is only ever displayed on the screen: it is never printed.

The option of the Page menu that puts a Form feed in for you is End page here. To see this in action, move the Text cursor just in front of the ↵ at the end of the second paragraph, pull down the Page menu and select End page here.

Notice how this time after you press [ENTER], you have two blank lines at the top of the next page – both of which you will want to get rid of. The Form Feed character makes the Carriage Return at the end of the line redundant. It also makes the (LastLine) code redundant – as you can see by rubbing out this code: once you have a Form Feed character at the end of the line, the page break is where you want it whether a (LastLine) code is present or not.

```
be a waste of effort for LocoSpell to pick out the B in
A B Smith as a spelling mistake!↧
```

```
↧
There are a number of different checks you can do. You can
```

(ii) Using keystrokes

You can insert both (LastLine) codes and Form Feed characters simply by using keystrokes.

- To put in a (LastLine) code, press [⊞] and then type LL
- To put in a Form Feed character, hold down the [ALT] key and keep it down while pressing [RETURN]. (Think of a Form Feed as being a 'Super' Carriage return.)

Suppose, for example, that you wanted to end the second page after the last line of the third paragraph. You could do this by placing the Text cursor somewhere on the last line of the third paragraph, pressing [⊞] and typing LL. That would give you a (LastLine) code on this line. Alternatively, you could move the Text cursor to the very end of the paragraph, hold down [ALT] and press [RETURN] to put in a Form Feed character.

Try these out both with Codes displayed and without.

Finally...

Finally, abandon editing this document. Then you can come back and work through this session again as if for the first time, whenever you want to check up on how to control Page Breaks and Line Breaks.

Session summary

In this session, you have seen:

- How to use Soft hyphens and Soft spaces to encourage a line break at a particular place
- How to use Hard hyphens and Hard spaces to stop line breaks at particular places
- How to tell LocoScript to keep a group of lines together on the same page
- How to tell LocoScript to move on to the next page at a particular point in your document

8809

The Professional touch – II: Headers, Footers and Page numbers

Headers and Footers – that is, special pieces of text at the top and bottom of every page – make documents very smart indeed. All professionally-produced books have Headers and Footers and so do magazines, if for no other reason than they are the best way of putting in page numbers. They can also be used to produce the effect of company headed notepaper on blank sheets of paper.

In this session, we show you how to set up the text for your Headers and Footers, including how to put in a slot for page numbers that LocoScript will fill in automatically for you. We also show you how to manipulate Headers and Footers so that you produce a special first or last page – or different odd-numbered and even-numbered pages so that you get the effect of left and right pages in a book.

The document we are going to use to show this is PCWINFO, which you will remember is stored in group 1 of your Examples disc. So the first thing to do is to open this document for editing.

Where do Headers and Footers go?

To cope with a Header at the top of the page and a Footer at the bottom, each page you print has to have three separate areas:

- a top area reserved for a Header – the Header Zone;
- a bottom area reserved for a Footer – the Footer Zone; and
- a middle area that is used for your document – the Text Zone.

As so far we have only been printing out the document itself each time, you probably think that we now have to take some special steps to create Header and Footer Zones – but in fact, this is something else that LocoScript has already set up for you. Indeed, as far as LocoScript is concerned you have printed everything so far with a Header that was blank and a Footer that was blank.

How big these three zones are is something that you can set. (We show you how to do this in the next session.) The example document has 3 lines reserved for a Header and 4 lines reserved for a Footer – leaving 54 lines on each page for your text. (Note: The lines referred to here are not actual lines of text but a way of measuring depths on the page. Each line is ⅙", so the depth of the Header zone here is ³/₆" = ½".)

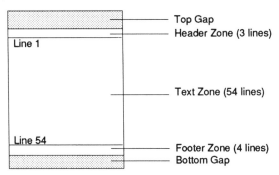

As you can see from this diagram, your page isn't simply divided into these three zones. There is also something called the Top Gap at the top of the page and a Bottom Gap at the bottom of the page.

When you use single-sheet paper, you need these two Gaps to mark the areas of the paper at the very top of the page and at the very bottom where your printer should not attempt to print – because the paper wouldn't be held properly by the printer mechanism. When you are using continuous stationery, the Gaps provide a very convenient way of ensuring (once the paper is properly adjusted) that you won't

---

print on the row of perforations that divide one page from another or on the backing paper between different labels.

We will be telling you more about Top and Bottom Gaps when we tell you about setting everything up for using different sizes of paper (Session 19).

Setting the Header and Footer text

Just having areas of the page reserved for a Header and a Footer is not enough. You also have to set up the text that you want to use for the Headers and Footers. This is sometimes called the Pagination text. The Header text we are going to set for the example document is General information about the PCW; and the Footer text is Session 16 Exercise.

The Header and Footer text are part of the Document Set-up – the fundamental set-up of your document – and so, to set them, you have to change the Document Set-up. This is done through the Document setup option of the Actions menu. As you will remember (or confirm by looking at the Information lines), you bring the Actions menu onto the screen by pressing [f1]. Do this now.

Select Document setup and press [ENTER]. This gives you a special screen – the Pagination Screen – set up ready for you to type in the Header and Footer text.

```
A: group 1/PCWINFO .    Document setup.           Printer idle. Using A: M:
Pagination    Pi12    LS1    CR+0    LP6                   Page ----  line --/54
f1=Actions  f2=Layout  f3=Style  f4=Size  f5=Page  f6=Printing  f7=Spell  f8=Options  EXIT
0.........|.........2.........|.........4.........|.........6.........|.........8...|....

━━end of header 1 : used for all pages━━━━━━━━━━━━━━━━━━━━━━━━━━━━━━━━━━━━

━━end of footer 1 : used for all pages━━━━━━━━━━━━━━━━━━━━━━━━━━━━━━━━━━━━

━━end of header 2 : used for no pages at all━━━━━━━━━━━━━━━━━━━━━━━━━━━━━━

━━end of footer 2 : used for no pages at all━━━━━━━━━━━━━━━━━━━━━━━━━━━━━━
```

This screen is divided into four sections because LocoScript allows you to have two sets of Pagination text. When you want the same Header and Footer on every page, you only need one set of Pagination text; but you will need two sets when you want different Headers and/or Footers on the left and right pages of a book – or when you want something special on the first or the last page.

But that's jumping ahead to something we will cover later in this session. For now, we are only interested in setting up Pagination text that will be used on every page – ie. in setting up text in the top two sections of this special screen.

9108

The first job is to type in the Header text – General information about the PCW. The slot for this is the top section of the Pagination Screen – as you will see from the legend on the line dividing this section of the screen from the next. The Text cursor is already at the beginning of this section – so to type in the Header text, just type. This text will be printed on the top line of the Header Zone. (If you don't want the text on the top line of the Header zone, start your Header text with one or two blank lines.)

As we said above, Headers and Footers are usually simple one-line pieces of text like this, but there's nothing to stop you having multi-line Headers and Footers if you want. The only limit is the size of the Header and Footer Zones: if you type more lines in the Header than there is room for, you will push the main document text out of position, possibly pushing the Footer over onto the next page. (The Header Zone in the example document can, in fact, accommodate up to three lines of Header text. We show you how to set the zone sizes in the next session.)

Now use the ⊡ key to move the Text cursor into the next section of the screen – ready to type the Footer text. You can't move to the next part of the screen by pressing ⌈RETURN⌋ because this just adds blank lines to the end of the Header text.

Footers are a bit more complicated than Headers because the Footer Zone starts **immediately below the last line of the document text**. Typically, you will want to leave at least one line between the document text and the Footer – which means that you must remember to start your Footer text with blank lines (one blank line for every line space you want to leave).

So to give your document a Footer of Session 16 Exercise on every page, separated from the document text by one blank line, type ⌈RETURN⌋ (to put in the blank line) and then type the Footer text.

You could now embellish this text in exactly the same way you can embellish individual words and phrases in the main part of the document. For example, you could make the whole of the Footer text bold by moving to the start of the line, pressing ⊞ and then typing B. (As you will remember, this set of keystrokes puts in a (+Bold) code.) Or you could put in the same code by using the Style menu. Both the Style menu and the Size menu are available here and work exactly as described in Sessions 9 and 10. There is also a Layout menu with much the same options as before (centring, right alignment, changing the layout – see Session 11) but this time you only have one layout to use, a special Pagination Text Layout.

Moreover, you don't have to worry about turning off any special styles you use at the end of your group of Headers and Footers. Each Header or Footer is treated like a separate document and styles turned on for the Headers and Footers and those turned on in the document itself are totally independent. You don't even need to put in a Carriage Return at the end of the Header or Footer text.

To move back to the Header text and embellish that, just press ⊡ to move the cursor up the screen. **Note:** You can't abandon changes you make to the Document Set-up, so it's important to get everything straight before returning to the document.

Note: If you want to clear away all the Header and Footer text that is set so far, you can do this through the 'Document Set-up' Actions menu – ie. the Actions menu that is available while your computer is displaying the Pagination Screen. Simply select the first option of this Actions menu, press [ENTER] to tell LocoScript to carry out this action and the current Pagination text will be cleared away.

When the Header and Footer text are as you want them, press [EXIT]. LocoScript then puts up a short menu:

Both of these options put into force the changes you have made and return you to the document. The only difference is whether you return to the beginning of the document or to the place you were working before you entered Document Set-up.

Once you have returned to the document, you can continue to make changes to the document itself. The Header and Footer won't be visible as you work on the document: they only appear at the top and bottom of each page when you print.

• Press [EXIT] and select Save and Print to see this Header and Footer in action. Then edit PCWINFO again – ready for the next refinement to the text.

Putting in page numbers

Something that you will often want to include in either your Header or your Footer is the current page number – so that each page you print has its page number on it. You might also want to include the total number of pages – so that you can give your pages labels like Page 3 of 5.

At the point you want to put the current page number or the last page number, you have to:

– put in a special code, and
– immediately follow the code with some special markers that mark out the space on the page you want the page number to occupy.

Without the special markers reserving room for the page number, no page number can be printed.

Note: Headers and Footers are the usual places to put page numbers but you can equally well put them into the main part of your document – by using the same keystroking that we describe here.

8809

Just the current page number

A common style of page numbering is – 1 –, – 2 – etc. centred at the bottom of every page. To achieve this, you need a Footer text that tells LocoScript to print at the bottom of each page the number of that page neatly centred between two hyphens and the whole neatly centred on the page.

The first thing to do is to bring the Pagination text onto the screen. As you will remember from earlier in this session, you do this by bringing the Actions menu onto the screen and selecting Document setup. The Pagination text that you set up earlier will now be displayed on the screen.

What we now want is the current page number centred between the hyphens, and centred in the middle of the Footer line – so the next step is to get rid of the existing Footer text. Move the cursor to second section of the Pagination Screen and delete the current Footer text – either by using the Delete keys or by marking it out as a Block and cutting it out, just as if it were text in the main part of the document. Leave the initial blank line, though – you will need that to separate the page numbers from the document text.

The page numbering we want looks more complicated than it is. The combination of word-processing codes and text you need to produce this style of numbering is just:

(CEntre) – (PageNo) *(some-special-characters)*–

The code that tells LocoScript to insert the current page number

The characters that mark out the space reserved for the page number

The hyphens are just straightforward characters that you type, and the (CEntre) code should be very familiar by now. The only complicated things are the (PageNo) code and the special characters.

The (PageNo) code is entered by typing a particular key sequence. This sequence is ▣ (as the code doesn't start with a –) followed by PN. (As always, you can just press ▣ and then wait or use the ▣ Help key to bring the associated Set menu onto the screen if you are not sure of the letters to type.)

LocoScript can only print the page number if some space has been reserved for it. To reserve space you must type a <, a > or an = for each character position you want to set aside for the page number – and you must set aside at least enough space for the largest page number you are going to use. If the biggest page number is 100, you must reserve at least three character positions – or you will lose part of the number. To reserve three character positions for the page number, you must follow the (PageNo) code with either <<< or >>> or ===. These are the special characters we referred to earlier.

Which of the three options you type depends on how you want the page number positioned within the space:

- type <<< if the number is to be positioned to the left
- type >>> if the number is to be positioned to the right
- type === if the number is to be centred

Page numbers like – 1 – have the number centred in the space; so type === *right up against the* (PageNo) *code* to reserve three character positions for the number.

Using the information we have told you here, try typing in the word-processing codes and text needed to give this style of page numbers. The finished Footer text should look like this:

With codes   Without codes

(CEntre)   -(PageNo)===-   -====-

Including the Total number of pages

Another common requirement is for Page n of m, say at the end of each Header. (n represents the current page number and m the total number of pages – ie. the number of the last page). This time the sequence of text and word-processing codes we want might be:

(RAlign)Page (PageNo)>> of (LPageNo)>>

The code that tells LocoScript to
insert the total number of pages

The characters that mark out the
space reserved for the page number

Again most of this is straightforward. The words Page and of are simple text, the (RAlign) should be very familiar, and the (PageNo) code and the >> characters are the ones we've just met. (The two > characters mark out two spaces and tell LocoScript to position the number over to the right in this space.) The (LPageNo) code, like the (PageNo) code, is also entered by typing a particular key sequence. This time the sequence is ▣ followed by LPN.

Try editing your existing Header text to give you this style of page numbering. The finished Header text should look like this:

With codes

..... (RAlign)   Page (PageNo)>> of (LPageNo)>>

Without codes

.....   Page >> of >>

8809

When you have these codes in your Header and Footer, return to the document as before. 'Save and Print' the document to see these page numbers in action – then open the document for editing again, ready for the next stage of this tutorial.

Lefthand and righthand pages

When you prepare something like a chapter of a book, you want odd-numbered pages laid out as righthand pages and even-numbered pages laid out as lefthand pages.

Much of the difference between right- and lefthand pages is in the Headers and Footers for the two types of pages. A lefthand page will have the Header and the Page number to the left of the page; a righthand page will have the Header and the Page number to the right of the page.

There are two phases to setting up the Headers and Footers
- setting up the Header and Footer text and the layout used for these; and
- telling LocoScript that you want to have one set of Pagination text for lefthand pages and another for righthand pages

The first phase of this is simply what we have been doing already this session. The only difference is that this time we need to set up two Headers and two Footers.

For the purposes of this tutorial, set up whatever Pagination text you like. Use all of LocoScript's positioning features – centring, right alignment, tabs etc. – to get the pieces of Header and Footer text in the right positions.

Setting how the Pagination text is used

How the Pagination text is used – ie. which pages a particular pair of Header and Footer appear on – is another aspect of the Document Set-up. So again, the route to setting this starts with selecting the Document setup option in the Editor Actions menu to display the special Pagination Screen. Do this now.

Once the Pagination text is displayed, the menu option you require is Header/footer options in the Page menu. Looking at the Information lines at the top of the Pagination Screen, you will see that this menu is brought onto the screen by pressing ⌐f5⌐. Press ⌐f5⌐ now; the following menu should be displayed:

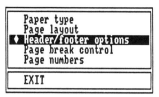

This Page menu is totally different from the 'Editor' Page menu that we used earlier in this tutorial to move directly to a particular page and to control page breaks. We shall be looking at the other options in this menu in later sessions of this tutorial, but for now we will just concentrate on Header/footer options.

Select Header/footer options in the usual way and press [ENTER]. LocoScript then immediately puts up a 'follow-on' menu of options – all to do with the different ways in which the Headers and Footers can be applied.

This menu is a 'Settings' menu – which, you will remember, means that you select the options you require by pointing at them with the Menu cursor and pressing [+]. The other feature of these menus to note is that setting an option will automatically clear any option that is incompatible with it. You will see this effect at work in this menu because you can only have one choice for how Header and Footer 1 are used.

As you can see, there are three sections to this menu – each of which you need to consider if you are going to get the results you require. The most important to get right is the setting you make in the top section of the menu because this sets the general rules for how the Headers and Footers are applied.

Setting for Left- and Right-hand pages

When you want separate Headers and Footers for lefthand and righthand pages, the first option to select is odd pages. This says that the first pair of Header and Footer texts are used for odd-numbered (righthand) pages. This automatically means that the second pair of Header and Footer texts are used for even-numbered (lefthand) pages.

Move the Menu cursor to odd pages and press [+]. Notice how the tick immediately moves from the current setting (all pages) to odd pages.

For the moment, leave the other settings as they are. Just press [ENTER] to tell LocoScript to confirm your choice of odd pages and then return to the document by pressing [EXIT], selecting from this Exit menu that appears and pressing [ENTER] – just as we did earlier in this session. Again, 'Save and Print' the document to see what effect specifying different Headers and Footers for odd- and even- numbered pages has had.

Special Headers and Footers for the beginning or the end of a document

There will be a number of occasions when you will want to treat the first and last pages of your document specially. For example, if you have a main heading on the first page, you probably won't want a Header there as well – even though you will want a Header on every other page. Similarly, you may want continues... at the bottom of every page – except the last.

8809

LocoScript has two features to help here:

- The option of using one of your two pairs of Header and Footer text specifically for either the first page or for the last page. (All the rest of the pages would then use the other set of Pagination text.)
- Independent selection of whether to have a Header and/or a Footer on the first page and on the last page, regardless of how Headers and Footers are used in the rest of the document. So if you didn't want a Header on the first page, you needn't have one.

Suppose for example you wanted:

- 1st page: No Header; Special footer
- Middle pages: Header and Footer
- Last page: Header; No Footer

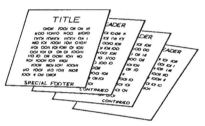

Analysing these requirements, you see that you want the same Header text everywhere (except for the first page where you have no Header) but you want two different Footers – one for the first page and the other for all the rest of the pages (except for the last which won't have any Footer).

The overall rule – for setting in the top section of the Header/Footer menu – is therefore one Header and Footer pair for the first page and the other pair for all the other pages. In other words, the option you require is `first page only`. (Header/footer 1 used on only the first page means that Header/footer 2 are used for every page except the first.)

To arrange that there is no Header on the first page and no Footer on the last page, you need to set options in the middle part of the menu.

There are four options in this part of the menu, each of which is 'true' when it is set (ticked) and 'false' when it is clear (no tick). So, for example, when `First page Footer enabled` is ticked, LocoScript will put the relevant Footer at the bottom of the first page but when this option is clear, no Footer will be printed at the bottom of this page.

What we want here is:

- No Header on the first page – ie. `First page Header enabled` clear
- A Footer on the first page – ie `First page Footer enabled` set
- A Header on the last page – ie. `Last page Header enabled` set
- No Footer on the last page – ie. `Last page Footer enabled` clear

Once again, set this up and press ⌷ENTER⌷ to confirm this combination. Then return to the document and 'Save and Print' to see the effect this has had.

The special case of One-page documents

As a footnote to this session, we shall stop for a moment and think about the Footer a single-page document should have.

The problem is that you will generally set up your documents expecting the beginning and the end of the document to be on different pages. However, a one-page document has both the beginning and the end of the document on the same page. It is pretty obvious that you will want the first page's Header at the top of this page – but whether you should have the Footer from the first page or the one from the last page at the bottom of the page, depends on the details of your document.

So LocoScript 2 leaves the choice up to you – and you make your selection through the last part of the same Header/Footer Options menu that we have been using to make all the other choices about how Headers and Footers are to be applied.

All this part of the menu does is ask you whether you would like the bottom of the one page document to be like the bottom of the first page or the bottom of the last page. If, say, you had a special Footer on the first page that listed all the Directors of the company – then you will probably want this as the Footer on one-page documents as well. In this case, the option to select is Use footer for first page. However, if you have the Footer continues... on all pages except the last, you will want Use footer for last page.

To select the option you want, just point to it with the Menu cursor and press [⊞] – in exactly the same way as you select any other options in the Header/footer options menu.

Session summary

In this session you have seen:

- How to set up Headers and Footers – that is, special text that is printed at the top and the bottom of every page of your document.
- How to give the pages of your document page numbers of various styles
- How to set up your document so that you produce lefthand pages and righthand pages
- How to set up special Headers and Footers for the first or the last page
- How to leave off the Headers or Footers from the first and last pages
- What the options are for Headers and Footers on a single-page document

---

LocoScript 2 User Guide: Tutorial

8809

Session 17

Changing the framework

In all the work we have done so far, you have been working within a framework that was set up for you – a framework that specified:
- which printer and paper you should use
- what the general rules were about laying the text out on the page

LocoScript set up this framework to save you the bother of making a number of complex settings before you could start doing any work. And as you know, the rules it set haven't got in the way of what you wanted to do. In fact, probably the only rule you have been aware of so far is that you have had to print everything on A4 paper.

The settings that make the rules are all part of the Document Set-up which we started changing in the last session. In this session, we are going to change some more of the framework to suit the documents you produce, specifically:
- how the page is divided up into a Header Zone, Footer Zone and Text zone
- what your set of Stock Layouts are
- what the general rules about page breaks in the middle of paragraphs are
- what the number of the first page is

We will be seeing how to specify the paper and the printer your document is set up for in Sessions 19 and 20.

The document we are going to work on in this session is MAIL1.TXT, which is stored in group 1 of your Examples disc. So to start, open this document for editing.

Note: Any changes you make to the Document Set-up must always be carefully thought out in advance because they affect the whole document.

Gaining access to the Document Set-up

The initial steps in changing the Document Set-up are the same ones we took in the last session to start work on the Header and Footer text. (The Header and Footer text is, after all, part of the Document Set-up.) You bring the 'Editor' Actions menu onto the screen, select Document setup and press [ENTER].

Do this now. (Look at the Information lines if you aren't sure how to bring the Actions menu onto the screen.) LocoScript then displays the special Pagination screen (see page 169), together with a special set of menus – the ones used to change details of the Document Set-up.

8906

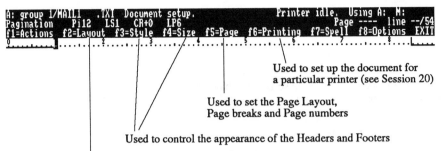

Used to set up the document for
a particular printer (see Session 20)

Used to set the Page Layout,
Page breaks and Page numbers

Used to control the appearance of the Headers and Footers

Used to lay out the Headers and Footers and to set up Stock Layouts

The menus we will be using in this session to set the sizes of Header and Footer zones, the rules about page breaks, the Stock Layouts, etc. are the Page menu and the Layout menu. We start this session by showing you how to set the first page number and the total number of pages.

Setting the page numbers

LocoScript initially makes the first page of your document Page 1. But this won't always be what you want. If your document contains an additional chapter for a book, for example, you will want its page numbers to follow on from the old last page of this book.

Similarly, LocoScript initially assumes that the total number of pages you want to quote when you put `Page n of m` on each page is the total number of pages in this document – when, in fact, the document could just be one section of a very much longer document.

You don't normally have to worry about setting either number, because there is a way of telling LocoScript that documents follow each other in a particular order before you print them. This sets up both the first page number and the Total Pages number for each document for you. We show you how this works in the next session. What we describe here is how to set both directly in the Document Set-up.

The menu you use to change both the first page number and the total number of pages is the 'Document Set-up' Page menu. To bring this menu onto the screen, press ⌴f5⌴. The option you want is `Page numbers`: so select this option and then press ⌴ENTER⌴. LocoScript then displays the Page numbers submenu:

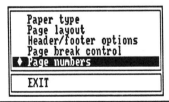

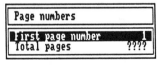

8809

This new menu is a Settings menu – but, as you have probably noticed, it is different from the other Settings menus you have met in that it has settable numbers, rather than a system of ticks marking selected items. You will see another menu like this later in the session.

The first line of the menu tells you the current page number for the first page. To change this number, check that the Menu cursor is on this line of the menu, type the number you want and press [ENTER]. Try setting the first page number to 21. Notice how the menu stays on the screen after you have pressed [ENTER] – in case you now want to change the Total Pages number. You have to press [ENTER] again to clear the menu off the screen.

The other line of the menu enables you to set a Total Pages number. If a Total Pages number is set, LocoScript will use this wherever you put a Last Page Number code (LPageNo) instead of the last page number it calculates from the First page number and the number of pages in the document.

The Total Pages number is set in exactly the same way as the First Page number. You just move the Menu cursor to this line of the menu, type in the Total Pages number you want (say, 42) and then press [ENTER]. Again, pressing [ENTER] just confirms the number you have typed and the menu stays on the screen – in case you want to change either number again. (If the Total Pages number has been set in the past and you want to clear it again, just point to the Total Pages line with the Menu cursor and press [□]: the entry then becomes ???? again.)

In general, there is no need to set the Total Pages number. You only need to worry about it at all if you have a string of documents and then only if you are using a page numbering style like Page *n* of *m*.

When you have finished setting the First Page and Total Pages numbers you want, press [ENTER]. This returns you to the Pagination Screen – so that you can now change other aspects of the Document Set-up.

Setting the page break rules

There are two basic rules about page breaks:
- whether page breaks are allowed to happen in the middle of a paragraph or only between paragraphs
- and, if so, whether Widows and Orphans are allowed

(Widows and Orphans are the names used to describe single lines separated by a page break from the rest of the paragraph – either at the bottom of the page or at the top of the next page.)

Unless you tell it otherwise (for example, by setting this in your template – see Session 21), LocoScript lays out the pages of your document assuming that it is OK to split a paragraph between one page and another but Widows and Orphans are not allowed – ie. if the paragraph is divided, then at least two lines of the paragraph must appear both at the bottom of one page and at the top of the next.

The menu option you use to change this is the Page break control option of the Page menu in Document Set-up – the same initial menu as you have just used to set the First Page and Total Pages numbers. Bring this menu onto the screen by pressing ⌈f5⌉, select Page break control and then press ⌈ENTER⌉.

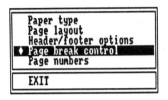
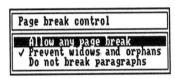

The submenu that appears is a 'Settings' menu offering three choices. If you don't care where paragraphs are split, then you want the first option (Allow any page break); if you don't mind paragraphs being split but you don't want any Widows and Orphans, select the second option (Prevent widows and orphans); if you don't want any paragraphs to be split, select the third option (Do not break paragraphs).

You can only ever choose one of these three, so just point to the option you want and press ⌈+⌉. This option then automatically becomes selected (with the tick beside it), with the other two options cleared. Press ⌈ENTER⌉ to tell LocoScript to go ahead.

Dividing up the page – the Page Layout

In this section, we are going to look at the process of changing the Page Layout – that is, the way lines on the page are allocated to the Header Zone, the Text Zone and the Footer Zone.

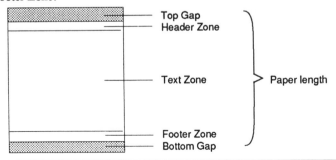

How many lines you have in these three zones depends very much on the type of paper you are using. When you are using A4 paper, each page is 11⅔ inches – or 70 standard lines – long. (Remember how pages are always measured in standard 6-Pitch lines?) When you use A5 paper (the size of paper used for this user guide), the page length is 8⅓ inches – or 50 standard lines. In other words, the page length is fixed by the type of paper the document is set up to use. (We show you how to use different types of paper in Session 19.)

The size of the three zones is also affected by the size of the Top and Bottom Gaps. As we explained in the last session, these gaps mark areas at the very top and at the very bottom of the paper that the printer can't print on or, in the case of continuous stationery, that you don't want it to print on. The size of the Top and Bottom Gaps are again a feature of the type of paper you are using. For example, on the built-in printer, you can't print on the top 1" or the bottom ½" of A4 paper.

This means you are left with a fixed number of lines in the middle that you can divide between the Header Zone, the Footer Zone and the Text Zone. For example, for the A4 paper you have been using, the total length of the page is 70 lines, the top gap is 6 lines (1") and the bottom gap is 3 lines (½") – giving you a total of 61 lines to divide between these three zones.

What you set is the depth of the Header zone and the depth of the Footer zone – the two distances marked on the above diagram. Setting these also sets how many lines can be used on each page to print the document itself, because the total is fixed by the page length and the two gaps.

The menu option to use to set these Zone sizes is the `Page layout` option of the Page menu in Document Set-up. When you select this option and press ⌈ENTER⌉, this menu appears:

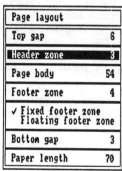

Page layout	
Top gap	6
Header zone	3
Page body	54
Footer zone	4
✓ Fixed footer zone Floating footer zone	
Bottom gap	3
Paper length	70

If you are not sure how long a page you have to work with and how big the top and bottom gaps are, then it's a good idea to bring this submenu onto the screen before you start working out how large you want the Header and Footer zones to be. As you see, included in the menu are details of the page length and the sizes of the gaps.

Working out where to put the Headers and Footers

To work out where to put the Headers and Footers, draw a little sketch of your sheet of paper and shade in the parts of the page covered by the Top and Bottom Gaps – because these can't be used in any of the three zones you are interested in. Now sketch out how you would like the rest of the page used. Remember to allow, not only for the length of Header text and the Footer text you want to use, but also for any blank lines that you want between the Header and Footer text and the main document text and between the Top Gap and the Header text.

Take the details of the Header and Footer Zone depths from this sketch. For example, your sketch might suggest that you have a Header Zone of 2 lines and a Footer Zone of 2 lines.

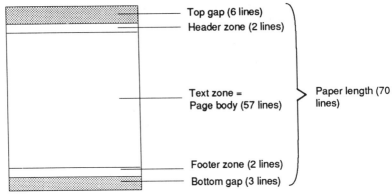

Top gap (6 lines)
Header zone (2 lines)

Text zone =
Page body (57 lines)

Paper length (70 lines)

Footer zone (2 lines)
Bottom gap (3 lines)

You now have the details you need to put into the Page Layout submenu. This is another Settings menu in which you type in the numbers you want. The current settings for the Header and Footer Zone are displayed. So to set the Header Zone to 2 lines, check that the Menu cursor is on Header zone and then type 2 [ENTER]; and to set the Footer Zone to 2 lines, check that the Menu cursor is on Footer zone and then type 2 [ENTER]. As you set these numbers, the Page body number also changes – so that you can see how many lines you are leaving for the Document Text.

The position of the Footer Zone

Beneath the Footer Zone setting in the Page Layout menu are a couple of options that we have ignored so far. These give you a choice of whether to keep your Footer text at a fixed position on the page or whether you want it to be immediately under the last line of text on the page.

Selecting a Fixed footer zone is the way to ensure that the Footer text will be at the same position on each page – which is what you will probably need. However, when your Footer text is something like continues... and ends, then you will want a Floating footer zone so that the ends (in particular) appears immediately after the last line of the document – wherever that comes on the page.

Set the option you require by picking it out with the Menu cursor and pressing [⊞]. Again, you can only have either a Fixed Footer Zone or a Floating Footer Zone – so setting one automatically clears the other.

When you have finished setting the Zone sizes etc., press [ENTER] again – to finish using the menu and return to the Pagination Screen.

Changing the document's Stock Layouts

A document's Stock Layouts are its supply of up to ten pre-prepared Layouts that can be used as patterns for the Layouts used in the document. These are stored in the Document Set-up.

Whenever you create a document, ten Stock Layouts are already set up for you. But these won't always be set up or named the way you want – and you obviously won't find them at all helpful until they are correctly set up. The menu option you use to do this is the Change Stock Layouts option of the Layout menu in Document Set-up – so the first step is to press ⌐F2⌐, select Change stock layouts and press ⌐ENTER⌐. LocoScript then displays a menu of the Stock Layouts – rather like the one you see when you use Stock Layouts (see Session 11).

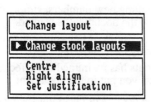
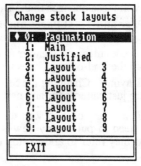

Now move the Menu cursor to the Stock Layout you want to change – say, the Justified Layout – and press ⌐ENTER⌐. This puts you into the Layout Editor and you can now change any aspect of the Stock Layout – margins, tabs, character pitch, line spacing, name, etc. etc. – exactly as if you were setting up the details you wanted in a new Layout code for use in your document. (The actions you use are described in detail in Session 11.) The only difference is that you can't set more than 15 tabs in a Stock Layout, whereas you can set up to 30 tabs in the Layout code.

Make whatever changes you want and then press ⌐EXIT⌐. This time, instead of going back to the document, you go back to the menu of Stock Layouts – so that you can now set up or change another of the Stock Layouts. If you want to change another Stock Layout, just pick this out with the Menu cursor and press ⌐ENTER⌐. If you don't want to set up any other Stock Layouts, press ⌐CAN⌐.

Saving the new Document Set-up

When all the changes you want have been made to the Document Set-up, press ⌐EXIT⌐ to tell LocoScript that you want to save these new settings and go back to working on the document text. As you will remember from the previous session, the menu that appears gives you a choice of the part of the document you want to return to –

---

either the start of the document or the place you were working when you selected the Document Set-up option. The main difference is one of speed: if you opt to go back to where you had been working, there could be a noticeable pause while LocoScript checks and adjusts the layout of the document up to that point.

As you have just changed the size of the Text zone, it is probably best to opt to return to the start of the document and then work through the document page by page, looking to see what effect the new Document Set-up has had on the document and whether you need to make any changes.

The effects of the new Document Set-up

What effect will these changes to the Document Set-up have had on your document?

- **First Page and Total Pages numbers:** Setting new numbers, simply changes any page numbers LocoScript inserts when the document is printed.
- **Page Break rules** and **Header and Footer Zones:** After you change either of these, all the End-of-page lines will probably have moved.
- **Stock Layouts:** Changing the Stock Layouts has no immediate effect because these are just patterns for any new Layouts you put in the document.

It's a good idea in any case to scan through the document checking the page breaks in case you need to put in any new Keep codes – to stop headings being divided from the text they refer to and to stop tables from being split across two pages (see Session 15).

Updating a document to use the new Layouts

The other thing you may want to do at this stage is update the Layout codes in the document so that it uses a more consistent set of Layouts.

Having a consistent set of Layouts is more aesthetically pleasing but there is a practical advantage as well. With the same Layout used for similar jobs throughout, it becomes more straightforward to move text around the document or between documents that use the same range of Stock Layouts – because when you insert the text in an area that uses the same Layout, you don't have to make sure that the text includes its Layout code. Whether the code is included or not, you will still get the same result.

The other reason you might want to use this feature is if you use one set of Layouts for the planning stage of a report, say, but another set when you come to fill out the outline report with detail. You could prepare your text initially in a document with one set of Stock Layouts and then insert the whole document into a new document with the other set of Layouts and then update all the Layouts to match the new set.

There are two possible ways of updating the Layout codes in a document.

One way is to work through each Layout code in turn, deciding whether you want to keep the Layout as it is or change it, either to the new version of the original Stock Layout or in some other way. This is called 'Exchanging' the Layouts, and it is the type of updating that you would use to get a more consistent set of Layouts throughout.

The other type of updating you can do is more automatic. This allows you to pick out a number of Stock Layouts and then tell LocoScript 2 to work through the document updating all the Layouts that were originally created from earlier versions of these Stock Layouts. This is called 'Replacing' the Layouts – and is the type of updating to use if you have different Layouts for your outline document and the finished article.

Exchanging Layouts

The process of exchanging Layouts is carried out forwards from the current position of the Text cursor – in very much the same way as Find and Exchange work forward from the Text cursor (see Session 13). So the first job is to position the Text cursor so that it is higher up the document than the first Layout you want to update – at the very beginning of the document, perhaps.

The menu option used here is the Layout Exchange option in the Layout menu. So the next step is to press [f2] to bring the Layout menu onto the screen, move the Menu cursor to `Layout exchange` and press [ENTER]. LocoScript then searches down the document for a (LayouT) code. When it finds this, it displays the message like that shown here:

The message tells you the name of the Layout LocoScript found and gives you a choice of actions. You can:

- replace the Layout by a copy of one of the Stock Layouts; or

- leave the Layout as it is – in which case LocoScript simply searches for the next Layout code; or

- change the Layout – with the aid of the Layout Editor, before going on and searching for the next Layout code; or

- abandon exchanging Layouts – in which case, you return to the document

To see how the Replace option works, select `Replace by stock layout` with the Menu cursor and press [ENTER]. LocoScript now displays a menu of Stock Layouts, exactly like the menu you see when you call up the Stock menu from within the Layout Editor.

In general, Stock Layout 0 will be pre-selected for you but if the Layout you are replacing was originally a copy of a Stock Layout, then this Stock Layout will be automatically selected. This means you just have to press [ENTER] when you want to replace the Layout code with a copy of the current version of the Stock Layout.

The first Layout in the example document is a copy of Stock Layout 2 and so Stock Layout 2 has been pre-selected – so to update it, just press [ENTER]. LocoScript then replaces the Layout code with a copy of the current Stock Layout 2, and goes on to search for the next Layout code. When it finds this, it displays the name of the Layout and the range of options – just as before.

Replacing Layouts

Replacing Layouts is the more automatic way of updating the Layout codes in your document. You specify which Layouts you want updated and LocoScript works forward through the document, replacing earlier copies of these Stock Layouts with copies of the current versions. The menu option you use to do this is the Layout Replacement option in the Layout menu.

Because the replacement is carried out forward from your current working position (rather like the Find and Exchange features we described in Session 13), you first move the Text cursor to just before the first Layout code that you want to update. When the cursor is in place, press [f2] to bring the Layout menu onto the screen, select Layout replacement and press [ENTER]. LocoScript now displays a menu of the Stock Layouts, for you to pick out the Layouts you want to update:

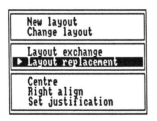 

The next step is to pick out these Layouts. To do this, you move the Menu cursor to each Stock Layout you are interested in and press [+] – putting a tick beside the name of the Stock Layout. (If you pick out one by accident or change your mind, point to it and press [-] in the usual way.)

When you are ready, press [ENTER] – to tell LocoScript to go ahead and automatically replace the old copies of these Stock Layouts with copies of the current versions. LocoScript then searches for Layout codes with the same names as the Stock Layouts you picked out and updates these for you.

Note: Updating in this way involves a lot of reformatting and so takes a little time.

8809

Session summary

In this session, you have seen:

- How to change settings held in the Document Set-up
- How to set the number of the first page and the Total Pages Number
- How to set the basic rules about page breaks
- How to set the sizes of the Header and Footer Zones and the position of the first line of the Header and the Footer
- How to change a document's range of Stock Layouts
- What effects changing these aspects of the Document Set-up have
- How to update existing Layout codes so that they match the current Stock Layouts

Session 18

Large documents

So far, what we have been dealing with have been reasonably small documents – two or three pages long at the most. What we look at in this session are the solutions LocoScript has to the problems of writing lengthy reports or a book:

- moving from one section to another quickly and easily in a long document
- running out of room on the disc, because the document you are working on is too large

The document we are going to edit is PCWINFO, which is stored in group 1 of your Examples disc, so the first step is to open this for editing. (Turn back to Session 5 if you are not sure how to do this.)

Moving around a large document

LocoScript gives you a number of ways of moving the Text cursor, as we have seen. Two methods are especially useful for moving around large documents:

- moving directly to a particular page by using the Find Page option of the Page menu (see Session 5), and
- LocoScript's system of Unit markers, which divide a document into sections (or Units) and help you to move from one section to the next.

How to insert Unit markers and then use these to move around your document is described below.

Note: Typically, these actions involve making some quite large jumps. While it makes such moves, LocoScript clears the screen and puts up a message telling you about the move it is making. If it's not the move you want, press [STOP], wait for LocoScript to pause and then press [STOP] again to stop LocoScript moving the Text cursor any further.

Unit markers

Using Unit markers is a two-stage operation:

- first you have to insert markers in the document at the beginning of each section you want to pick out;
- then you use the markers to move the Text cursor quickly to the start of the next section or to the beginning of the previous section.

8809

Inserting a Unit marker

The example document has three distinct sections – the first part up to Section 1, Section 1 itself and Section 2. The way to make it easy to move to the beginning of any of these sections is to put Unit markers at the beginning of Sections 1 and 2.

A Unit marker is, in fact, just another word processing code – represented on the screen by (UniT). As well as being a marker, this code has the action of a ↵ – so typically you replace the ↵ immediately before the start of the section of text by the Unit code.

This particular code can't be inserted through a menu: it can only be inserted by keystroking (or through the associated Set menu). The keystroking to use is [⊞]UT. So to insert a Unit marker at the beginning of Section 1, you move the Text cursor to the beginning of this section, delete the ↵, press [⊞] and type UT. LocoScript then inserts a (UniT) code in the document.

Exactly the same steps are used to put the second Unit marker at the beginning of Section 2. Move the Text cursor to the beginning of Section 2, press [⊞] and then type UT. LocoScript then inserts another (UniT) code in the document – marking the start of another Unit of the document.

Unit key

Moving to a Unit marker

You move the Text cursor to a Unit marker by pressing the [UNIT] key. To see how this works, start by moving the Text cursor somewhere in Section 1.

To move the Text cursor to the beginning of the next Unit, press [UNIT] – ie. [SHIFT]+[PARA]. Do this now: the Text cursor will move to the start of Section 2. (Do it again, and you will move to the end of the document.)

To move the Text cursor to the beginning of the previous Unit, hold down [ALT] as you press [UNIT]. Place the Text cursor somewhere in Section 2, press [ALT]+[UNIT]: and it will move to the start of Section 2. Do it again, and the Text cursor will move to the start of Section 1. (Do it again, and it will move to the start of the document.)

Over-size documents

A document becomes over-size when there is no longer room on the disc to edit it. (There has to be at least as much free space on a disc as the size of the document you want to edit so that the new version can be stored before the old version is thrown away – an obvious safety precaution, if you think about it.)

If there isn't room on the disc to save a new version of the document you pick out for editing, LocoScript 2 spots this and puts up a message like this:

8809

A more traumatic effect of working with an over-size document is that you may run out of disc space while you are in the middle of editing the document. LocoScript saves away portions of your document to disc while you are working and if you have been adding a lot of new text to your document, you might easily find yourself running out of space on the disc. You can also run out of space on Drive M if you have a lot of text copied into Blocks. When either of these happen, you will see a message like this:

```
ERROR in:  Drive M:

Disc is full

▶ Run disc manager
   Cancel operation
```

Short-term solutions

The short term solution to both of these problems is to spend some time throwing away any documents on the disc you don't need and moving others to a different disc until you have made enough room.

As you would expect, you use the Disc Manager both to erase documents and to move them. If the problem happened as you tried to edit or copy a document, you are already using the Disc Manager. When it happens in the middle of editing a document, your best course of action is to make a note of which drive the message is telling you is affected, and then take the Run disc manager option. Selecting Cancel operation (or pressing the [CAN] key) is not a good idea unless you really know what you are doing, for the simple reason that it throws away all the editing that you have done so far and returns you to the Disc Manager Screen.

If you select Run disc manager, LocoScript temporarily replaces your document by the Disc Manager Screen. (You can tell it hasn't abandoned the document you're working on by looking at the top Information line: this still shows the details of your document.) You can now pick out documents and use the File menu to erase them or to move them to a different disc – exactly as if you were doing this before you had started editing the current document.

If you run out of space on Drive M, you can erase files from here as well but in some cases you may be prevented from erasing the file because it is "in use". In particular, you may not be allowed to erase certain 'printer files' (with names ending .PRI or .#xx). There is, however, a procedure you can use to 'release' these files: this is explained in Appendix V, in the section on 'Trouble while editing'.

Another way in which you can make space on Drive M is to use the Show blocks option in the f1 Actions menu and the ⌷⊟⌷ key to remove Blocks that you no longer need. The steps are similar to the ones used to clear Phrases (see page 148).

But whatever you do, **don't remove the disc you are working on** – the Examples disc – from its drive and replace it by another disc. If you want to move a document off your current disc to another disc and you only have a single-disc machine, move it to Drive M.

Stop moving and erasing documents when you have made enough free space, bearing in mind the original size of your document and the changes you want to make to it. You will need at least 1k more free space for every 1000 characters and codes you want to add to the document. (You can see how much room there is on the disc by looking up at the relevant drive summary towards the top of the screen.)

Press ⌷EXIT⌷ to return to editing the document.

• Before you go on to the next part of this tutorial, finish the current edit (ie. select the Finish edit option from the Exit menu).

Long-term solutions

Repeatedly finding documents to move or erase whenever the disc is full is far from an ideal solution. What you probably need to do is to split your large document into smaller parts. Editing one of these smaller parts doesn't need anything like the same amount of free space on the disc – and, as we shall show you later in this session, you can get LocoScript to ensure that the page numbers are consecutive. There is really no need to work with large documents at all.

Splitting a large document into smaller documents

There are two ways of splitting large documents into a number of smaller documents.

One method is to make a copy of the original document for each new smaller document and delete all the text from this copy except the section you want to keep. Because you produce these by copying the original document, the new documents all share the same basic page layout – without any extra effort on your part.

The other method is to store each section in a separate Block and paste each Block into a separate new document. The advantages of this method are that it is neater and that it requires less free space on the disc when you start. However, you may have to set up the page layout afresh for each of these documents (though not if you make use of LocoScript's Template feature – see Session 21).

We shall now illustrate both these methods.

Suppose you wanted to split the example document into three smaller documents – the section up to Section 1, Section 1 and Section 2, ie. the three sections we marked earlier with Unit markers. We will call these new documents INTRO.TXT, SECTION1.TXT and SECTION2.TXT.

Move the File cursor to PCWINFO, press ⌐f3⌐ to bring the File menu onto the screen, select Copy file and press [ENTER]. Assuming that there is room on the disc, don't pick out a different group – just press [ENTER] again. This gives you a Copy menu with the same name for the copy. You will have to give the copy a new name because you can't have two documents with the same name in the same group. If there isn't room on the disc, you may have to store the copy on Drive M – the Memory disc.

Give the copy the name SECTION1.TXT – then edit it.

The first job is to mark out the part up to the beginning of Section 1 as a Block (Block 0) and delete it, using the techniques we used in Session 6. Remember, now you have the Unit marker marking the beginning of Section 1, you can move the Text cursor to the end of the Block simply by pressing [UNIT].

Then move the Text cursor to the beginning of Section 2 (again, make use of the Unit marker you inserted earlier), mark all the text between here and the end as Block 2 and delete it from the document. That leaves just Section 1 in the document, which is what you want. So press [EXIT] and save Section 1.

Now create a new document called SECTION2.TXT and paste in Block 2 (by pressing [PASTE] and then typing 2). This gives you a document containing just Section 2 – which is again what you want – and as the document you are working with uses the standard page layout, there isn't even any tidying up to do. Just press [EXIT] and save Section 2.

Finally, either edit PCWINFO, delete both Section 1 and Section 2, and rename it INTRO.TXT – or create a new document called INTRO.TXT and paste in Block 0. Either way, you get a third document that contains just the introduction part of the example document.

You now have three smaller documents where before you had one larger document.

Giving documents consecutive pages

Preparing a large document as a number of separate documents means that you get several Page 1s – unless you set up the First Page numbers of each document so that the page numbers run consecutively. What we are going to show you here is how to get LocoScript 2 to set up all the First Page numbers for you – and the Total Pages number as well, if you want.

Suppose INTRO.TXT, SECTION1.TXT and SECTION2.TXT were the chapters of a book that you had been working on and were now ready to print. (It's not really worth setting all the page numbers until you have finished preparing the text – because if you change something that makes the page numbers change, you may find yourself re-setting the numbers later!)

The first job is to set all the First Page numbers but before you get going, it is a good idea to check that the first chapter you are going to pick out (ie. INTRO.TXT)

8809

has the right First Page number to start with. This is important because you use this number to set the initial value of the counter that LocoScript will use in its calculations. LocoScript automatically starts the counter at its most recent value – so that, for example, you can set the page numbers for the documents you have on one disc; stop and change discs; and then carry on the sequence with documents you have stored on another disc.

The easiest way to check the First Page number is to display the Disc Manager Screen and use the Inspect option in the Document menu. (We used this option in Session 7 to set up and inspect short descriptions of documents.) Pick out the document you want with the File cursor, then press [f5] and [ENTER] and LocoScript displays a range of details about the document, including its First Page number. (Press [ENTER] when you have finished checking this.) If the First Page number isn't the one you want, correct this now by editing the Document Set-up.

Setting the First Page numbers

Setting First Page numbers also uses the Document menu, but before you display this menu, you must pick out the first document of the sequence with the File cursor.

The document to pick out, as you might expect, is the first chapter of your book or the first section of your report. In our example case, this means picking out INTRO.TXT – so move the File cursor to INTRO.TXT; then press [f5] to display the Document menu.

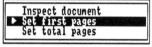

The option you want here is Set first pages, so select this with the Menu cursor and then press [ENTER]. LocoScript 2 now displays a Selection menu, giving details of the document you have picked out.

At the bottom of the menu are two 'Command' options, Set counter=first page and Set first page=counter. For the first document in the sequence, the option to pick is normally Set counter=first page which sets the counter to match the First Page number in the document. (You are unlikely to want Set first page = counter at this point because the counter will be set to the last value it had, which probably won't be the value you want.) Select the Set counter option and press [ENTER].

(Note: If the current First Page number is wrong, then cancel setting the page numbers temporarily, edit the document and set the correct First Page number in its Document Set-up – as described in Session 17.)

Next, you will see a message on the screen telling you to pick out a document. Move the File cursor to the second document in the series – SECTION1.TXT – and press [ENTER]. This document happens to be in the same group as the previous document but this doesn't have to be the case. You can pick out any document you like from the ones currently available on the Disc Manager Screen.

Once again, you now see the Selection menu – but with a difference. The difference is that you just get one option at the bottom of the menu – to Set first page = counter. This time, the counter is correctly set to one more than the last page number of the previous document.

Press [ENTER] to take the Set first page=counter option and once again, the message asking you to pick out a document will appear. This time, move the File cursor to SECTION2.TXT before pressing [ENTER]: you will then see the details of SECTION2.TXT and the new value for the counter. Press [ENTER] to set the First Page number to the counter.

That's the last document in the series – so this time when the message appears asking you to pick out a document, press [CAN]. You are then returned to the Disc Manager Screen. All the First Page numbers have now been set so that the pages are consecutive.

Note: If you accidentally pick out the wrong document at any stage in this process – don't panic. You don't have to go back to the beginning and start again. Instead, just press [CAN] (which takes you back to the Disc Manager Screen), pick out the **right** document with the File cursor, then open the Document menu and select Set first pages as if you were starting afresh. LocoScript then displays the version of the Selection menu with two 'Command' options at the bottom of the menu. The option to select is Set first page=counter – because the counter will be showing the right value. You can then carry on setting the page numbers as if nothing had happened.

Setting the Total Pages number

If you use a numbering scheme like Page n of m, you also need LocoScript 2 to set up the Total Pages number for each document. Do this immediately after you set the First Page number of the last document in the sequence – so that you know that the counter will be set to the right value.

Again this is carried out from the Disc Manager Screen and again you need the Document menu – but this time the option to pick is Set total pages. Pick out one of the documents from the sequence – say INTRO.TXT. Then press [f5] to bring the Document menu onto the screen, select Set total pages and press [ENTER].

This time it doesn't matter which order you pick out the documents because they will all be given the same Total Pages number. However, in practice it may well be easiest to remember which documents to pick out if you do pick them out in order!

LocoScript 2 then displays a Selection menu giving all the details of INTRO.TXT – ie. of the document you have picked out and the current setting of the counter – just

8809

like the ones you saw while you were setting the First Page numbers. However, this time the counter shows the number of the last page of the last document you picked out in the sequence.

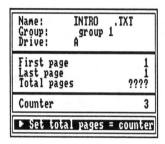

This time, you just get the one option, Set total pages=counter. This sets the Total Pages number to the counter: press [ENTER] to tell LocoScript to do this.

You then see the message asking you to pick out a document again. Move the File cursor to the next document you want to set (say, SECTION1.TXT) and press [ENTER]; then press [ENTER] again to tell LocoScript to set the Total Pages number; and so on until you have set all the Total Pages numbers. When you have picked out all the documents – press [CAN] when you are next asked to pick a document.

If you like, you could now check that this has been done properly for INTRO.TXT, SECTION1.TXT and SECTION2.TXT by printing these out. (The documents should contain suitable header and footer text from the use of the same example document in Session 16.)

Note: Once again, you can press [CAN] if you accidentally pick out the wrong document – just as you could when you were setting First Page numbers. When you are returned to the Disc Manager Screen, pick out the right document with the File cursor, select the Set Total Pages option – and carry on as if nothing had happened.

Revising the page numbers

To finish, we'll take a quick look at what you do when you need to change some of the page numbers you have set up – because you have made some change that has given you a different number of pages than you had before or you have decided to change the order of some of the sections.

Suppose, for example, that you had made some change to SECTION1.TXT that meant that it had one less page than before. This puts out the First Page number of SECTION2.TXT and makes the Total Pages number wrong for all three documents.

Move the File cursor to **the first document in the sequence that now has a different number of pages**. In our example case, that means moving the File cursor to SECTION1.TXT.

Press [f5] to bring the Document menu onto the screen and then select Set first pages. Even if you have only changed the total number of pages, you still have to start by selecting Set first pages so that you can set the counter. Press [ENTER].

The usual Selection menu then appears. Because the change is within this document, its current First Page number is correct and doesn't need to be changed. What you need to do here is to set the counter to this number to get the ball rolling. So move the Menu cursor to Set counter=first page and press [ENTER].

Back comes the message asking you to pick out a document. You now need to work through the rest of the documents in the sequence in order, just as if you were setting their First Page numbers for the first time. Not only are these numbers likely to be all wrong, you also need to work through to the end if you have to correct the Total Pages numbers.

If you are using the Total Pages number, you will need to work through **all** the documents in the sequence – just like you did before. Do this when you have finished setting all the First Page numbers.

Session summary

In this session, you have seen:

- How to put in section markers (Unit codes) and how to move forward to the next section marker or back to the last one
- How documents can become over-size and how LocoScript tells you that this has happened
- What short-term solutions you have to the problem of an over-size document
- What you should do in the long term
- How to split a large document into a number of smaller documents
- How to set the first page number of a series of documents so that the pages of the documents follow on from one another

9108

Session 19

Using different types of paper

In all the sessions up to now, we have been telling you to use A4 sheets of paper every time you printed any of the example documents.

We insisted on A4 in this way because we knew that both the part of the software that controls the printer and the documents you were printing were set up for A4 sheets of paper.

If you are happy to go on using A4 for every document you ever print, that's fine – but you will be restricting yourself unnecessarily. LocoScript 2 is well equipped to handle a wide range of different sizes and types of paper – labels, 11" fanfold paper, large A3 sheets, small A5 sheets to name but a few.

A number of these different types of paper are available as standard. If you have a special paper requirement, you just describe the paper to LocoScript 2 and it will use it properly. You can even add this type of paper to its list of standard types.

To use these different types of paper, both the software controlling the printer and the document that is going to be printed on this paper need to be set up for it. In this session, we are going to show you how this is done by setting up one of the Example documents (SPELL.TXT) for printing on A5 paper and then print it out first on A5 paper and then on A4 paper. (A5 paper is half the size of A4. The pages of this user guide, for example, are A5.)

Why set up the printer?

The printer needs to be set up for the type of paper you want to use so that each piece of paper is fed through the mechanism properly. Different types of paper need different handling.

For example, when you use 11" continuous stationery, you want the printer to advance the paper exactly 11" between the top of one page and the top of the next sheet. Similarly, you want the printer to 'know' how many lines it can print on a single sheet of paper. If it doesn't, it may try to print in the area at the bottom of the page where the paper is no longer held firmly by the printer mechanism. Text printed in that part of the page is very unlikely to be straight.

Having the printer set up for the type of paper you intend to use is crucial. You should never mislead LocoScript about the paper you are using in the printer.

8809

Why set up the document?

You set the type of paper you want to use in the document because LocoScript divides up your documents into pages for you. In order to do this properly, LocoScript needs to know the number of lines that you can put on each page – and that is fixed by the size of the paper. (Remember, how when we were setting up Header and Footer zones in Session 17, we said that the page length was fixed by the type of paper?) In other words, you set the type of paper you want to use in the document so that it is divided up into pages correctly.

However, your document only needs to be set up for the paper you ultimately want to print it on – that is, the paper you will use when you print the final version. While you are preparing the document, you can produce Draft versions on different (cheaper) paper. For example, you can always use 11" continuous stationery to print Draft versions of documents set up for A4, as we shall see below.

The key concept – Paper Type

All the details that LocoScript 2 needs in order to lay out and print your documents correctly on a particular type of paper are described by this paper's Paper Type. This Paper Type fixes:

– whether the paper comes in single sheets or as continuous stationery
– the length of each sheet
– the width of each sheet (single sheet stationery only) – to tell LocoScript the length of each sheet when the paper is used widthways in the printer; and
– the size of the Top and Bottom Gaps – ie. the areas at the top and the bottom of the sheet on which the printer never prints

LocoScript 2 is set up to know about certain types of paper – typically, A4 and A5 single sheet stationery and 11" continuous stationery. LocoScript 2 keeps the details of these Paper Types in its store of 'Settings', which also holds details of the printer(s) you use – as we shall see in the next session. These Settings are recorded in the SETTINGS.STD file on your Start-of-day disc, which is automatically read each time you load LocoScript.

Using one of the Paper Types is very straightforward. Essentially all you have to do is pick out the name of the Paper Type you want to use, and LocoScript 2 does all the 'difficult' part of setting up the details of this type of paper for you.

However, this doesn't mean that you always have to use one of these standard types of paper because you can specify your own Paper Types as well. LocoScript 2 can handle up to 10 different 'standard' Paper Types. And when you want to use a special type of paper for one particular document, you can set up a 'special' Paper Type for the document, with its own details of length, width etc.

Seeing what Paper Types you have

As we said above, LocoScript 2 keeps all the information about the Paper Types in its store of Settings.

You have access to this information through the Disc Manager Screen's Settings menu, which is brought onto the screen by pressing ⌐f6¬ (as you can see from the Information lines at the top of the screen). So to see what Paper Types you have, display the Disc Manager Screen and then press ⌐f6¬ to display the Settings menu.

This menu is a Commands menu but it is different from most of the Commands menus you have used up to now in that the selected option is marked with a diamond ♦ rather than an arrow ▶. You met this type of menu before in Session 12 when you used the Left offset menu to adjust the position of the print head for Direct Printing. Once again, the diamond tells you that when you press ⌐ENTER¬, LocoScript will carry out the command and then return you to this menu so that you can pick out either the same command again or a different one.

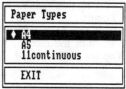

The option you want here is Paper Types. Select this option with the Menu cursor and press ⌐ENTER¬. LocoScript then displays a menu showing the names of all the Paper Types it knows. Typically, each name will give you a pretty good idea of the paper it refers to. For example, A4 refers to standard A4 paper (single sheets, 11⅔ inches long and 8⅓ inches wide); 11continuous refers to 11" continuous stationery (fanfold paper, each sheet 11 inches long).

To see the details of a particular Paper Type, point to this Type and press ⌐ENTER¬. For example, to see the details of A4 paper, move the Menu cursor to A4 and press ⌐ENTER¬. The following menu is then displayed. This gives the current specification for the Paper Type you picked out. Most of the details are self explanatory. Single Sheet is ticked because A4 paper comes as a number of separate sheets. The Height and Width of the paper give physical dimensions of the paper. The Top and Bottom Gaps, as you remember, are the parts of paper on which you don't want LocoScript to try to print – either because the paper isn't held firmly enough by the printer mechanism or to avoid the line of perforations between one page and the next.

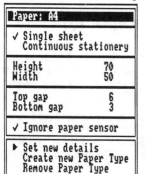

The Height and Width of the paper and the Top and Bottom Gaps are all given as a number of lines. These 'lines' are standard 6-Pitch lines (6 lines to the inch) – just as the Paper Length and Header and Footer Zone sizes you used in Session 17 were.

A4 paper is 11⅔ inches long and 8⅓ inches wide, so its Height is 11⅔ x 6 lines (ie. 70 lines) and its Width is 8⅓ x 6 lines (ie. 50 lines). The printer cannot print on the top 1" of the page or on the bottom ½" – so the Top gap is 6 lines and the Bottom Gap is 3 lines.

Why you give the Width as a number of lines is probably puzzling you but, in fact, the job of the Width is to tell LocoScript how many lines it will be able to fit in down the page when the paper is used widthways rather than lengthways. If you think about it, the width of a sheet of paper is its length when it is turned on its side. **Note:** The Width setting is **not** used to ensure that the width of your text is appropriate to the paper you are using. You need to ensure this yourself by setting the margins in your Layouts (see Session 11).

When you have finished looking at these details, press [ENTER]. LocoScript then re-displays the list of Paper Types, so that you can inspect the details of another Paper Type if you wish. So if, say, you now wanted to look at the details of 11continuous, you would move the Menu cursor to this option and press [ENTER]. But if you have seen all the Paper Types you want, select the EXIT option at the bottom of the menu – the quick way to do this is to press [EXIT] – and press [ENTER]. You are then returned to the Disc Manager Screen.

Using a Paper Type

OK, LocoScript 2 knows about all these different Paper Types, but how do you use one for a document?

The answer is that you set up the document itself for your chosen Paper Type. Once this has been done, LocoScript 2 helps you to ensure that the printer is set up correctly for you to print the document on this paper.

To demonstrate the steps, we are going to set up SPELL.TXT for printing on A5 paper and then print it out on this paper. So to start, open this document for editing.

Setting up a document for a particular Paper Type

The Paper Type is one of the pieces of information recorded in Document Set-up, so setting a different Paper Type means changing the Document Set-up – which, as you will remember, means selecting the Document setup option in the Actions menu. Press [f1] to bring the Actions menu onto the screen, select Document setup and press [ENTER] now.

Once the Pagination Screen is displayed, you have access to the Document Set-up and you also have an array of menus to help you change this. The one you want here is the Page menu (brought onto the screen by pressing [f5]) and the option you want from this menu is Paper type. Select this option, press [ENTER] and the following menu is displayed:

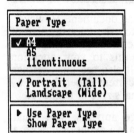

Which Paper Type?

The first job is to select the Paper Type you want. This part of the menu is a Settings menu, with a tick beside the Paper Type that is currently selected. What we want here is A5, so move the cursor to this option and press [⊞] to select it.

Portrait or Landscape?

When you select a type of paper that comes in single sheets (such as A4 or A5), you then need to specify which way round you will want to use the paper. The choices are Portrait or Landscape. Portrait means the paper is used lengthways in the conventional way; Landscape means the paper is used widthways. Here, select Portrait.

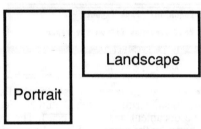

Note: Only select **Landscape** if your paper can be passed widthways through your printer or if you have a Laser printer which can print in either orientation on the page.

Details of the Paper Type

If you know that the Paper Type properly describes the paper you want to use, all you do now is press [ENTER] to tell LocoScript to use this Paper Type. If, however, you want to check or change any of the details first, move the Menu cursor to Show Paper Type and press [ENTER]. LocoScript then displays a menu like the one we saw when we were inspecting the details of the different Paper Types – giving the current specification for the Paper Type you picked out. A5 paper is 8⅓ inches long and 5⅚ inches wide, so its Height is 8⅓ x 6 lines (ie. 50 lines) and its Width is 5⅚ x 6 lines (ie. 35 lines). Again, the printer cannot print on the top 1" of the page or on the bottom ½" – so the Top gap is 6 lines and the Bottom Gap is 3 lines.

The menu is a standard 'Settings' menu – so you can, if you need, change any of these settings. We will show you how this works shortly. But as we just want to use standard A5 paper, we will leave everything as it is and just press [ENTER]. LocoScript then returns you to the previous menu: this time, move the Menu cursor to Use Paper Type and press [ENTER] to confirm the details you have selected.

Note: If you do change any details at this point, you in fact create a 'special' Paper Type (see page 213). To avoid confusion later, it is best to change its name as well.

Normally, that is all there is to setting the paper type for the document. However, there will be occasions when the paper type you select is too short for the size of Header and Footer zone you have set up in the document's Page Layout (see Session 17). When this happens, LocoScript will bring this to your attention immediately through the following Alert message. You will also see this message when you set a Page Layout that is incompatible with your current Paper Type – by choosing Header and Footer Zones that leave a Page Body that's zero or negative.

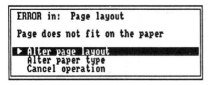

When this message appears, you must either change the Page Layout or choose a different Paper Type. Simply select the option you want in this Alert message and LocoScript will display the appropriate submenu so that you can put this right.

• After you have finished setting the Paper Type in the Document Set-up, press [EXIT] to finish working on the Document Set-up, select the option to return to the start of the document and press [ENTER]. The fact that you have changed the Paper Type is shown by the number of lines LocoScript says you have to a page (written at the end of the second Information line). When the document was set up for A4, you had 54 lines of document text on every page; now you have just 34.

Before you finish editing the document, you should check that the righthand margin you are using does not exceed the width of the paper. Work out where the righthand edge of the paper is on the Ruler Line by multiplying the width of the paper (in inches) by the Scale Pitch used in the document. (You may need to select Change layout from the f2 menu to find out what the Scale Pitch is.) If necessary, adjust all the margins in the document. Finally, press [EXIT] and save the document.

Printing on the correct paper

We now have SPELL.TXT set up for A5 paper – and we can load A5 paper into the printer. (If you don't have any A5 paper, prepare a couple of sheets by tearing a sheet of A4 in half.) What we haven't done yet is set up the printer for A5 paper.

As we shall see later in this session, there are some special steps that you can take to set the printer up. But in fact, you rarely have to do this. As you will see, when you have the document set up for the type of paper you want to use, LocoScript 2 helps you either to use the current printer paper or to set up the printer to match the document. All you have to do to start the process is print the document.

Check that the File cursor is on SPELL.TXT; then go through the steps to print one copy of this document (ie. press P and then [ENTER]). Because the printer isn't set up for the same paper as the document, LocoScript puts up the following Alert message:

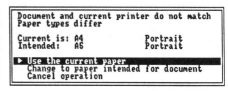

8809

We want to print on the paper the document is set up for, so the option to take here is to Change to paper intended for document. LocoScript 2 then displays the details of the set-up you have selected, together with the option to Proceed or to Cancel the operation altogether. Assuming that you choose to proceed, LocoScript then sets up the Printer for the same Paper Type as the document before printing the document.

This is a very useful feature of LocoScript 2. If you think about it, it means you never need to worry about setting up the printer for the same paper as the document you are about to print. If the document is not set up for the paper you have just used, LocoScript 2 first puts up an Alert message reminding you which paper the document is set up for and then gives you the option of automatically setting up the printer for the same type of paper. All you need to do is feed the right paper into the printer!

Select the option to Proceed and then feed a sheet of A5 paper into your printer. Now that the printer has been set up for A5 paper, this is what you must use. Press [EXIT] to leave Printer Control State – and LocoScript 2 will start to print your document. The document should print perfectly.

Drafting on the 'wrong' paper

As we said earlier, LocoScript doesn't force you to print a document on the paper it has been set up for. After all, it is very reasonable to want to produce Draft versions of reports on 11" continuous stationery, rather than on A4 sheets of paper.

However, when you want to do this, you have to remember to arrange that the printer is set up for your Drafting paper **before** you start to print the document. The only Paper Type that LocoScript 2 can set up the printer for on your behalf is the Paper Type set in the Document Set-up.

If you have just been printing on this type of paper, that's fine – the printer is already set up for this type of paper. If you haven't, then you need to set up the printer as follows:

Setting up the printer for a chosen Paper Type

As with any action that involves setting the printer, the first step is to put LocoScript into its Printer Control State – by pressing the [PTR] key. Do this now.

Once you are in Printer Control State, you have an array of menus to help you set up any aspect of the printer. The one you want here is the Paper menu which, as you see, is brought onto the screen by pressing [f3]. Press [f3] now and the following menu appears:

This looks familiar because it has exactly the same design and contains exactly the same sort of information as the Paper Type menu you have just used to set the Paper Type information in the Document Set-up. Moreover, it works in exactly the same way.

As we said earlier, what is most important here is that the Paper Type you set accurately describes the paper you are going to use. So to produce your Draft version on 11" continuous, say, you move the Menu cursor to 11continuous and press [⊞]. In this case, we are going to print a document set up for A5 on A4 paper.

So select A4 paper and tell LocoScript that you will use this paper Portrait. Then, as the Paper Type specifies the paper correctly, just press [ENTER] to tell LocoScript to set up the printer for this Paper Type. If it didn't, you would move the Menu cursor to Show Paper Type and set the details you want, exactly as you would to get the document set up correctly for the paper.

Finally, press [EXIT] so that you leave Printer Control State and return to the Disc Manager Screen.

Printing on the chosen paper

Now the printer has been set up specifically for the paper you want to use, you are ready to print SPELL.TXT (the document we have set up for A5 paper) on A4 paper.

Check the File cursor is on SPELL.TXT and press P and then [ENTER] to print one copy of this document exactly as before. Because the paper set in the Document Set-up is not the paper the printer is set up for, LocoScript puts up its Alert message:

Whenever you are printing the document on the wrong paper quite deliberately, the option you want is Use the current paper. Select this option now, press [ENTER] and feed some A4 paper into your printer. This paper must be A4 paper – ie. the paper the printer is set up for. You can't just use any piece of paper you happen to have

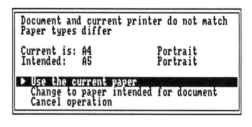

because, as we explained before, it is essential for the printer to be set up for the paper you actually use – or it won't handle the paper properly.

The example document will now print. As you see, each page that you earlier printed on A5 paper is now printed on a separate sheet on A4 paper. This is because LocoScript retains the way the document is divided up into pages.

9007

Obviously, printing on longer sheets of paper is fine because the printer can easily fit each page onto a separate sheet of paper. But what happens when the paper you use is shorter? The answer is that LocoScript still keeps the document divided up into its pages and if there is room for the text on a single sheet of the paper, then it will be printed on just this sheet. Otherwise, it uses two (or more) sheets of paper for every page of the document.

Setting up a new Paper Type

The supplied Paper Types cover the commonest types of stationery, but are unlikely to cover all the sorts of paper you use. If you use a particular type of labels, for example, you should set up a Paper Type which describes these labels. (You can have up to 10 different Paper Types in all.) To show you how you tell LocoScript about other sorts of paper, we shall now set up a Paper Type for 1½" labels on continuous backing paper. In practice, the ideal time to do this is immediately after you have set up either a document or the printer for this type of paper because then most, if not all, of the information you want will be set up already for you.

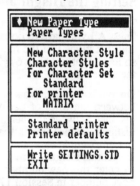

As you will remember, all the information about your Paper Types is held in LocoScript's store of Settings – which is recorded in SETTINGS.STD on the Start-of-day disc. So the first stage is to display the Disc Manager Screen, insert the Start-of-day disc in Drive A and press [f7] to tell LocoScript that you have changed discs. When you are ready, press [f6] to bring the Settings menu onto the screen.

The option you want this time is New Paper Type. This is the option that is pre-selected for you, so all you have to do is press [ENTER]. LocoScript now displays a special version of the Paper Type menu:

As you see, this menu is already filled in. These are the details of the 'current' Paper Type – that is, either the last Paper Type you picked out from the Paper Types menu (see 'Seeing what Paper Types you have', above), or the Paper Type you have just set up a document or the printer for. What changes you make to these settings is up to you, but you must ensure that you give LocoScript an accurate picture of the paper.

8809

Continuous or Single Sheet

The first item to set is whether the paper is Single Sheet or Continuous. If your paper is supplied as separate sheets, you must ensure that Single Sheet is selected – but if it comes as a continuous roll or 'fanfold', you must select Continuous stationery. This is covered by the top section of the menu.

Labels stationery is continuous, so move the Menu cursor to Continuous and press [⊞] to select this. If Single Sheet was selected before, you will see the menu change. The previous version had a Width entry – but the new menu doesn't because it describes Continuous stationery. Continuous stationery can only be used one way round and so its width is irrelevant.

Instead, LocoScript inserts the option to set the Left Offset – ie. the distance the print start position is moved to the right of its normal start position. This is used to ensure that your printer always prints on the part of the continuous stationery you want it to and never, in the case of rolls of labels, on the backing paper – assuming that you always keep the paper holders on the tractor feed unit in the same place.

Setting the Height and Width

The Height is the length of each page, expressed as a number of standard 6-pitch lines. All you have to do is measure a sample sheet of paper in inches, multiply by 6 and that gives you the number of lines. For example, A4 paper is 11⅔ inches long, so its Height is 11⅔ x 6 = 70 lines. The Width of Single Sheet paper is calculated in the same way.

On fanfold paper, what you need to know to work out the Height is the distance between the lines of perforations. This is, in fact, how the paper is specified. The distance between the perforations on 11" continuous stationery is 11". On labels, the distance to measure is that between the top of one label and the top of the next. In our example case, this distance is 1½" so the Height you want is 1½ x 6 = 9 lines. To set this Height, move the Menu cursor to Height and type 9. Then press [ENTER] to 'enter' this new number – in exactly the same way as you 'entered', say, a new First page number in Session 17.

Setting the Left Offset

The Left Offset you set will be the number that gives the distance you want the printing to be displaced in tenths of an inch.

However, finding out the number you need involves some trial and error because it depends on precisely where you have chosen to put the paper holders on your printer's tractor feed unit. There is nothing that you can measure until you try printing out with some initial Left Offset – say, ½" – and then see how you need to adjust this to get the text in the position you want.

In our example case, we want a Left Offset of ½", ie. 5 tenths of an inch. So move the cursor to Left Offset and type 5, followed by [ENTER] to 'enter' this number.

Setting the Top and Bottom Gaps

The Top and Bottom Gaps, as you remember, are the parts of paper on which you don't want LocoScript to try to print – either because the paper isn't held firmly enough by the printer mechanism or to avoid the line of perforations between pages.

With continuous stationery, you have a completely free choice as to how large you make these Gaps. If you want a rule that you never print on either the first or the last three lines of the page, you simply set the Top Gap to 3 and the Bottom Gap to 3. If you want to get as many lines as possible on the page, then you might make both Gaps 0 – though then you run the risk of printing on the line of perforations.

With single sheet stationery, the Top and Bottom Gaps are largely set by the mechanism for feeding sheets of paper through the printer. For example, the PCW printer cannot print on the top six lines or on the bottom three lines of each sheet of paper. Other printers will have similar restrictions.

You still have a great deal of freedom in setting the Top and Bottom Gap – but the Gaps you set must always be at least as big as the Gaps needed by your printer. So when you are setting the Paper Type for single sheet paper used in the PCW printer, you must always make the Top Gap at least 6 and the Bottom Gap at least 3.

For labels stationery, you could set both Gaps to zero because it is continuous stationery but this risks printing on the backing paper. We suggest setting both Gaps to 1 line to prevent this from happening. Set these Gaps in exactly the same way as you have set the Height and the Left Offset – by moving the Menu cursor to the relevant line of the menu and typing the number of lines, followed by [ENTER].

Choosing whether to Ignore the Paper Sensor

The other option you can set is Ignore paper sensor. The sensor this refers to is built into the printer and it detects the end of the paper. This is very useful when you are using continuous stationery because it stops the printer from trying to print beyond the last sheet of the roll. However, it gets in the way of using single sheet stationery because it signals the end of the paper before you have printed the last few lines of the page.

So, when you are using single sheet stationery, you want to set (ie. tick) Ignore paper sensor (so that the signals from the sensor are ignored) but when you are using continuous stationery, this option should be cleared so that LocoScript responds when the sensor signals the end of the roll.

As the labels stationery is continuous, check that Ignore paper sensor isn't ticked – because otherwise you will have to be prepared to stop the printer in the nick of time before it prints off the end of the paper. If Ignore paper sensor has been selected, move the Menu cursor to this option and use the technique of pressing either [←] or the Space Bar to clear it.

Naming the Paper Type

That's set all the details of the Paper Type except one – its name. You must set a name because this is used to identify the Paper Type. This name can be up to 12 characters long and you can use a wide range of characters in it – not just the standard A...Z, a...z and 0..9. For example, you could call the Paper Type you have set up for 1½" labels, 1½" Labels. (The full list of characters is given in Appendix III.) The name you choose can't have been used already for another Paper Type.

Move the Menu cursor to Paper, press [□] to clear away the current name and type your chosen name.

Storing the New Paper Type

When you have set all the details you want, press [ENTER]. This selects the single command option Create new Paper Type in the bottom section of the menu. You are then returned to the previous menu, so that you can now create another New Paper Type or inspect the current Paper Types or make some other change to the Settings file (see Session 20).

To leave the Settings menu, move the Menu cursor to the EXIT option (remember, the quick way to do this is to press [EXIT]) and press [ENTER]. LocoScript now displays a special message, which offers to update your SETTINGS.STD file. The point is that you have done the work of creating a new Paper Type and LocoScript has modified the version of the Settings file it is currently using, but if you want to have this Paper Type available the next time you use LocoScript, you have got to update the SETTINGS.STD file on your Start-of-day disc. If you don't, your new Paper Type will be lost.

To take this option, check that you have your Start-of-day disc in Drive A and then press [ENTER]. When you press [ENTER], LocoScript writes the SETTINGS.STD file on the disc in Drive A. (It's up to you to check that you have the right disc in the drive.) You are then returned to the Disc Manager Screen.

Getting rid of a Paper Type

We have just shown you how to set up a new Paper Type – so we will now show you how to delete a Paper Type you don't need. You may need this to keep within the limit of 10 Paper Types. Again, this means changing LocoScript's store of Settings – so display the Disc Manager Screen and bring the Settings menu onto the screen by pressing [f6].

The option you want is Paper Types – so move the Menu cursor to this option and press [ENTER], exactly as you did when you were seeing which Paper Types you have. This brings the list of Paper Types onto the screen.

Move the Menu cursor to the Paper Type you want to delete (say, the 1½" Labels you have just set up) and press [ENTER] – again, exactly as you did when you were inspecting the Paper Types. But this time when the menu appears, move the Menu cursor to the Remove Paper Type option right at the bottom of the menu. Normally, you would now press [ENTER] to tell LocoScript to go ahead and delete this Paper Type. For the moment, however, just press [CAN] – partly because you may well want to have a Paper Type for 1½" labels, but also because we need this Paper Type for the next part of the tutorial!

You are then returned to the Settings menu, which you can leave by selecting the EXIT option and pressing [ENTER]. Again, you have changed the Settings file and so LocoScript reminds you to save the new version on your Start-of-day disc. You must do this if you are to get rid of this Paper Type permanently.

Special Paper Types

Earlier in this session we set up a document for printing on one of the Paper Types. However, there will be occasions when you want to use some other type of paper. For example, you may want to use special 2" labels stationery just for ADDRESS.LST (one of the Example documents). What do you do then?

In fact, the steps are very similar. Again, you need to set up the document for your chosen paper by setting up the Paper Type in the Document Set-up. That done, you can get LocoScript to set up the printer for you when you print the document on the special paper.

Because we set this information in the Document Set-up, the first step is to open ADDRESS.LST for editing and then display the Pagination Screen by selecting the Document setup option in the Actions menu ([f1]). Do this now. Once the Pagination Screen is displayed, you have access to the Document Set-up and you also have an array of menus to help you change this. As before, the menu you want is the Page menu (brought onto the screen by pressing [f5]) and the option you want from this menu is Paper Type.

What to select from the Paper Types menu?

The first job is to select a Paper Type – just as before. The one to choose is the Paper Type that is most like your chosen paper: then you will have the least to do to make it precisely the Paper Type you want. In particular, it's always better to choose a Single Sheet paper type if your special paper is supplied as separate sheets of paper, but choose a Continuous Paper Type if it is supplied as a continuous roll or as fanfold paper.

The labels we want to set up here are most like the 1½" labels we have just set up, so simply move the cursor to 1½" labels and press [+] to select it. The option you have selected is a continuous type of stationery – so the part of the menu that deals with whether you want to use the paper Portrait or Landscape disappears.

Now move the Menu cursor to Show Paper Type and press [ENTER].

Setting the details

LocoScript now displays the details of the Paper Type you picked out. This gives the current specification for the Paper Type you picked out. To create your special Paper Type, you just change some of these details – exactly as you did earlier in this session when you were setting up a new Paper Type. In this case, simply change the Height to 12 lines.

Naming the Special Paper Type

When you create a special paper type, LocoScript automatically gives your special paper type essentially the same name as the standard type you selected to start with, but it adds ?. So the name of the paper type you have created by changing the specification for 1½" labels would be 1½" labels?.

If you don't want to use this name, you can change it. Just move the Menu cursor up to the Paper line of the menu, press [⊡] to clear away the current name and then type your new name. Once again, this name must be no more than 12 characters (letters and digits) long. For example, call the new Paper Type 2in Labels. LocoScript will still add ? to this name in the Paper Type menu, just to point out that this is not one of the standard Paper Types.

• If you copy a LocoScript document that someone else has set up on their own machine, they may well have selected a paper type for the document that is standard on their system but not on yours. This is particularly true of documents set up abroad where the standard paper sizes are very different.

This is not the problem that it at first seems. LocoScript simply treats the paper type that's been selected as a Special Paper Type that has been set up for the document. You can set a different Paper Type – or leave it as it is because, as you will remember, it is not essential for the Paper Type set in the document to match the Paper you print on. However, once you select a different Paper Type, you will have to set up the original Paper Type afresh if you need it again. LocoScript only retains the details of special Paper Types while they are actually in use.

Session summary

In this session, you have seen:

- How to set up a document to work with a particular type of paper
- How you can readily get the printer set up for the same type of paper as the document you are about to print
- How to set up the software controlling the printer for a particular size of paper
- What happens when you print a document on a different type of paper to the one is it set up for
- How to set up new Paper Types
- How to set up a Special Paper Type for a document

Using different printers and fonts

So far in this tutorial, whenever you have printed a document, you have done this on the PCW's built-in printer and in its 'Standard' font. In fact, one of the most powerful aspects of LocoScript 2 is that you aren't tied to using either one particular printer or even one particular font on that printer. Instead, you can choose which printer and which font to use, even for individual documents.

This session starts by showing you how to choose different fonts to use on the PCW's built-in matrix printer, then goes on to show how you can extend these techniques to printing with a different printer. If you only have one printer – the PCW's built-in printer – and you only want to use the Standard font on this printer, you need never worry about this side of using LocoScript 2. All the software and all your documents will automatically be set up for this printer and this font without you doing anything. You will, however, be missing the chance to make your documents more stylish!

Note: If you have a PCW8256 or a PcW9256 with only 256k of memory and you have the LocoSpell spelling checker on your system, you have too little space on Drive M to use either different fonts or different printers. Perhaps now is the time to upgrade your PCW's memory. Contact Locomotive Software for further details.

Using a different font

LocoScript 2 comes supplied with two fonts – 'Standard' and 'Sans Serif'. 'Standard' gives a similar style of text to that provided in LocoScript '1'; 'Sans Serif' is a more modern-looking typestyle which doesn't have any of the decorative lines ('serifs') at the tops and bottoms of characters (hence its name).

Standard

Further to my letter of the 13th June, I confirm
my order for 25 fittings with screw threads.
Please ensure that these are delivered no later
than the 28th July.

Sans Serif

A detached executive house close to open
countryside, yet convenient for the town
centre. Just 5 minutes drive from the
railway station (Waterloo 35mins).

In addition, if you buy the LocoFont disc for your PCW, you can add a whole range of other fonts to your system from decorative 'Script' styles, suitable for producing stylish invitations, to formal styles suitable for business letters and the like.

Having the font available

Before you can use any font on the built-in printer, the font has to be 'available' – and to be 'available', two conditions have to be met.

The first condition is that the file containing details of the font must be in group 0 on Drive M at the time you want to use the font. This is not so hard to arrange as you might be imagining. Provided the fonts have been correctly installed on your system, the files you need will be automatically copied to Drive M for you as part of the process of loading LocoScript.

Load LocoScript now and then look across at group 0 on Drive M. You should see two files called MATRIX.#-something in this group – MATRIX.#SS and MATRIX.#ST. These files provide the Sans Serif and Standard fonts respectively. They were copied to Drive M automatically at Start-up from group 0 on your Start-of-day disc. (If you insert your Start-of-day disc (and press [f7]) you should see these same two files in group 0 of that disc.)

(*Note:* You also need to have the main file that drives the built-in printer either loaded into memory or in group 0 on Drive M. This file is called MATRIX.PRI but you'll rarely be conscious of its presence because it is one of LocoScript's Hidden files. Normally, you won't need to worry about this file: LocoScript takes care of loading it for you – but if LocoScript does ever declare that the MATRIX printer is unavailable, then one thing to check is that MATRIX.PRI is in group 0 on Drive M.)

The other condition which has to be met before a font is available is that its name must be recorded in the current Settings file, SETTINGS.STD. This should have been done for you in this case, but you won't get any such automatic service either when you install the LocoFont fonts or extra printers. Updating the Settings file to record any fonts or printers you add to your system is an important part of the installation procedure and must on no account be neglected.

Setting up a document for the chosen font

Although not essential, it is a very good idea to set up each document for the font that you intend to use when you print the document.

For a start, you will generally get a noticeably better finished result. When the document has been set up for the font in which it is printed, LocoScript has had access to the correct character widths in working out where to position the characters and how much space to leave between the words in justified text. When you print a document in some other font, LocoScript does its best to adapt the document to the different character widths of the new font but it is constrained to keep the same line breaks and page breaks. As a result, words can look too squashed or too widely spaced (depending on whether the new font has wider or narrower characters) and in some cases, lines may be impossible to justify.

The other advantage of setting the font in the document is that then LocoScript will automatically prompt you to select this font if you are about to print in some other font. It can even help you change the printer over to your required font. (Just as valuably, if you set a document up for your chosen font, LocoScript won't prompt you to change font when you already have the right font selected!).

To show you how to set up a document for a particular font, we shall now set up MAIL.TXT (an example document on the Examples disc) for the Sans Serif font.

The font for which a document is set up is recorded in its Document Set-up, so the first step is to open MAIL.TXT for editing. Once the document is on the screen, press ⌈f1⌉ and select Document setup in the usual way to gain access to the Document Set-up (see Session 17).

Once the Pagination Screen is displayed, you have an array of menus to help you change the Document Set-up. The one you want here is the Printing menu which, you will see, is brought onto the screen by pressing ⌈f6⌉.

The Printer Selection menu that appears shows the details of the printer set-up currently defined for the document, its so-called 'Intended' printer set-up. Ignoring for the moment the Character Style setting (which is only an important factor when working with a daisy-wheel printer), you will see this menu tells you that the document is currently set up for the MATRIX printer and the Standard Character Set. 'MATRIX' is the name by which LocoScript knows the built-in printer, while 'Character Set' is the term used within LocoScript for a font. So this confirms that the document is set up for the Standard font on the built-in printer.

Move the Menu cursor to the Character Set line and press ⌈ENTER⌉. You then see a new menu.

This menu is essentially just a list of the fonts that are currently 'available' for the MATRIX printer – ie. recorded in Settings file and currently in group 0 on Drive M. You can have up to 10 fonts listed here. Simply move the cursor to your new selection (Sans serif in this case), press [+] to tick this and then press [ENTER] to return to the Printer Selection menu. Note how this menu now specifies Sans serif as the current Character Set.

Press [EXIT] followed by [ENTER] to leave the Printer Selection menu, and then again to leave Document Set-up and return to the document itself. Finally, exit from the document and save the new version to disc. Before closing the document, LocoScript works through the text, re-laying it. Changing the font gives LocoScript a new set of character widths to work with – which might change how the text is laid out. (In fact in this particular instance, there will be no change because the Sans Serif and Standard fonts have identical character widths but this is somewhat of a special case.)

Note: When you select the Character Set menu, the current font may be shown with ? beside it. This tells you that this font isn't 'available' at the moment – ie. either its file is not on Drive M or its name is not in the current Settings file. You can continue editing with the document set up for such a font but won't be able to print in this font (or to re-select it after changing to a different font) until the font has been restored.

Printing the document

The steps used in printing a document in its Intended font are essentially just the ones you will be used to from earlier in the Tutorial.

To see this, print MAIL.TXT at High Quality. (You need to select High Quality to see the font properly. When you print at draft quality, the characters are not as well formed and so there is either no difference between different fonts – as is the case with Standard and Sans Serif – or the difference is barely perceptible. Draft quality is only intended for producing drafts after all!)

The difference in the action is that, before it prints the document, LocoScript displays the following message:

```
Document and current printer do not match
Character Set and/or Style differ

Current is: Standard    /Standard    PS
Intended:   Sans serif  /Standard    PS

  Use the current Set/Style
▶ Change to Set/Style intended for document
  Cancel operation
```

To understand why this message has appeared, you need to understand a bit more about how LocoScript works with printers.

All the time you are using LocoScript, it is set up for a particular combination of printer, Character Set and Character Style known as 'Current' printer set-up. This is the printer set-up LocoScript currently expects to use when you next ask it to print.

What's happened here is that LocoScript has spotted that the document you have asked it to print is set up for a different Character Set. So it displays this message, simply to ask whether you want to use Current Character Set (Standard) or the "Intended" one set in the document or cancel (which allows you to select something different).

To print in the Intended font, move the cursor to the Change to intended option and press [ENTER]. The Intended Character Set then becomes the Current Character Set.

There aren't any further differences for it to report, but before going ahead, LocoScript shows the following "Check-out" message for you to check. This gives full details of the printer set-up LocoScript is about to use. Press [ENTER] to say OK and the document prints.

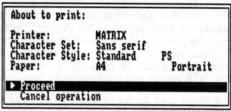

```
About to print:

Printer:          MATRIX
Character Set:    Sans serif
Character Style:  Standard      PS
Paper:            A4            Portrait

▶ Proceed
  Cancel operation
```

Before you go on to the next part of this session, print MAIL.TXT again. The thing to notice is that this time, LocoScript doesn't display any message. Since changing to the Intended Character Set on the previous printing, the Current and Intended Character Sets now match and so there is no need for any message.

Note: The option to Change to intended is only offered if the Intended font is available. If this font isn't available, you are simply offered the choice of printing in the Current font or cancelling.

Setting up LocoScript for a particular font

The alternative way of arranging that a document is printed in a particular font is to ensure that this is the Current Character Set before you start. Then when the message appears telling you that the Current and Intended Character Sets don't match, you simply have to select the Use current option to get the required result. The steps are very like the ones you use to set up the printer for a particular Paper Type, as we shall now see. (**Note:** You can only carry out these steps we are about to describe when the printer is idle: LocoScript won't allow you to change the Current Character Set while it is still printing the last document.)

We should however emphasise that the following steps should not be treated as your standard method of arranging that the document is printed in the font you require. The layout of the document is worked out when it is edited and so all the calculations are based on whatever font is selected as the Intended Character Set. The result is in fact OK in case of Standard and Sans Serif because the two fonts have exactly the same character widths in proportional spacing and so the choice of the seriffed or the unseriffed font doesn't affect how the document is laid out. Normally, however, the character widths in the two fonts will be very different and the printed document will suffer either from variable line lengths or from excessively small or large word spacings (or perhaps from both!).

9010

To show the steps involved, we'll set the Current Character Set back to Standard.

As with any action that involves making an adjustment to the printer, the first step is to go into Printer Control State – by pressing the ⌈PTR⌉ key. Do this now. Once you are in Printer Control State, you have an array of menus to help you specify any aspect of the printer. The one you want here is the Printer menu which, as you see, is brought onto the screen by pressing ⌈f5⌉. Press ⌈f5⌉ now.

The menu that appears should look familiar because it has exactly the same layout as the Printer Selection menu that you have just used to tell LocoScript which font you wanted the document set up for. Again it shows a summary of the printer set-up that is currently selected (ie. the built-in MATRIX printer and the Sans serif Character Set).

```
┌─────────────────────────────┐
│ Printer selection           │
├─────────────────────────────┤
│   Character Style           │
│     Standard        PS      │
│ ◆ Character Set             │
│     Sans serif              │
│ Printer                     │
│     MATRIX                  │
│                             │
│   EXIT                      │
│   Remove Current Set        │
└─────────────────────────────┘
```

The menu also works in exactly the same way. In other words, all you have to do to set the Current Character Set you require is to move the cursor to the Character Set line of the menu and press ⌈ENTER⌉. When the list of available fonts appears, use the ⌈⊞⌉ key to tick the required font (Standard in this case) and then press ⌈ENTER⌉ to return to the Printer Selection menu. This menu should now be showing Standard as the Character Set. Finally, press ⌈EXIT⌉ followed by ⌈ENTER⌉ to leave the Printer Selection menu; then press ⌈EXIT⌉ to leave Printer Control State. Standard is now the Current Character Set.

If you want to prove that these steps have had the prescribed effect, all you have to do is to print MAIL.TXT again. Before the document prints, you should once more see the message telling you that the Current and Intended Character Sets don't match. This time, however, just check that the Use current option is selected and press ⌈ENTER⌉. The document should then be printed in Standard font. (**Note:** LocoScript doesn't display any 'Check-out' message this time because the Current printer set-up is unchanged.)

Making your chosen font the main font

LocoScript is initially set up so that when you switch on in morning, it is automatically primed to print in the Standard font. The reason Standard is selected is that this is the 'Default' Character Set on the built-in printer.

If you want, you can set up LocoScript so that a different font (such as Sans serif) is the default and thus the font automatically selected at Start-up. The steps you take to arrange this are as follows:

From the Disc Manager Screen, press ⌈f6⌉ to display the Settings menu. When this menu appears, move the cursor to Printer defaults and press ⌈ENTER⌉. A new menu then appears, the Printer defaults menu. This starts at the top with the name of the printer for which defaults are displayed; then below it gives a summary of the current defaults for this printer.

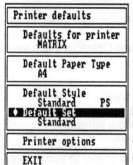

Before you go any further, it is important to check that the printer shown at the top of the menu is the MATRIX printer. If it isn't then you must select the Defaults for printer line of the menu, press [ENTER], use [⊞] to select the MATRIX printer from the list that's offered and then press [ENTER] again. If some other printer is specified at the top of the menu, any further steps you take will set the Default Character Set for this printer, not for the built-in printer that is our aim.

With the correct printer selected, move the cursor to Default Set and press [ENTER]. You will now see the by now familiar list of the fonts available for your printer. Simply use [⊞] to tick the required font and then press [ENTER] to return to Printer defaults menu, where the font you picked should now be selected as the Default Set.

Press [EXIT] followed by [ENTER] to return from the Printer defaults menu to the Settings menu; then again to leave the Settings menu. When LocoScript offers to write the new SETTINGS.STD file on the disc in Drive A, insert your Start-of-day disc in Drive A (if you load from a sequence of Drive A Start-up discs, insert the first disc in the sequence) then press [ENTER] to accept this offer.

The new Default Character Set is then both recorded in the current Settings file and saved on disc for when you re-load.

LocoScript 2 and External printers

There are lots of different printers that you could use as an alternative to the PCW's built-in printer – dot-matrix printers, daisy-wheel printers, even laser printers and such exotic things as bubble-jet printers.

Dot-matrix printers, like the one supplied with the PCW, and laser printers produce characters by making patterns of dots on the paper. Daisy-wheel printers take all their characters directly from a 'printwheel'. The wheel has a number of 'petals', each with a different character on it, and looks rather like a daisy – hence the name 'daisy-wheel'.

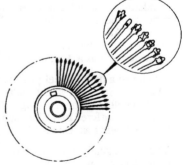

A printer that you use instead of the built-in printer is referred to as an 'External printer' and you can set up your system for up to three 'External' printers at the same time, giving you a choice of four printers to work with.

Unfortunately, using an External printer is not just a matter of attaching the printer to the PCW by a suitable cable. Printers have similar facilities – some more, some less – but the instructions they respond to and characters they print vary considerably even among printers that their manufacturers describe as 'compatible'.

Printwheels have different characters on the ends of the petals (or a different arrangement of characters on the petals); fonts on dot-matrix and laser printers typically offer similar but different ranges of characters. Even where the printers offer the same characters, these inevitably have different character widths, even on the same printer: LocoScript needs the correct width information for any set of characters it prints with in order to get the document's layout correct.

So before you can print a document on an external printer, LocoScript needs to know:

- what commands the printer requires
- which characters the printer can produce and their widths (for proportional spacing): this is known as the 'Character Set'
- details of the 'Style' of these characters – in particular, the Character Pitch they were designed to be used at

About Character Sets

A Character Set is a list of all the characters that are available in the set and the codes the printer uses to refer to each character, together with the width information needed so that characters are positioned correctly in proportionally-spaced text.

The characters that are in a particular Character Set vary from printer to printer and, in the case of daisy-wheel printers, they may vary from printwheel to printwheel. A number of Character Sets are based on the standard ASCII characters – a . . . z, A . . . Z, 0 . . . 9 and a range of common punctuation marks. Others have 'specialist' uses – for example, there are some Character Sets that have been specifically designed for technical reports and others for text in foreign languages.

It's obviously impractical to talk about a Character Set by listing the characters it contains, so instead we just use its name. Some of these names are reasonably standardised, so the characters in one 'ASCII' Character Set will be very much the same as those in another 'ASCII' set. However, there may be differences even between ASCII Character Sets: in particular, the different 'language' versions of ASCII cover slightly different ranges of characters. For example, the US ASCII character set has a # and no £, whereas the English version has a £ and no #.

If you use a daisy-wheel printer, you will probably work with a number of different Character Sets, but a dot-matrix printer will often only have one Character Set, corresponding to the full range of characters that can be printed. Sometimes, though, you will be offered two Character Sets – one being the set of 'standard' characters and the other being an 'extended' set, often including some accented characters.

You will usually have to turn to the manual on your printer to find out which characters you will be able to print.

About Character Styles

With a daisy-wheel printer, you can have a number of printwheels which have exactly the same arrangement of the characters on their petals. What is different about these wheels is the design of the characters themselves. For example, one wheel might have upright characters, while another has slanted (italic) characters; one wheel could have typewriter-style characters, while another has characters that imitate handwriting. The other important difference will be the Character Pitch they have been designed to be used at – ie. the actual size of the characters on the wheel.

These wheels are described by the same Character Set, and so aren't distinguished that way. Instead they are distinguished by their Character Style. Each Character Style identifies the design of the characters plus the pitch they were intended to be used at (though not necessarily the only pitch that they can be used at). LocoScript needs to know this pitch so that it can ensure that characters are underlined correctly. So Character Styles have two-part names, made up of a descriptive title and a pitch: for example, Prestige PS and Courier 10 – Prestige and Courier describing the look of the characters, PS and 10 defining the design pitch. PS means that the wheel is intended to be used for proportionally-spaced text.

Character Styles are therefore chiefly a way of describing different printwheels that have the same characters on them but have been designed for use at different Character Pitches. For consistency, all Character Sets have a Character Style associated with them but often just one. In the case of dot-matrix printers, there is no need for separate Character Styles covering different pitches because LocoScript can work out everything it needs to position characters accurately, simply by scaling.

About Printer files

LocoScript supports these different options by having separate files of information about printer commands for each printer and for each font/printwheel on this printer.

The principal Printer File any printer needs is the one containing the information on how to select the different facilities of the printer. Files containing this kind of information are identified by the filetype PRI. For example, the file called JUKI6100.PRI contains information on how to control a Juki 6100 printer (or some other printer that works in the same way as the Juki 6100).

To print a document, LocoScript also needs to know which characters can be printed. So the .PRI file also contains the details of a Character Set that is used on the printer. This Character Set is usually some sort of ASCII Character Set. For example, the JUKI6100.PRI file contains details of this printer's US ASCII 100 printwheel.

The character details in this .PRI file, though they can be used (up to a point) with other printwheels, only describe one Character Set you might use on a Juki 6100. So, alongside each .PRI file, LocoScript uses a second type of Printer File – the Character Set file. Character Set files share the same main name as the .PRI file but have filetypes which start with a #.

LocoScript 2 User Guide: Tutorial   **223**

Session 20: Using different printers

Each .# file contains details of a Character Set that can be used as an alternative to the one in the .PRI file. Alternative Character Sets are particularly relevant when you are using a daisy-wheel printer because each printwheel that has a different selection or arrangement of characters on it. The JUKI6100.#02 file, for example, contains details of the Triumph Adler 'Group 2' printwheels used on the Juki printer.

The precise details of the Printer Files you need depend on the printer you want to use and, if this is a daisy-wheel printer, on the printwheels you have. You will always need at least a .PRI file for your printer because this contains the information LocoScript needs to 'drive' the printer.

Ideally, the Printer Files to use are ones specifically intended for your printer. You can find out which these are from the PCW External Printers Guide. These files will enable LocoScript to use all your printer's features as it prints out your documents. They also ensure a proper match between the characters you enter into the document and the ones printed in the finished document (particularly in the case of daisy-wheel printers). There are some Printer Files on the LocoScript 2 Master disc but for the full range, you will need the Printer Support Pack, available from Locomotive Software.

If no Printer Files are available specifically for your printer, do not despair. You may well be able to use the .PRI file designed for a similar printer. In particular, you may be able to use one of the .PRI files supplied on your LocoScript 2 disc. A number of printers are compatible with the printers for which these files were designed. Similarly, you may be able to use a .# file that contains details of a Character Set that doesn't exactly match the characters on your printwheel.

However, using files for printers or printwheels other than those for which they are intended can affect the way your documents are printed on this printer.

i) You won't necessarily be able to use all your printer's features. For example, if you use the FX80 files, you won't be able to produce 15 pitch characters, even if your printer has this facility – because the Epson FX-80 printer for which these files are intended does not have a 15 pitch option. (In this case, LocoScript will in fact print any 15-pitch text in 17 pitch because this is the nearest alternative supported by the FX80 Printer Driver.) Similarly, if you use the D630 file with a daisy-wheel that uses 100-petal wheels, you won't be able to use four of the characters on your printwheels because the D630 file is intended to be used with 96-petal printwheels.

ii) The widths and positions of characters like] and } are not the same on every printwheel. Using a Character Set intended for a different wheel can mean that to print #, say, you actually have to put { in your document. You may also find that the letters won't be spaced properly when you are using proportionally-spaced text.

If you just use the common ASCII characters, the 'deficiencies' caused by using the wrong Character Set won't affect your documents too much. However, using the wrong Character Set may be less than ideal if you use non-ASCII characters and/or use PS wheels, particularly if slight inaccuracies in the positioning of characters do matter to you. All you need to rectify this is a Printer File containing the correct details for the printwheel you are using. This file can also be prepared with the aid of the Printer Support Pack.

Using an external printer

To print on a particular printer in your chosen font or using your chosen printwheel, you need both to attach this printer to your PCW and get it ready to use and to direct LocoScript to use the correct Printer Files.

In order to make these Printer Files available to LocoScript, you first have to go through a procedure known as 'installing' the printer.

This procedure does two things. Firstly, it places the Printer Files for this printer on your Start-of-day disc in such a way that these files are automatically available to LocoScript immediately after loading – you don't need to organise this yourself. Secondly, it records the name of the printer plus the names of the various fonts or printwheels you have on this printer in the Settings file, SETTINGS.STD. Before you can use any printer, font or printwheel, its name must be recorded in the Settings file.

Then when you want to print on this printer, you need to tell LocoScript which printer, Character Set and (where appropriate) Character Style you want to use for the document – in much the same way as you did earlier in the session to use different fonts on the built-in printer.

• *The remainder of this Tutorial describes how to use an external printer to print documents. This is only worth working through after you have installed such a printer on your system as described in the PCW External Printers Guide. When you return to this Tutorial, you will, of course, have to substitute the actual name of your printer and its associated Character Sets and Styles for names used here (D630, UK ASCII 96 and Vanilla 10).*

Note: Part III of the PCW External Printers Guide covers the same actions that are described here, so there is no need to study that section of the Printers Guide as well as this Tutorial.

Having the printer etc. available

Just as each font you want to use on the built-in matrix printer has to be 'available' before you can use it in any way, so your external printer and its fonts or printwheels have to be available before you can use them.

The conditions for availability are also pretty much the same.

The first condition is that you must have the appropriate files in group 0 on Drive M at the time you want to use the printer etc. One difference, however, is that this time you don't just need the appropriate .PRI and .#*xx* files in this group. You also need to have the additional .DRV file that provides the interface between LocoScript and the printer files. In most cases, the file you need is called INSTALL.DRV but if your printer is being used in 'Download mode', the .DRV file you need is called LQ24.DRV.

9010

As with the built-in printer's fonts, arranging that these files are on Drive M is not as hard a task as you might imagine. Provided you followed the installation procedure correctly, all the files you need will have been stored in group 0 either on your Start-of-day disc or on a Start-up disc. From there, these files will be automatically copied to group 0 on Drive M when you load LocoScript, leaving them ready and waiting for when you want to use your external printer.

(If you like, you could check this now by re-loading LocoScript and then checking that the list of files that have been copied to group 0 on Drive M includes the correct .DRV file, your printer's .PRI file and any .#xx files you installed. If any of these files are missing, either you didn't install this printer correctly or you have a hardware problem: sort this problem out by consulting the Troubleshooting section of the PCW External Printers Guide.)

The second condition that has to be met – as with the built-in printer's fonts – is that the name of the printer, its Character Sets and Character Styles are recorded in the Settings file, SETTINGS.STD. Again, all should be well provided you have installed your printer correctly.

However, while these two conditions were the only ones needed in the case of the built-in fonts, there is an extra condition that has to be met before you can print using an external printer. You must have had the appropriate Interface attached to the back of your PCW when you loaded LocoScript. If the Interface was missing or doesn't work, LocoScript assumes that you don't want to use an external printer and doesn't load any of the appropriate software. You won't however be prevented from selecting the printer you want to use in a document, once you have copied the appropriate .PRI or .#xx file to group 0 on Drive M.

Setting up a document for a particular printer

The task of setting up a document for a particular printer also uses much the same steps as setting up a document for a font on the built-in printer. And again, setting up your documents for the printer, font or printwheel that you intend to use is strongly advised as this ensures that LocoScript has the correct character width information to work with in laying out the document. The finished document will be noticeably better as a result. Setting the correct printer details in the document also allows LocoScript to prompt you to select the correct printer, font or printwheel when you are about to print using some other combination.

To show how it's done, we will now go through the steps used to set up the example document MAIL.TXT for a 10 pitch ASCII printwheel on a D630 printer. Similar steps are used to set up a document for any printer, font or printwheel, so simply work through these steps picking out your printer, its Character Sets and Character Styles instead of the D630 printer, UK ASCII 96 Character Set and Vanilla 10 Character Style shown in the illustrations.

The printer, Character Set and Character Style that you intend to use for a particular document are recorded in its Document Set-up, so the first step as before is to edit

MAIL.TXT. Once the document is on the screen, press ⬜️f1⬜️ and select `Document setup` to go into Document Set-up in the usual way (see Session 17), then press ⬜️f6⬜️ to display Printer Selection menu exactly as before. Again, this menu displays the printer etc. for which the document is currently set up. The only difference is that this time, we are going to change rather more of these settings.

```
Printer Selection

Character Style
   Standard      PS
Character Set
   Standard
♦ Printer
   MATRIX

EXIT
```

Selecting the printer

The first thing to set is the printer. Whenever you want to change the printer for which a document is set up, you need to select this first because the Character Sets and Character Styles available to choose from depend on the printer that is selected.

```
Printer

✓ MATRIX
   D630
```

To set the printer, move the Menu cursor to the `Printer` line of the menu and press ⬜️ENTER⬜️. A new menu then appears. This Printer menu is essentially just a list of the printers that are currently available (ie. name recorded in the Settings file *and* the relevant Printer Files in group 0 on Drive M), with a tick beside the printer the document is currently set up for. Simply move the cursor to the printer you require and press ⬜️+⬜️ to select it.

(Note: If the current printer is shown with ? beside it, this means that printer isn't 'available' at the moment – ie. either the appropriate Printer File is not on Drive M or its name has been removed from SETTINGS.STD. You can continue editing with the document set up for this printer and indeed may be able to select a Character Set to use on this printer but you won't be able to print on it until the appropriate Printer Files have been restored.)

Press ⬜️ENTER⬜️. LocoScript then returns you to the Printer Selection menu, so that you can check and if necessary change the Character Set and the Character Style. Notice how this now specifies the printer you selected. You may also notice that the other details in the menu have also changed – to the defaults defined for this printer (see Part I of the PCW External Printers Guide), provided these are available.

Selecting the Character Set

It could well be that the Character Set and Character Style that are now selected are the ones you require. This will almost certainly be the case if your printer only has one font or one printwheel! If not, you now need to select the appropriate Character Set – and then an appropriate Character Style if this is not selected by default. Again, the Character Styles offered depends on your choice of Character Set so it is important to select the Character Set first.

```
Character Set

✓ UK ASCII 96

For printer
   D630
```

To set the Character Set, move the Menu cursor to `Character Set` and press ⬜️ENTER⬜️, just as you did earlier in this session to select a different font on the built-in printer. LocoScript then displays a list of Character Sets available for the printer listed at the bottom of the menu (ie. the printer selected in the Printer menu). Again, the selection of Character Sets you see is limited to ones that are both available in group 0 on Drive M and recorded in the Settings file, and again a ? beside the current Character Set means you can continue with this Character Set but you won't be able to print using it until the appropriate file has been restored.

As usual, the current selection is marked with a tick. When you have just set a different printer, this will be either the default Character Set for this printer or, if the default isn't available, the one at the top of the list. The Character Set that was set before you selected the printer is forgotten. That's why it's important to follow your selection of a printer by selecting the Character Set. Simply move the cursor to the Character Set you require and press ⌷ to select it.

Now press ⌷ENTER⌷ – to return to the Printer Selection menu, so that you can now check and if necessary change the Character Style that you have been given.

Selecting the Character Style

Character Style

✓ Vanilla 10
PrestigePica 10

For Character Set
UK ASCII 96
For printer
D630

This time move the Menu cursor to Character Style and press ⌷ENTER⌷. The menu that appears displays the different Character Styles recorded in the Settings file for your chosen printer and Character Set (shown at the bottom of the menu). The number given alongside each style name tells you the Character Pitch the character style was designed for.

Again the menu works in exactly the same way as the previous ones – with the current selection marked with a tick, but as you have just selected a new Character Set, this is simply the default Character Style for this Character Set which is also the one at the top of the list.

With a dot-matrix printer, you will probably be offered just one Character Style but with a daisy-wheel printer, you may see a number of different Styles corresponding to the different printwheels you have with the same Character Set on them.

The Character Style to choose (where you have a choice) is the one that describes the printwheel you intend using when you print the document. If you can't decide between two that offer similar characters and the same typestyle but at different pitches, choose the printwheel that matches the character pitch used in the document. For example, for documents that use 10-pitch characters, use a 10-pitch wheel; for documents that use 12-pitch characters, use a 12-pitch wheel. (If the document uses a mixture of these character sizes, then it will probably be best to choose the 10-pitch wheel because it is better for the 12-pitch sections to look closely spaced than for the 10-pitch sections to look excessively spaced.)

Select the Character Style you want as before – by pointing to it with the Menu cursor and pressing ⌷. Then press ⌷ENTER⌷ to return to the Printer Selection menu. This should now be set up for the printer, Character Set and Character Style you require.

9010

Leaving the menu

Leave the Printer Selection menu by moving the Menu cursor to the EXIT option and pressing [ENTER]; then press [EXIT] followed by [ENTER] to return to the document itself. Finally, exit from the document and save the new version on the disc. Before closing the document, LocoScript works through the text, re-laying it. The steps you have just taken have given LocoScript a new set of character widths to work with – which might change how the text needs to be laid out.

• *When you want to set up the document for a different printwheel or a different font, you don't need to select the printer again – just the Character Set and the Character Style, or in the case of a printwheel, maybe just the Character Style. You still use the Printing menu but this time you just select the Character Set or the Character Style option as appropriate. You don't have to start by selecting the printer.*

Printing the document

These steps have set up MAIL.TXT for your external printer. To see what happens when you print this, simply select MAIL.TXT on the Disc Manager Screen and print it in the normal way. (**Note:** We suggest selecting Draft quality printing here. For a start, on a daisy-wheel printer or a laser printer there is no difference between high quality and draft; secondly, it is usually faster.)

As before, differences between the 'Current' printer set-up and the 'Intended' printer set-up defined in the document cause LocoScript to display messages – first about differences in the printers (if any); then about differences in the Character Set/Style (ie. fonts); and lastly about differences in the Paper Types (see Session 19).

```
Document and current printer do not match
Current is not the intended printer

Current is: MATRIX
Intended:   D630

    Use the current printer
▶ Change to printer intended for document
    Cancel operation
```

Immediately after loading, the printer defined in the Settings file as the Standard printer is automatically selected as the Current printer. Assuming that this is the built-in printer, the first message you will see now will be one telling you 'Current and Intended printer do not match'.

When this Alert message appears, it normally offers three options – printing on the 'Current' printer (ie. the one LocoScript is currently set up for), printing on the 'Intended' printer (ie. the one set in the Document Set-up) or cancelling the operation. However, the option to change to the Intended printer won't be offered unless:

– the Intended printer is one of the printers recorded in the Settings file;

– the Printer Files it needs are currently in group 0 on Drive M; and

– the interface for the printer was present when LocoScript 2 was loaded

All three conditions have to be met before LocoScript can prepare itself for your chosen printer.

To change to the printer specified in the document, you just select the Change to intended option and press [ENTER]. Do this now (assuming that it is offered). The Intended printer then becomes the Current printer, and the Current Character Set, Character Style and Paper Type all change to the defaults defined for this printer.

LocoScript then carries on its comparison of the Current printer set-up against the Intended printer set-up, displaying further Alert messages as necessary. To print on the Intended printer set-up (as we want you to do here), you need to select the Change to intended option in each message that is displayed.

Finally, LocoScript displays a 'Check-out' menu specifying the details that you would then be setting, and giving you the option of either proceeding or cancelling the operation altogether. Before proceeding, check that the printer set-up specified in this message corresponds to the actual printer set-up that LocoScript is about to use and then press [ENTER]. LocoScript now sets itself up for this printer and then prints the document on the 'right' printer. This printer set-up then becomes your Current printer set-up – until you either load LocoScript 2 again or you set it up to use another printer.

IMPORTANT: You should always check that the printer that LocoScript is expecting is actually connected to your machine and, if this is a daisy-wheel printer, that you have the correct printwheel on the printer. LocoScript has no way of detecting which printer is attached and so will assume that it is the correct one. If you don't check, you might just print rubbish.

Handling single sheet stationery

The document you are printing, MAIL.TXT, is set up for A4 single sheet paper.

While it is printing, LocoScript 2 keeps track of its position on the paper. When LocoScript 2 knows the sheet of paper is finished, it stops printing and waits for you to insert the next sheet. Only when it knows the next sheet is available will printing continue. By keeping track of what is going on in this way, LocoScript 2 avoids printing on the platen or otherwise losing part of your document.

While you are using the built-in printer, this is all nice and simple. LocoScript detects you pulling back the bail bar to load the next sheet. LocoScript then automatically enters Printer Control State and, because it knows you are loading paper, it cancels the 'Waiting for paper' state. Once you are sure the paper is straight, you simply press [EXIT] and LocoScript continues printing.

All this is no different in principle with any other printer, but unfortunately it is not possible for LocoScript to know when you have put the next sheet of paper in. Not all printers can sense paper; there is no standard way of signalling paper or the bail bar state; and the CPS8256 interface doesn't implement the Centronics 'Paper Out' signal anyway. As a result, the steps needed to handle single sheet stationery are somewhat different on an external printer – and they differ again, depending on:

- whether you have a sheet feeder on your printer
- whether this sheet feeder is an integral part of the printer or an attachment you fit on as an extra
- or you have to feed single sheet stationery by hand.

If your printer has a sheet feeder

If your printer has a sheet feeder built into it (as many laser printers have) and you are using the Printer Driver that we recommend for this printer, there is nothing to do except to make sure that there is paper in the sheet feeder. In your case, MAIL.TXT should already be printing because the information that the printer has a sheet feeder is recorded in the Printer Driver and so LocoScript is automatically set up to use it.

Where the sheet feeder is an optional extra which you add to the printer, you need to proceed as follows:

The first step is to fit the sheet feeder to your printer and make any settings that are required on the printer itself. There may be an option switch or some 'front panel' settings that you need to change. See your printer manual for details.

Once the sheet feeder is fitted, press [PTR] to go into Printer Control State. Quickly check that the correct printer and paper are selected (this is shown on the second information line) and then press [f8] to display the Options menu.

Move to the Sheet feeder option in this menu, press [⊞] to select this and then press [ENTER] to close up the menu. Sheet feeder should now be added to the second Information line. Finally, press [EXIT] to leave Printer Control State: the document should now print. All you have to do now is keep the printer supplied with paper.

When you want to use the printer without the sheet feeder – for example, to print on continuous stationery – you will need to clear the Sheet feeder setting. The formal way to do this is to display the f8 Options menu in Printer Control State, move the cursor to the Sheet feeder option, press [⊟] to clear this option, and then press [ENTER] and [EXIT] as before. However, simply setting up LocoScript for continuous stationery is sufficient. Because sheet feeders can only handle single sheet stationery, LocoScript responds by displaying an Alert message which gives you the choice of: changing the Paper Type (to allow you to select the single sheet stationery used in the sheet feeder); confirming that the sheet feeder has been removed and the printer is now set up for continuous stationery; or cancelling. If you select the second of these options, LocoScript clears the Sheet feeder setting for you.

• If you intend to keep the sheet feeder attached to the printer, then you should use the f6 Settings menu to set Sheet feeder as one of the default printer options for this printer. Then, whenever you select this printer, the Sheet feeder option will automatically be selected for you. How you do this is described in Part II of the PCW External Printers Guide.

When hand-feeding single sheet stationery

The steps taken when you hand-feed paper into an external printer depend on whether your printer can sense when it has paper in it or not.

• *If your printer is capable of detecting whether it has paper in it*

– you should pretend to LocoScript – though not to your printer – that you have a sheet feeder fitted to the printer. The steps to take are those described in the previous section (except you don't actually have to fit anything to the printer!). This shifts the task of detecting what is happening to the paper from LocoScript to the printer, and you just have to keep the printer supplied with paper.

• *If your printer doesn't have this facility*

– then the following happens when you hand-feed paper:

1 LocoScript 2 keeps track of its position and stops printing at the end of the page.

2 LocoScript 2 enters 'Waiting for paper' state and the top line of the screen changes to display Paper please.

Note: If your printer stores text in an internal buffer before printing it, this stage may be reached before the entire page has been printed.

3 You now load new paper.

4 Press [PTR] and enter Printer Control State.

5 Press [⊞]. This both clears 'Waiting for paper' and leaves Printer Control State.

6 LocoScript 2 continues printing.

This is the same sequence of events as on the built-in printer except you have to enter Printer Control State and clear 'Waiting for paper' by hand, because LocoScript cannot detect you performing Step 3.

Note: On all printers LocoScript automatically assumes a 'Top of Form' position based on where it expects single sheet stationery to be left ready to print. Normally, this will be Line 7 (corresponding to an inch down the page), but it may assume some other figure if the printer is known to load paper to a different position. If you find that when you use single sheet stationery your text is printed either too high up or too low down on the page, then in your case the paper is being loaded to a different position. You can readily discover the true Top of Form position as follows:

With LocoScript set up to use single sheet stationery (and if appropriate, the sheet feeder), press [PTR] to go into Printer Control State and use the f3 Paper to modify the Current Paper Type to give it a Top Gap of 0 (see 'Setting up the printer for a chosen

Paper Type' in Session 19 of this Guide). Load a fresh sheet of paper (with a sheet feeder, you can use the Feed to top of form *option in the f1 Actions menu within Printer Control State to do this) and then use Direct Printing to print something –for example, a line of text or a line of underlines. Take the paper out, measure how far from the top of the paper this line is (in inches), multiply by 6 and round to the nearest whole number, and this will tell you the Top of Form setting you need. Set this figure in the f8 Options menu in Printer Control State (and as a default printer option in the f6 Settings menu).*

Setting up LocoScript for a particular printer

Finally in this session, we look at the steps you need to take when the printer you want to use is neither the one LocoScript is currently set up for nor the one specified in the document. In such cases you need to set up LocoScript yourself for the printer you intend to use. The steps are very like the ones you used earlier in this session to set up the built-in printer for a particular font.

Again, the steps we are about to show you are not recommended as the standard way of arranging that your document is printed on the printer you require. As we explained when discussing fonts on the built-in printer, the layout of the document is determined while the document is being edited and so is based on the Intended Character Set. If you then print it on a different printer or using a different Character Set, LocoScript does its best to adjust for the differences in the character widths but there are inevitably some compromises in the quality of the result. In particular, the spaces between words may either be very big or very small and the righthand edge of justified text won't necessarily be straight.

However, setting up LocoScript for your chosen printer is a quite reasonable thing to do when you want to draft documents on a faster printer or to print a document prepared on a different system when you don't want to upset its layout.

Just as you can arrange that your document is printed in particular font by making this the Current Character Set before you start and selecting Use current when the Alert message appears, so you arrange that a particular printer is used by making this Current printer and selecting the Use current option when this is offered.

Start as before by pressing PTR to go into Printer Control State and selecting the f5 Printer menu.

As we mentioned earlier, this menu has exactly the same layout as the Printing menu you used earlier to tell LocoScript which printer you wanted to set up the MAIL.TXT document for, and moreover, it works in exactly the same way. In other words, you start by selecting the Printer option, which gives you a menu of the printers that are currently available.

You then select the printer you want and move on, through the Character set option, to the menu of the Character Sets available for the printer you have picked out – and so on to the Character Style menu. The only difference is that there are never any ?s in the list. No printer or Character Set can appear in the menu unless it is fully available – ie. recorded in the Settings file, its Printer Files are stored in group 0 on Drive M and the interface for the printer was attached when LocoScript was loaded.

Use these menus to set up the Printer software for the D630 printer, UK ASCII 96 Character Set and the Vanilla 10 Character Style or the equivalent set of options for your own printer. (Again, you may just want to change the Character Set or the Character Style. In this case, use the Printer menu as described above but select the Character Set or the Character Style option as appropriate. You don't have to start by selecting a printer.)

When all is set as you require, select the EXIT option and press [ENTER] to leave the menu. LocoScript then selects your printer – you will see the printer name on the second Information line change – and resets it. (You should see the message Resetting printer, followed by Ready on the Information line. If the message stays locked at Resetting printer, something is wrong with your printer's set-up and you need to consult the Troubleshooting section of the PCW External Printers Guide.)

Finally, press [EXIT] to leave Printer Control State and then select the document to print in the usual way. When LocoScript displays the Alert message telling you that the Current and Intended printers do not match, simply make sure that you select the Use current option.

Note: For safety, LocoScript won't let you change the Printer, Character Set or Character Style until everything you have asked it to print has been printed.

Session summary

In this session, you have seen:

- How to print in different fonts on the built-in printer
- The hardware and software you need to print LocoScript documents on a printer other than the built-in printer
- How to set up a document for a particular printer, Character Set and Style
- Why it is a good idea to print each document on the printer set-up that the document is set up for
- What happens when LocoScript is set up for a different printer etc. to the document
- How single sheet stationery is handled on external printers
- How to set up LocoScript to work with a particular printer

Using one document as a pattern for another

In this session, we look at the feature of LocoScript which means that you can always use the same style of document for a particular type of job. You set up in a document all the details you want:

- the Stock Layouts
- the Headers and Footers
- the type of paper and how the page is laid out
- the printer you use
- text that will appear in every document – your address, for example

...

and LocoScript will arrange that this document is used as the pattern for every other document of the same type. And if you put a little effort into designing this document – for example, using a special style of text for the address – you will get very professional-looking results in all your documents without any extra effort.

The document you have to prepare is a perfectly normal LocoScript document. You can print it, edit it ... and everything is set up within it exactly as we have described in the earlier sessions of this tutorial. The only thing that is special is the document's name: it must be called TEMPLATE.STD. (A template is something used in woodwork or metalwork as the pattern for particular piece of work.)

If a group contains a document called TEMPLATE.STD, then it is used as the pattern for each new document created in that group. In fact, the new document is simply a copy of the TEMPLATE.STD document in every detail.

What this means is that you can have up to eight different templates on one disc – one in each group. So, for example, you could have a separate template for:

- letters on A4 paper
- letters on A5 paper
- memos
- reports
- articles for magazines
- meeting agendas
- labels; and
- acknowledgements

---

all on the same disc. And each new document that you create will have exactly the same Layouts, etc. as the template for its group.

What we are going to do in this session is work out all the details that you would need in the templates for two common types of document – letters on A5 paper and 3" address labels – and then show you how to put such a design into practice by working through creating the template for the A5 letters. We'll store the new template in the second group of your Examples disc: so, if necessary, replace the disc in your drive by your Examples disc. (As always, remember to press ⌐f7⌐ after changing discs.)

Stage 1: Planning

As we have pointed out a number of times in this tutorial, sitting down and planning precisely what you want to do pays off – and this is particularly true when you are preparing a TEMPLATE.STD. Get the TEMPLATE.STD right in every detail and you will get the documents you prepare based on this template right as well. You won't have to do any time-consuming adjusting of such things as Stock Layouts or Header and Footer Zones. Instead, you will be able to concentrate on your text.

There are a lot of things to decide on:

- what printer and paper to use
- how large a Header and Footer Zone you want
- what rules you want to set about page breaks
- how the Headers and Footers are to be applied
- what layout you want for the Header and Footer
- whether either the Header or the Footer will be the same for all documents prepared with this template
- what margins etc. you want to have at the beginning of the document
- what Stock Layouts you want and how these are going to be used
- what standard text you want in the template

– in short, just about everything that we have covered in this tutorial comes into creating the TEMPLATE.STD you want.

But having said that (and probably frightening you rigid), these are only the decisions that you make, one way or another, for every single document you work on – and anyway, in many cases you will just want a setting that is already in the TEMPLATE.STD document, particularly when you want to print on A4 paper in the built-in printer. LocoScript's TEMPLATE.STDs let you think about all these details once (for each type of document you want to produce), get it right and then know that every document is set up correctly for ever more.

Moreover, the chances are that you already have a document with enough of the right characteristics that you can readily create a perfect template from it – just by making a copy that you call TEMPLATE.STD and then editing it.

However, even if you have a document ready to copy, you still need a clear idea of what you want in the template – if only as a checklist while editing the copy. One way of sorting out what you require is through a Question and answer session:

	A5 Paper	Labels
Which printer and print wheel should the documents be set up for	The PCW dot-matrix printer (so the print wheel is irrelevant)	The PCW dot-matrix printer (so the print wheel is irrelevant)
What paper do you want to use	A5 single sheet – that's 8½" long (50 lines) and 5¾" wide	long
How large a Header and Footer Zone do you want	3 lines each – and as you won't be able to print on the top 6 lines or the bottom three lines, that leaves 50–6–3–3–3=35 lines for document text on each page	None
What rules do you want to set about page breaks	No split paragraphs	Don't care
How are the Headers and Footers to be applied	First page – Special Header and Special Footer; Other pages – Header only	Irrelevant
What layout you want for the Header and Footer	Margins at character positions 10 and 60; character pitch PS, line spacing 1, CR extra spacing 0, line pitch 6	Irrelevant
Are any Headers and Footers the same for all documents	The First Page Header and Footer will be the same	Irrelevant
What margins etc. do you want set in Stock Layout 1	Margins at character positions 10 and 60, a simple tab at character position 15, character pitch PS, line spacing 1, CR Extra Spacing ½, line pitch 6, justified	Margins at character positions 5 and 50, no tabs, character pitch PS, line spacing 1, CR Extra Spacing 0, line pitch 6, unjustified (ragged)
What are the details of Stock Layouts 2 and 3	Layout 2– as Layout 1 but character pitch 10 and CR Extra Spacing 0; Layout 3 – as Layout 1 but simple tab at character position 30	Irrelevant
What standard text do you want in the template	The company's address, the words Ref:, Your ref: and Dear, and the Yours sincerely 3" continuous – that's 18 lines	None

Stage 2: Creating a new template

TEMPLATE.STD documents are perfectly standard LocoScript documents and so can be created by using LocoScript's Create New Document facility, just like any other document. Just create it in the group that you want to use it as the pattern for (see Session 3). Or alternatively, as we mentioned above, copy an existing document that has a lot of features of the template you want to create, call the copy TEMPLATE.STD and edit it (see Session 7).

Copying an existing document is often a very attractive option – potentially saving you a lot of effort, particularly if the original document is already set up for the right paper and has the right Stock Layouts and Pagination text. However, it is still best to work through steadily checking every detail – just as if you were setting the document up from the word go.

For practice – and to convince you that it isn't such an enormous job as it seems – we shall opt for creating a new document. So move the Group cursor to group 2 on the Examples disc, create a new document and call it TEMPLATE.STD.

Because LocoScript didn't have a template to copy, the document is set up in its default way for printing on A4 sheets of paper – inch-wide margins, no tabs, etc. You now change this set-up to fit the documents you want to create in future.

Stage 3: Check and correct the Document Set-up

The first aspect of the template to set is everything to do with the Document Set-up, ie:
- the printer and printwheel
- the paper type
- the Header and Footer zones
- the way the Header and Footer text is applied
- special rules about page breaks
- the Stock Layouts
- the layout used for the Header and Footer text
- and, finally, the Header and Footer text itself

These can be set essentially in any order but it is a good idea to set the paper type before you set the Header and Footer zone sizes. (As you will remember, the page length and gaps quoted in the Page Layout menu are that of the current Paper Type – so by setting the Paper Type first, you ensure that you see the right numbers in the Page Layout menu.) It is also a good idea to get the Pagination text layout sorted out before you type any Header and Footer text.

Work through checking and setting up all of these for the A5 letters we have just described. This is easily the best way of seeing how straightforward a task this really is – and how, in the event, there is often little work to do.

As everything we are setting here is an aspect of the Document Set-up, the first step is to gain access to the Document Set-up – which, you will remember, you do by selecting the Document Set-up option in the Actions menu (see Session 17). Press ⌐f1⌐ to bring the Actions menu onto the screen and select Document setup. As well as displaying the special Pagination Screen, this gives you access to all the menus that help you change how the document is set up.

If you are using this session to help you set up your own templates, you should ignore the details of what we set here and substitute the settings you want. What we describe here are the settings for our example A5 letter template.

1) The Printer and the Print wheel (Session 20): Our design specifies the built-in printer, which should already be set. However it is always best to check – so pull down the Printing menu and check that the printer specified in this menu is MATRIX. If it is, there's nothing to set – so just press ⌐CAN⌐.

2) The Paper Type (Session 19): Pull down the Page menu and select Paper Type, to bring the Paper Type menu onto the screen. The Paper Type you want – A5 – is one of the standard paper types, and so can be selected directly. Do this now; then check that the Portrait option is selected, to say that you will use the page lengthways rather than widthways. Press ⌐ENTER⌐ to confirm this choice.

3) The Header and Footer Zone sizes (Session 17): Also from the Page menu, select Page layout to bring the Page Layout menu onto the screen.

Set a Header Zone size of 3 and then set a Footer Zone size of 3. The Page body this leaves should be 35 lines. Also select the Fixed footer zone option so that the Footer will always appear in the same position on the page. Press ⌐ENTER⌐.

4) How the Headers and Footers are used (Session 16): Again from the Page menu, select Header/footer options to bring the follow-on menu onto the screen.

In the top section of the menu, select first page only – so that one Header/Footer pair is used for the first page and the other pair is used for all other pages. In the middle section, set all but the last option – Last page footer enabled – so that the first page will have both a Header and a Footer, but the last page will only have a Header.

Finally select Use footer for first page, so that single-page documents have the special Footer you set up on the first page as well as longer documents.

Press ⌐ENTER⌐.

5) Page Break rules (Session 17): Finally from the Page menu, select Page break control and press [ENTER]. Select Do not break paragraphs – to ensure that no paragraph is split between one page and another, and press [ENTER].

6) The Stock Layouts (Session 17): Pull down the Layout menu, select Change stock layouts and press [ENTER]. The Stock Layouts to set up are:

– Stock Layout 1, which will be used for most of the text
– Stock Layout 2, for the Address part of the document; and
– Stock Layout 3, for Yours sincerely, etc.

Select each of these in turn and press [ENTER]: this puts you into the Layout Editor.

In each case, you will need to set justified text and margins at character positions 10 and 60, and to check that you have a Line Spacing of 1, a Line Pitch of 6 and that you will use the unslashed zero. (How to make these settings is described in Session 11.) The other settings to make are:

– Stock Layout 1: a simple tab at character position 15, Character Pitch PS and CR Extra Spacing ½

– Stock Layout 2: a simple tab at character position 15, Character Pitch 10, CR Extra Spacing 0 and the name Address

– Stock Layout 3: a simple tab at character position 30, Character Pitch PS, CR Extra Spacing ½ and the name Yours etc.

Press [EXIT] after you have finished setting up each Stock Layout so that you can pick the next one. Press [EXIT] and then [ENTER] when you have finished setting all of the Layouts.

7) The layout for the Header and Footer text (Session 16): Pull down the Layout menu and select Change layout to use the Layout Editor to change the Pagination text layout.

Set the margins at character positions 10 and 60, with the help of the Margins menu. Clear any tabs with the help of the Tabs menu. Set the character pitch to PS, the Line Spacing to 1, the CR Extra Spacing to 0 and the Line Pitch to 6 with the Size menu. Finally use the Options menu to make sure that the text won't be justified and that the correct style of zero is used (the one without a slash).

8) The standard Header and Footer text (Session 16): Type in the special Header text and the special Footer text for the first page in the slots of the Pagination screen for Header/Footer 1.

• That's checked and adjusted all aspects of the Document Set-up. You should now press [EXIT] and return to the start of the document text.

Stage 4: The standard text

The remaining task is to set up the text that you will want in every document that uses this template. In our case, this is the Company address, the 'Ref's and the final Yours sincerely.

Type these exactly as you would in any other document – remembering, of course, to type:

- ⊞LT2 on the line above the address so that you use the Address layout for this

- ⊞LT1 at the end of the address to that you use the Main layout for the main part of the document; and

- ⊞LT3 on the line above the Yours sincerely so that you change to the Yours etc. layout for this.

Stage 5: Save the template

Once you've set everything up, all that's left to do is to save this template – exactly as you would any other document.

• Exactly the same procedure is used to set up other templates – one for each of the groups on the disc. Work out what type of documents you will want to store in each group and the template for this type of document and then set it up.

Working with templates

The presence of a document called TEMPLATE.STD in a group means that this will be used as the pattern for every new document that is created in that group. So if you wanted, you could have a different template in every group on every disc that you use.

Maybe this is what you want. However, you are much more likely to want to use a just few different templates across a number of discs. How do you go about arranging that?

The answer is that you put copies of the templates you want to use, one per group on Drive M – because if there isn't a template in the group you are actually working on, LocoScript will look instead for a template to copy in the corresponding group on Drive M. So if, say, you organise your work such that you always put A4 letters in the first group on the disc (group 0), A5 letters in group 1, and memos in group 2, you don't have to have a copy of each TEMPLATE.STD document on every disc – you just need on Drive M a copy of the A4 letter template in group 0, a copy of the A5 template in group 1 and a copy of the memo template in group 2.

If instead you want all the documents on a disc to have the same pattern, then you just need to have one template on this disc – in group 0. And if you want the same pattern for all your documents, then you just need one template – in group 0 on Drive M.

All these options are the result of the order in which LocoScript searches for a template to use when you create a new document. It looks first in the same group as your new document, then in the corresponding group on Drive M, then in group 0 of the current disc and then in group 0 on Drive M. Only if there isn't a TEMPLATE.STD file in any of these places is the built-in default template used.

To make things even easier for you, you don't actually have to copy the templates to Drive M yourself. If you store your templates in the right groups on your Start-of-day disc, LocoScript will automatically copy each template to the corresponding group on Drive M as part of the process of loading LocoScript 2. You don't have to do a thing!

Session summary

In this session, you have seen how LocoScript searches for and uses one document as a pattern for another, and how you can make use of this by:

- Setting up the documents to be used as the pattern for other documents of the same type

- Arranging to store these documents so that the right one is used as the pattern for the particular document you want to create

Postscript

Getting the best out of LocoScript 2

The tutorial you have just completed has introduced you to all the features of LocoScript 2. You now know how to use LocoScript.

But before you rush on to using LocoScript to prepare all your letters, articles, invoices etc., it's worth sitting down and thinking about how you are going to put LocoScript to good use. You have been introduced to all the various facilities of LocoScript; how are you going to ensure that these help you in your own work?

Organising your work

The aspect of using a word-processor that cannot be emphasised too much is how much easier everything is if you have a system of working and organise yourself accordingly. Decide what you are going to use LocoScript for, what printers you are going to use, what stationery you are going to need, how many discs you will need, ... – and you save yourself a lot of time and effort in the long run.

So:

• Decide which printer you are going to use for most, if not all, of your work – and make sure that you have all the necessary cabling, interfaces and Printer files for this printer (see Session 20).

• Make sure that you have a copy of each of the Printer files you need in the first group (group 0 or the SYSTEM group) of your Start-of-day disc.

• Make sure that all the standard types of paper you plan to use and all your Print wheels are specified in the Settings file, SETTINGS.STD (see Sessions 19 and 20).

• Plan how you are going to use your discs. Do you want to devote one disc to letters, one disc to memos, one disc to articles (say) – or do you want to keep each disc as a record of all your work between one date and another, and so have a mixture of letters, memos and articles on each disc.

• Plan how you are going to make use of LocoScript's system of groups. Do you want to always use the same group (for example, group 2) for a particular type of document (say, A4 letters)? Remember, if you do always use the same group for a particular type of document, you can store the template for this group in the corresponding group on your Start-of-Day disc – and LocoScript will automatically arrange for this template to be used for all new documents created in this group.

- Set up the templates you want for your new documents and store these in the appropriate group either on the Start-of-Day disc or on the appropriate disc (see Session 21).

- Set up files containing the standard phrases you expect to use (see Session 14).

- In short, get everything set up ready and on the right disc.

Note: Although it really is a very good idea to get all these things sorted out before you start, you shouldn't feel that you must get everything right first time. Everything you set up can be changed, files can be moved to different discs and to different groups, templates can be edited, etc. etc. – as you develop and improve your systems of working. However, do try to set up as many of these aspects as possible. The more documents you create in an unstructured way, the harder it gets to sort everything out.

Spotting the word-processing tools to use

The Tutorial was designed to build up the number of tools you know how to use, step by step – so that you gradually increased the range of features that you can give your documents. But even so, you can feel a little lost in deciding which of LocoScript's facilities to use when it comes to preparing your own work.

There isn't any need to lose sleep over this. As we have seen, one of the beauties of LocoScript is that you can produce very professional-looking results without using anything like the full range of word-processing tools that are provided.

To a great extent, knowing what to do comes from trying things out and seeing what gave you good results and what was an absolute disaster – and from seeing what other people do. So, to finish we give some examples of documents you might want to produce and which word-processing tools that you might use in preparing these.

Business letters

- 'Pseudo' Letterhead – by setting up your company name and address either as the Header text for the first page or just setting it as initial text in a Template. Make them attractive by using different character pitches, stylings such as bold and italic, and by positioning the text using (CEntre) and (RAlign)
- Letter starting beneath Letterhead on printed stationery – by setting the Header Zone
- List of Directors across the bottom of the page – set in the Footer text for the first page
- Letter to ..... at the beginning of continuation pages – by setting this as the Header text for all pages except the first
- Addressee's address in the right place for window envelopes – by setting a start position for this in the Template
- Standard positions for the date and for reference numbers – by setting these in the Template
- Special styling for addresses etc. – by using the different character sizes and print styles available in LocoScript
- Standard names in the 'Copies to' list – by setting their names up as Phrases
- Copy letters – by telling LocoScript how many copies you want to print
- Corrected spelling – by using LocoSpell
- Personalised versions of the same letter to different people – by using LocoMail or by editing the original version

Memoranda

- The word MEMORANDUM written across top of the page in large bold letters – by selecting Character Pitch 10 Double-width, using Bold to style the word and using the (CEntre) code to position it
- Standard positions for To:, From:, Date:, Copies: – by setting these in the Template or by storing these together with the word MEMORANDUM in a Phrase
- Line across the page – by creating a line made up of a (+UL) code, a (RAlign) code, a space, a (-UL) code and a Carriage Return. This, too, can be stored as a Phrase.
- Names in the 'Copies to' list – by storing these as Phrases
- Multiple copies – by telling LocoScript how many copies to print
- Standard Memo paper – set up as one of LocoScript's Paper Types and specified in the 'Memo' Template

---

Reports and Magazine articles

- Making major revisions – by using the Block Editing techniques
- Inserting text from other articles or reports – either via the Blocks or by inserting whole documents, including ASCII versions of text produced on a different word-processor
- Double-spaced text – by setting the Line Spacing to 2
- Producing draft versions on cheaper paper – by setting up the document for the final paper but setting up the printer for the cheaper paper
- Correcting individual pages of the final version – by reprinting just the pages you want
- Moving quickly around a long document – by using Find page ?? and/or by putting in Unit markers at strategic points in the document
- Numbering the pages – by setting up a Header or Footer that includes the (PageNo) code
- Putting Copyright details at the bottom of each page – by including the Copyright symbol (typed by pressing [ALT] C) in the Footer
- Writing sections of text in Greek or Russian – by using the Greek and Cyrillic modes of the keyboard
- Correcting the spelling – by using LocoSpell
- Counting the number of words – by using LocoSpell

Technical reports

- Preparing tables – by setting up a Layout with an appropriate range of tabs
- Drawing horizontal lines across tables – by using (+UL) at the beginning of each line and finishing the line with a (RAlign) code, a space, a (-UL) code and a Carriage Return
- Drawing vertical lines in tables – by using either the Vertical Bar character ([EXTRA] §) or the Modulus character (Symbol Super Shift: §)
- Ensuring that tables are not split over two pages – by inserting Keep codes on the first line and/or the last line of the table
- Inserting text from other reports – either via the Blocks or by inserting whole documents, including ASCII versions of text produced on a different word-processor
- Using the Page n of m style of page numbering – by setting up a Header or Footer that includes both the (PageNo) code for n and the (LPageNo) code for m
- Preparing complex technical formulae – by using LocoScript's symbol characters
- Typing non-standard fractions – by setting the numerator as a 17 pitch superscript and the denominator as a 17 pitch subscript

---

Books

- Brief title of each chapter at the top of every page except the first – by preparing each chapter as a separate document, setting this brief title as Header text and disabling the Header on the first page
- Left and right pages – by using Header/Footer text 1 on odd pages and Header/Footer text 2 on even pages and setting these up to suit righthand pages and lefthand pages, respectively
- Numbered pages – by including the (PageNo) code in either the Headers or the Footers
- Major changes – by using the Block Editing techniques either to move text around within the same document or to transfer text from one chapter to another
- Leaving spaces for illustrations at the top or the bottom of a page – by putting in strategic End-page-here characters ([ALT] [RETURN]), followed by lots of carriage returns when you want to leave space for a picture at the top of a page.
- Special Paper – by setting up a Paper Type and setting this Paper Type in the Document Set-up
- The same Page Layout etc. for each chapter – by setting up this layout first in a Template
- Standard styles for Headings, Subheadings, Notes etc. – by setting up Stock Layouts for these in the 'Chapter' Template
- Consecutive page numbers in chapters that are prepared separately – by using the Set First Pages procedure
- Corrected spelling – using LocoSpell

Invoices

- Standard way of setting out the invoice – set up through a Template that is a standard invoice or a Master invoice that can be filled in using LocoMail
- Have special ways of setting up parts of the invoice – by setting up appropriate Stock Layouts in the 'Invoice' Template
- Standard items that appear on invoices – stored as Phrases, in one or more Phrases file. These Phrases could include the one-off price so that you don't have to remember this or look it up specially
- Copy invoices – by telling LocoScript how many copies you want
- Do arithmetic on information in the invoices – by using LocoMail

Club administration

Meetings:

- Produce this month's agenda – by copying last month's and editing it, for example using Exchange to change the date of the meeting throughout
- Have pre-prepared standard items for discussion, eg. the Christmas lunch – stored as Phrases
- Have a standard style for both agenda and minutes – by setting these up in Templates. In particular, set up Stock Layouts for Agenda Items, Questions, Replies, etc.
- Shorthand versions of the names and positions of Committee members – by storing these as Phrases
- Producing copies for every member – by telling LocoScript to print the number of copies you want
- Producing labels so that copies of the agenda, etc. are sent to every member – by creating a document set up for your Labels stationery with each name and address on a separate page, or by setting up a Label master and using LocoMail
- Members' details recorded and updated – using LocoFile

Circulars:

- Producing copies addressed to every member of the club – prepare a document in which the club address, date etc. is set up as the Header for every page, the text of the Letter is set up as the Footer and make the text of the document the names and addresses of the members – one on each page – or better, set up the circular as a Master document and use LocoMail to prepare copies for each member

Newsletters:

- Produce a professional-looking newsletter – by using character sizes and line spacings to produce attractive text and by using (CEntre) and (RAlign) to position it
- Make special items of news stand out – by using a special character size or bold and italic to style it differently from other items
- Standardise on a selection of different text styles – by storing these as layouts or by storing combinations of Pitch, Line Spacing, Bold and Italic codes in Phrases
- Draw lines across the page – by creating a line made up of a (+UL) code, a (RAlign) code, a space, a (-UL) code and a Carriage Return. This can be stored as a Phrase for re-use.

Appendix I

Using a PCW

This appendix gives brief details of the basic actions involved in using your PCW – such as switching on, switching off, handling discs, loading paper into the printer, putting a new ribbon into the printer. Full details are given in your PCW guide.

The PCW

Switching on

The procedure for switching on the PCW is as follows:

1. Press the Eject button(s) on the drive(s) to release any discs that are at present in your machine's floppy disc drive(s). Withdraw any disc from the drive.

2. Plug your machine into the Mains supply – if it is not already plugged in.

3. Press in the Power Switch on the front of your machine. This switches your PCW on.

4. Hold the disc holding the software you want to use (ie. the LocoScript 2 Start-of-day disc) by its labelled end and insert it in Drive A. On a PCW8256 or a PcW9256, Drive A is the only drive; on a PCW8512, Drive A is the upper drive.

Note: On an 8000 series machine, you need to insert your Start-of-day disc with Side 1 to the left.

Push the disc in until it clicks home. However, this should require no more than gentle pressure: if the drive appears to be resisting the disc, stop. Whatever you do, don't force it in.

If you have problems:

– check that there isn't another disc – or anything else   in the drive
– check that you are trying to put the disc in the right way round

5. When the disc is inserted, the disc drive motor should automatically turn on. (You should hear a gentle whirring sound.) If it doesn't, press the Space Bar.

You should now see a pattern of horizontal lines on the screen as the software is read in from the disc. If instead, your PCW bleeps or the screen flashes, the disc is either damaged or not a Start-of-day disc.

9108

Release the disc from the drive and check that you inserted the disc you meant to use. Then try again – by inserting the disc and, if necessary, pressing the Space Bar as above. If you continue to have problems, consult your dealer.

6. All the software has been read from the disc when the disc drive light stops flashing. Do not release the Start-of-day disc from the drive until the disc light stays off.

Switching off

1. Press the Eject button(s) in to the drive(s) to release any discs that are at present in your machine's floppy disc drive(s). Withdraw any disc from the drive.

2. Press the Power Switch on the front of your machine. This switches your PCW off.

Wait at least 5 seconds before switching on again.

Resetting your PCW

Resetting your machine is essentially the same as switching it off and then on again and it is much better for it!

1. Place the disc holding the software you want to use (ie. the LocoScript 2 Start-of-day disc) in Drive A.

2. Hold down the [SHIFT] and [EXTRA] keys and keep them held down as you press [EXIT]. The software should now be read off the disc, exactly as it is during start-up after the PCW has been switched on.

3. All the software has been read from the disc when the disc drive light stops flashing. Do not release the Start-of-day disc from the drive until the disc light stays off.

Cleaning your PCW

Use an aerosol anti-static foam cleaner to clean both the screen and the PCW's plastic case. Under no circumstances should spirit-based cleaners be used.

9108

About discs

The type of discs to use

The PCW8256 and the PCW8512 use only 3" Compact Floppy Discs; the PcW9256 uses only 3½" Floppy discs.

You are recommended to always use labelled discs from a leading manufacturer: such discs should give good service. Avoid cheap, unlabelled discs because using these represents a false economy. Not only is data transfer between discs likely to be unreliable, but in the worst case, use of such discs can damage your disc drives and so might also damage all the other discs used in these drives.

Handling discs

Discs are highly sensitive – to dust, to temperature, to moisture and to magnets. So:

- Don't poke anything into the disc's casing: in particular, don't scratch the part of the disc that is exposed through the reading window.
- Don't try to force the plastic casing open.
- Don't store the discs anywhere they could get damp or very hot or very cold. *Note:* The fact they get warm while they are used is nothing to worry about.
- Don't store them anywhere near a magnet – and that includes the magnets in such pieces of equipment as your audio equipment, your telephone or your TV.
- Never put discs into your disc drives before you switch on and never turn your PCW off while there are still discs in the drives. Take the discs out first.
- Never take a disc out of a drive while your PCW is reading from it or writing to it – ie. while the disc light is either fully on or flashing on and off.

What to do with a new disc

New discs are typically supplied in boxes of ten.

Before you can use a new disc, it has to be prepared ready to have information stored on it. This preparation is called formatting and we recommend you to format all new discs that you buy, essentially as soon as you get them home, so that they will be ready for use when you want them.

Discs and PCW8512s

On an 8000 series PCW with two floppy disc drives, the upper disc drive (Drive A) is a 'normal-capacity' disc drive but the lower disc drive (Drive B) is a 'high-capacity' disc drive.

CF2 discs are used in both drives but the discs used in Drive A are formatted in a different way to those used in Drive B. The formatting makes them either single-track

---

'discs for Drive A' or double-track 'discs for Drive B'. Double-track discs can only be used in Drive B. Single track discs can be read in either drive, but can only be written in Drive A. If you use a disc in an unsuitable drive, you will see an error message.

Inserting a disc in the drive

1. Release and withdraw any disc that is at present in the drive.

2. Hold the disc by its labelled end.

3. Insert the disc into the drive slot until it clicks home.

On an 8000 series machine, you need to insert the disc with the side you want to use to the left. *Note: High-capacity (720k) discs should always be inserted in Drive B with Side 1 to the left.*

Note: This should require no more than gentle pressure. If the drive seems to resist the disc, stop: whatever you do, don't force it. Press the Eject button on the drive in case there is a disc already in the drive. If you can't find out what the trouble is, consult your dealer.

Removing a disc from a drive

1. Look at the 'Using' message in the top righthand corner of the screen. If the message says that the drive holding the disc is in use, **don't** remove the disc.

2. Press the Eject button on the drive. This releases the disc and partly ejects it from the drive.

3. Withdraw the disc the rest of the way.

Write-protecting a disc

With the Write-protect hole on a particular side of the disc closed, data can be written to that side of the disc. With the hole open, attempts to write to the disc will only generate an error message telling you that the disc is write-protected.

The method used to open (and close) the hole varies from disc manufacturer to disc manufacturer. Many discs have a shutter arrangement that can be opened and closed with your thumbnail. Others have a small lever, set into the edge of the disc casing by the hole, which can be moved with (for example) the tip of a ball point pen.

Important: Opening a write-protect hole only secures the data on that side of the disc against overwriting or erasure. To secure both sides, both write-protect holes must be opened.

The PCW printer

Paper for the printer

The printer will handle ordinary bond paper provided it is not too flimsy (less than 50gsm) or too stiff. It can also handle copy paper (40gsm) at the same time as a top copy on bond paper is being printed.

Any size of paper can be used, up to 9" wide.

Autoloading a single sheet of paper

The printer is set up so that paper resting in the paper guide can be automatically fed into the printer and left so that printing will begin in the correct position.

1. Place the sheet of paper in the paper guide so that its top edge rests against the back of the printer platen (the rubber roller).

Align the lefthand edge of the paper with your paper position marker – or if you don't have any such mark, place the paper so that its lefthand edge is approximately ¾" from the lefthand end of the platen.

2. Turn the Paper Loading Knob one quarter of a turn towards you. The printer should now feed the paper in.

If the printer doesn't feed the paper, you have inserted the paper in too far by hand. Turn the Paper Loading Knob back to its original position, take the paper out and then try again.

3. Turn the Paper Loading Knob back to its original position.

4. If the paper needs any further adjustment, you can do this now.

Note: Loading paper automatically puts your PCW into Printer Control State. You will have to press [EXIT] before anything can be printed.

Setting up the printer to use continuous stationery

1. Remove the paper tray by hingeing it until it is vertical and then lifting it off.

2. Hold the tractor feed unit with the white cog-wheel (underneath the unit) to your left. Lower the unit so that the two small hooks at the front fit into the two small holes (slightly forward of the platen) on the top of the printer. Then clip the back of the tractor feed down into position.

3. Feed the paper from behind the back of the tractor unit as if it were single sheet stationery (ie. rest the top edge against the back of the platen and then turn the Paper Loading Knob a quarter turn forward so that the paper feeds in).

4. Turn the Paper Loading Knob back to its original position and then turn the Paper Feed Knob so that the paper is fed through a further few inches.

5. Open the covers of the paper holders and adjust the position of the paper (and, if necessary, the position of the tractors themselves) so that the sprocket holes on the paper fit over the tractor cogs. The paper should be straight.

6. Close the covers over the paper.

7. Turn the Paper Feed Knob until the print position is approximately ⅛" below the next line of perforations.

Note: Loading paper automatically puts your PCW into Printer Control State. You will have to press [EXIT] before anything can be printed.

Changing the ribbon

Note: When you buy a printer ribbon, you should ask for an Amstrad Printer Ribbon (PR-1).

1. Lift the dust cover up gently. It is hinged, but you need to release it from its hinges.

2. Take hold the fin on the top of the old ribbon cassette and lift this out.

3. Hold the new ribbon cassette with its fin uppermost and the ribbon away from you. Turn the Ribbon Feed Knob to the left of the fin in the direction of the arrow to remove the slack.

4. Slot the cassette into position, taking care that the ribbon itself passes between the print head and the ribbon guide – as illustrated on the cassette. Be careful not to twist the ribbon.

Do not touch the print head: if you have just been printing a document, the head could be very hot.

5. Press down gently on both sides of the cassette so that it is properly located. Check that the ribbon is properly positioned in front of the print head and remove any slack in the ribbon by gently turning the Ribbon Feed Knob.

6. Replace the dust cover.

Adjusting the print head

1. Hinge the dust cover forward and locate the Head Adjustment Lever on the inner righthand side of the printer.

2. Select one of the five settings on the Head Adjustment Lever. Use the lower settings for thinner paper; the higher ones for multiple thicknesses (for example, a top copy plus two flimsies). Position 2 should be right for a single thickness of ordinary paper.

Appendix II

Glossary

Alert	A type of message that LocoScript displays to draw your attention eg. to an error
ASCII	(American Standard Code for Information Interchange). System of codes used by most computers to represent characters. Consists of the upper and lower case letters, the numbers 0...9 and a range of punctuation symbols.
ASCII file	A file containing only simple ASCII text characters
Back-up copy	A copy of a disc, made as a reserve copy for use in case of accidents
Bail bar	The bar on the printer that holds the paper against the platen (rubber roller)
Block	An area of memory used to hold sections of text, ready for pasting into a document
Block editing	Changing the text by copying sections of text into Blocks and then pasting them back into the document in different positions
Bold	A way of styling text that makes characters darker when printed (each character is printed twice with the second printing shifted slightly to the right – cf. Double-strike)
Bottom Gap	The area at the bottom of a page in which the printer never prints
Booting LocoScript 2	Loading the LocoScript 2 program into the PCW's memory
Byte	Unit of storage space either in memory or on a disc. Each byte can hold one character
Caps Lock	Special key combination ([ALT]+[ENTER]) that tells LocoScript to automatically convert any lower case letters you type from here on to upper case – until you type [ALT]+[ENTER] again
Case (of a character)	Whether the character is a capital letter (upper case) or a small letter (lower case)
Centre tab ↔	Tab that aligns text segments so that the centre of each text segment is at the tab position

8809

Centring (of a line)	Positioning the text on the line centrally between the margins
Centronics port	A connector into which you can plug a printer which has the Centronics type of interface. Also known as a Parallel port
Character keys	The keys on the keyboard that produce text characters
Character Pitch	The number of characters that can be typed per inch along a line
Character Set	The range of characters available
Character Style	The appearance of the characters – in particular, the Character Pitch they were designed for
'Commands' menu	A menu offering a choice of actions. An arrow or a diamond marks the action that will be carried out when [ENTER] is pressed
Continuous stationery	Paper on a continuous roll or 'fanfolded' with pages divided by a line of perforations
Carriage Return (↵)	Special character that tells LocoScript to start a new line
CR Extra Spacing	Additional line spacing following a Carriage Return
Cursor	Area of highlighting used either to mark what you are working on or to pick out items on the screen
Cursor keys	The four 'Arrow' keys – used to move Cursors
Daisy wheel printer	A printer that produces characters by hitting the 'petals' of a print wheel with a hammer
Data discs	Discs used to store documents and data files (cf. Start-of-day disc)
Decimal tab	Tab that aligns numbers in such a way that their decimal points are at the tab position
Default Layout	The Layout (ie. margins, character pitch, line spacing, etc.) that LocoScript uses when no other Layout has been specified
'Disc for Drive A'	Disc prepared for use in Drive A of an 8000 series PCW, the upper 'normal-capacity' drive
'Disc for Drive B'	Disc prepared for use in Drive B of an 8000 series PCW, the lower 'high-capacity' drive
Disc Manager Screen	The display showing the documents, etc. on the discs currently in your disc drives
Document	The text of a letter, chapter of a book, report etc. as stored in memory or on disc

Document Set-up	Information stored alongside the text of a document that specifies eg. which type of paper the document has been prepared for
Dot matrix printer	A printer that produces characters by making patterns of dots on the paper
Double-spaced text	Text that has a blank line between each line of text
Double-track disc	Disc prepared for use in Drive B, the 'High-capacity' drive
Double-strike	Making text darker by printing each character twice in the same position (cf. Bold)
Draft quality	The quality of text produced quickly by using a low density of dots (dot matrix printers only)
Drive M	The area of the PCW's memory used to store documents and data files (temporarily)
Editing	Changing the text of a document
End-of-page line	Special line used on the screen to mark the end of each page of the document
End-page-here (↓)	Special character which tells LocoScript to start a new page. Also known as a Form Feed (typed by holding down ALT and pressing RETURN)
Exchange Text	Text that LocoScript will substitute for examples of the Find Text in the document (see Find Text)
Fanfold paper	Continuous stationery with the pages divided by lines of perforations and folded
File	Collection of related data or the text of a document, as stored in memory or on a disc
File Cursor	Band of highlighting on the Disc Manager Screen used to pick out the document or file you want to work with
Find Text	Text that you supply which LocoScript tries to match against the text in the document
Fixed Pitch text	Text in which the characters all take up the same amount of space along the line
Footer	Optional text printed at the bottom of one or more pages of your document
Footer Zone	Section of the page reserved for the Footer
Form Feed (↓)	Special character which tells LocoScript to start a new page. Also known in LocoScript as the End-page-here character (typed by holding down ALT and pressing RETURN)

Formatting	The process of marking out a new blank disc ready to store data and documents
Function keys	Keys on the keyboard marked f1, f2 etc. used in particular to bring menus onto the screen
Group	Group of documents and data files on a disc. You can have up to eight different groups on each disc
Group cursor	Band of highlighting in the upper part of the Disc Manager Screen used to pick out the group you want to work with
Hard hyphen	Special type of hyphen that tells LocoScript not to break the line at this hyphen (typed by pressing ⊞ and then typing a hyphen)
Hard Space	Special type of space that tells LocoScript not to break the line at this space (typed by pressing ⊞ and then typing a space)
Header	Optional text printed at the top of one or more pages of your document
Header Zone	Section of the page reserved for the Header
Hidden files	Files on the Start-of-day disc which are vital to the running of LocoScript and so have been hidden to protect them against accidental erasure
'High-capacity' disc	Disc prepared for use in Drive B of an 8000 series PCW – the 'High-capacity' drive
High Quality	The quality of text produced using a high density of dots. Also known as NLQ or 'Near Letter Quality' (dot matrix printers only)
Indent tab (↪)	Special character that tells LocoScript to use the next tab position as the left margin for the text until the next Carriage Return (typed by holding down [ALT] and pressing [TAB])
Information lines	The three lines at the top of the screen, displaying details of the current task and of the facilities that are available
Italic	A way of styling text in which the characters are slanted
Justification	Increasing the spaces between words so that the righthand edge of the text is straight as well as the left
K	A Kilobyte or 1024 bytes. Used to express the size of files, the amount of storage space on a disc etc.

Landscape	Orientation of a sheet of paper widthways instead of lengthways (see Portrait)
Layout	The specification of the margins, tabs etc. used to lay out text in the part of the document that uses this layout
Layout Editor	The part of LocoScript that helps you set up or change the Layout for the current text
Left Offset	The distance the print start position is moved to the right of its normal start position
Limbo files	Files that have been 'erased' but remain on disc until the storage space they occupy is needed to store another file
Line Break	The point in continuous text at which LocoScript decides to move onto the next line
Line Pitch	The number of standard lines per inch down the page – normally either 6 or 8
Line Spacing	The number of standard lines the printer advances between printing one line and printing the next (but see CR Extra Spacing)
Loading LocoScript 2	The process of loading the LocoScript 2 program from the Start-of-day disc into the PCW's memory so that you can start using the program.
LocoMail	The program that works alongside LocoScript, merging information eg. from data files into documents
LocoSpell	The program that works alongside LocoScript, checking words against dictionaries of standard spellings
Lower case characters	Small letters (cf. Upper case characters)
Menu cursor	Band of highlighting used to pick out options in menus
Memory disc	Section of the PCW's memory used as a temporary store for files and documents (see Drive M)
NLQ (Near Letter Quality)	The quality of text produced using a high density of dots. Also known as High Quality
'Normal-capacity' disc	Disc prepared for use in Drive A of an 8000 series PCW – the 'Normal-capacity' drive
Num Lock	Special key combination ([ALT]+[RELAY]) that sets/clears the use of the Textual Movement Keys as a numeric keypad

---

Page Break	The point in the text at which LocoScript decides to move onto the next page (shown on the screen by an End-of-page line)
Pagination Screen	The display showing the Header and Footer texts, from which any aspect of the Document Set-up can be changed
Pagination text	Text for use at the top and bottom of one or more pages of the document (see Header and Footer)
Paper Type	Specification of Height, Width, etc. of a particular type of paper
Paragraph	Block of text separated from other text by one or more lines of 'white'
Parallel Port	A connector into which you can plug a printer which has a 'Parallel' interface. Often described as a Centronics port
Phrases	Short pieces of text, including word-processing codes, stored on disc for easy insertion into documents
PHRASES.STD	File of Phrases that are automatically made available as part of loading LocoScript 2
Pitch	Number of characters per inch on a line
Platen	Rubber roller in the printer against which paper is held
Portrait	Orientation of the paper lengthways (see Landscape)
Printer Control State	Phase of using LocoScript in which all actions affect how the printer is set up (entered automatically when you load paper into the printer or by pressing [PTR])
Printwheel	Interchangeable unit on a Daisy wheel printer with characters on each 'petal'
Proportional Spacing	System of positioning characters so that wide characters take more space on a line than narrow characters – equivalent on average to 12 characters per inch
Relaying	Re-adjusting how the text is laid out to take account of changes that have been made
Resetting	Restarting LocoScript 2 by pressing [SHIFT], [EXTRA] and [EXIT]. Equivalent to switching off and switching on again

Reverse	A way of styling text so that words are shown on the screen as dark text against a light background
Right Aligning	Positioning text so that the last character is at the righthand margin
Right tab	A tab that marks the position of the last character in any segment of text using this tab
RS232 Interface	The standard type of Serial Interface (see Serial Port)
Ruler Cursor	Marker on the Ruler Line showing how far across the page you are working
Ruler Line	Line displaying the current set of margins and tabs
Scale	Character Pitch used to mark out the Ruler Line
Scrolling	Moving the screen display up, down, left or right to see other parts of the document or other lines of files
Serial Port	Socket into which you can plug a printer that has a serial (RS232) interface
Selection menu	Menu that displays details of the document(s) you have picked out to work on, so that you can confirm your selection
Settings	File of general information about the facilities of your system (stored as SETTINGS.STD on the Start-of-day disc) – in particular, it records the types of paper you use and the printer and paper LocoScript is initially set up to print on
Settings menu	Menu of options that can be either 'Set' or 'Cleared'. Ticks mark the options that are set
Simple tab	A tab that marks the position of the first character in any segment of text using this tab
Single sheet stationery	Separate sheets of paper
Single-spaced text	Text that has no extra space between the lines
Single-track disc	Disc prepared for use in Drive A, the 'Normal-capacity' drive
Soft Hyphen	Special type of hyphen that can be inserted into a long word, giving LocoScript the option of breaking the line at this hyphen. The hyphen only appears when the line is broken at this point (typed by pressing [⊡] and then typing a hyphen)
Soft Space	Special type of space that can be inserted into a long word, giving LocoScript the option of breaking the line at this space (typed by pressing [⊡] and then typing a space)

8809

Appendix II: Glossary

Start-of-day disc	Disc holding the programs and data files read into memory when LocoScript 2 is loaded (cf. Data discs)
Stock Layout	Pattern for a Layout stored as part of the Document Set-up
Subscript	Character written below the normal line of the text
Superscript	Character written above the normal line of the text
Super Shift	Special key combination that puts the keyboard into a particular character mode, eg. Greek or Symbol (typed by holding down ALT and pressing one of Function keys)
System files	Special files that LocoScript uses, usually stored on Drive M. Details of these files are never displayed.
Template (TEMPLATE.STD)	Document used as the pattern for new documents, especially those in the same group
Text Cursor	Marker showing the point in the document at which you are currently working
Textual Movement Keys	Keys on the keyboard marked Para, EOL etc. used to move the Text cursor through the document
Toggle	Using the same action to switch from 'Set' to 'Clear' or from 'Clear' to 'Set'
Top Gap	The area at the top of a page in which the printer never prints
Tractor Feed	The part of the printer designed for handling continuous stationery
Typestyle	Alternative set of character shapes, provided on the built-in printer through a MATRIX.#xx Character Set file
Underline	Underlining both words and spaces (cf. Word Underline)
Upper case characters	Capital letters (cf. Lower case characters)
Widows and Orphans	Single lines of paragraphs separated from the rest of the paragraph by a page break
Wildcard character (?)	Special character used in Find Text to match any character including space
Word processor codes	Special codes embedded in text to tell LocoScript how the text should be laid out and styled
Word Underline	Underlining of the words but not the spaces between the words (cf. Underline)
Word Wrap	Automatic movement of parts of a word onto the next line because there isn't room for the whole word on the current line

Appendix III

LocoScript 2 Characters

LocoScript 2 supports a very wide range of characters and symbols, making it possible to type not only in English but also mathematical equations and text in almost every European language. All of these characters can be displayed on the screen, but the range of characters you can print depends on the printer you use.

To type each character, you have to press one of the Character keys on the keyboard, often together with another key. You can see how to type the commonest characters just by looking at the keyboard. The letters a...z, the digits 0...9 and characters like hyphen, comma and full stop are typed by just pressing the key marked with this character. Other common characters – in particular, the capital letters A...Z – are typed by holding down the [SHIFT] key while pressing the key marked with the appropriate character. Where the key has two characters engraved on it, the lower character is the one that is typed when the key is pressed on its own: the upper one is only typed when [SHIFT] is held down as well.

Further characters are typed by holding down the [EXTRA] key or the [ALT] key at the same time as pressing either the Character key on its own or together with [SHIFT]. Characters that you produce in this way are not engraved on the keys themselves: they are the ones listed in the table below with a key combination starting [EXTRA], [ALT] or [SHIFT] [ALT]. Taking an example from the top of the table, the key combination for an upper case ae diphthong is given as [SHIFT] [ALT] A – telling you to hold down both the [SHIFT] and the [ALT] keys at the same time as pressing the 'A' letter key.

The key combinations using [SHIFT], [ALT] and [EXTRA] enable you to type the vast majority of the characters – but not all of them. To type Greek characters, Cyrillic characters and a number of special symbols, you have first to put the keyboard into a special mode known as a 'Super Shift'. With each Super Shift, different characters are produced when you press the key on its own, or with either [SHIFT], [ALT] or [SHIFT] and [ALT]. The characters produced when you press the key with [EXTRA] stay the same. For example, if you put the keyboard into its Greek mode, pressing the A key types a lower case alpha – not a lower case a – but pressing [EXTRA] E still gives you an acute accent.

The characters for which you need to put the keyboard into a Super Shift can be picked out from the table below by looking for Greek:, Cyrillic: or Symbol: at the beginning of the key combination or in the heading to the section. For example, the heading for the section of the table on Greek letters tells you that the keyboard has to be put into its Greek mode before you type any of the given key combinations.

Putting the keyboard into its 'Greek' mode doesn't mean that all you can type are Greek letters. You can still type standard Roman Script letters and many of the special letters and symbols – but you will generally have to use a different key combination.

9010

All the characters that were typed by just pressing the key or the key together with [SHIFT] can be typed, simply by holding down [ALT] at the same time as pressing the given key combination. And as we mentioned above, all the characters that are typed by pressing a key together with [EXTRA] can still be typed using the same key combination. However, the characters that are typed by holding down [ALT] or [SHIFT] and [ALT] at the same time as pressing the key are temporarily 'lost' to you. To type these again – and to use the usual key combinations for the common characters – you have to put the keyboard back into its 'Normal' mode.

The keyboard is put into a different mode by pressing a special key combination called a 'Super-Shift' as follows:

- Symbol: [ALT] [f7]
- Cyrillic: [ALT] [f5]
- Greek: [ALT] [f3]
- Normal: [ALT] [f1]

So if, for example, you wanted to type a line of Greek in the middle of your document, you would press [ALT] [f3] immediately before you wanted to type the Greek characters and [ALT] [f1] when you had finished.

Note: Moving the Text cursor to a part of a document where you earlier used one of the special modes of the keyboard doesn't automatically put the keyboard into this special mode. So if you want to add to your line of Greek, say, you will have to put your keyboard into its Greek mode by pressing [ALT] [f3] as before.

The full character set

The following table gives all the characters that it is possible to type using LocoScript 2, together with details of the keys you have to press to type these characters. Where the key combination starts with Greek:, Cyrillic: or Symbol:, this means that you have to be using the keyboard with this Super Shift.

The 'normal' keyboard is laid out as a standard English keyboard, while the Greek keyboard is designed to match keyboards used in Greece. The Cyrillic keyboard is Russian Mnemonic (Phonetic), based on the recommendations of the AATSEEL Ad Hoc Committee on Standardisation of Computer Keyboards for Cyrillic.

Among the characters listed here are 16 'user definable' characters. Which characters these are and how to define new characters is explained in the booklet on 'Designing your own characters'.

Note: The table gives the key combination only for the lower case version of any letter. To type the corresponding Capital letter, hold down [SHIFT] and then press the key combination for the lower case letter.

Alphanumerics

Symbol	Description	Key combination
a...z	Lower case letters	Unshifted letter
0...9	Numerals	Unshifted number
		(Also Greek and Cyrillic)
0	Zero (no slash)	[ALT] 0
æ	ae diphthong	[ALT] A
œ	oe diphthong	[ALT] Z

Note: Upper case versions of these letters are typed by holding down [SHIFT] as you press the key combination given for the lower case letter.

Accents

Note: Accented letters are entered, without leaving the Super Shift you are working in, by typing the accent followed by the letter you want to apply the accent to. LocoScript 2 automatically 'amalgamates' the accent with the letter, both on the screen and when the document is printed on the built-in printer. Another printer won't necessarily be able to print the accent you want and it won't amalgamate the accent with the character in the same way – but the accent should still be printed with the letter.

´	Acute	[EXTRA] E (Greek: ;)
`	Grave	[EXTRA] T (Greek: [SHIFT]])
^	Circumflex	[EXTRA] U
¨	Umlaut or diaeresis	[EXTRA] W (Greek: [SHIFT] [ )
ˇ	Caron or hacek	[EXTRA] I
˙	Dot	[EXTRA] Q
~	Tilde	[EXTRA] P
˘	Breve	[EXTRA] S
˝	Double acute	[EXTRA] R
˚	Ring	[EXTRA] A
¯	Macron	[EXTRA] O
˶	Double grave	[EXTRA] Y
¸	Cedilla	[EXTRA] D
˛	Ogonek	[EXTRA] F
،	Latvian tail	[EXTRA] G
.	Dot below	[EXTRA] H
/	Stroke	[EXTRA] /

Note: (i) LocoScript also supports a complete range of Greek breathings and other accents associated with Greek language. Details of these are given on the next page.

(ii) Latvian lower-case g-tail's have the accent **above** the letter – not below.

9010

Greek characters (typed using the Greek Super Shift)

Symbol	Description	Key	Symbol	Description	Key
α A	Alpha	A	σ Σ	Sigma	S
β B	Beta	B	ς		W
γ Γ	Gamma	G	τ T	Tau	T
δ Δ	Delta	D	υ Y	Upsilon	Y
ε E	Epsilon	E	φ Φ	Phi	F
ζ Z	Zeta	Z	Φ		SHIFT W
η H	Eta	H	χ X	Chi	X
θ Θ	Theta	U	ψ Ψ	Psi	C
ι I	Iota	I	ω Ω	Omega	V
χ K	Kappa	K			
λ Λ	Lambda	L	F F	Digamma	-
μ M	Mu	M	ϙ ϙ	Qoppa (koppa)	=
ν N	Nu	N	ϲ Ϲ	Lunate sigma	Q
ξ Ξ	Xi	J		Thousands mark	SHIFT 6
ο O	Omicron	O	ϡ	Sampi	SHIFT 7
π Π	Pi	P	ϛ	Stigma or numerical	
ρ P	Rho	R		digamma	SHIFT 8

Symbol	Description	Key combination
ϊ	Iota diaeresis	[
ϋ	Upsilon diaeresis	]
ᾳ	Alpha with iota subscript	SHIFT 3
ῃ	Eta with iota subscript	SHIFT 4
ῳ	Omega with iota subscript	SHIFT 5

Additional Greek accents (available from any Super Shift)

ʽ	Rough breathing	EXTRA L
῞	Rough breathing with acute	EXTRA X
῝	Rough breathing with grave	EXTRA V
῟	Rough breathing with circumflex	EXTRA N
῏	Rough breathing with tilde	EXTRA ,
ʼ	Smooth breathing	EXTRA K
῎	Smooth breathing with acute	EXTRA Z
῍	Smooth breathing with grave	EXTRA C
῏	Smooth breathing with circumflex	EXTRA B
῀	Smooth breathing with tilde	EXTRA M
῀	Greek circumflex	EXTRA J

Note: Upper case versions of these letters are typed by holding down SHIFT as you press the key combination given for the lower case letter.

9010

Cyrillic characters (typed using the Cyrillic Super Shift)

Symbol	Description	Key	Symbol	Description	Key
а А	A	A	п П	P	P
б Б	B	B	p P	R	R
в В	V	V	с С	S	S
г Г	G; H (BR, U)	G	т Т	T	T
ґ Ґ	G (BR, U)	–	у У	U	U
д Д	D	D	ф Ф	F	F
е Е	E; Ye (BR, R)	E	x Х	Kh	X
є Є	Ye (U)	½	ц Ц	Ts	C
ж Ж	Zh	§	ч Ч	Ch	H
з З	Z	Z	ш Ш	Sh	W
и И	I (Blg, R); Y (U)	I	щ Щ	Shch; Sht (Blg)	]
й Й	Y (postvocalic)	J	ъ ъ	hard sign; A (Blg)	=
і І	I (BR, U)	/	ы Ы	Y (postcon. BR,R)	Y
к К	K	K	ь ь	soft sign	;
л Л	L	L	э Э	E (BR, R)	#
м М	M	M	ю Ю	Yu	[
н Н	N	N	я Я	Ya	Q
о О	O	O	№	Number	SHIFT 3

Note: (i) Blg = Bulgarian, BR = Byelorussian, R = Russian, U = Ukrainian.

(ii)Upper case versions of these letters are typed by holding down SHIFT as you press the key combination given for the lower case letter.

Other special language characters

Symbol	Description	Key combination
đ Đ	D stroke	ALT D
ð Đ	Eth	ALT F
ħ Ħ	H stroke	ALT H
ı	Dotless i (Turkish)	ALT I
ĳ Ĳ	IJ	ALT J
ĸ Κ	k (Greenland)	ALT K
ŀ Ŀ	L dot	ALT .
ľ Ľ	L'	ALT ,
ł Ł	L stroke	ALT L
ℓ	Curly l	SHIFT ALT I
ŋ Ŋ	Eng	ALT N
ø Ø	O stroke	ALT O

Note: Upper case versions of these letters are typed by holding down SHIFT as you press the key combination given for the lower case letter.

9010

Symbol	Description	Key combination
ß	Scharfes S	[ALT] S or [SHIFT] [ALT] S
þ Þ	Thorn	[ALT] P
ŧ Ŧ	T stroke	[ALT] T
Ď	D hacek	[SHIFT] [ALT] E
ď	Alternative form of d hacek	[ALT] E
Ť	T hacek	[SHIFT] [ALT] Y
t'	Alternative form of t hacek	[ALT] Y

Textual Symbols

Symbol	Description	Key combination
−	Hyphen	Unshifted -
,	Comma	Unshifted , (Also Greek and Cyrillic) or [SHIFT] , (Also Greek)
.	Full stop	Unshifted . (Also Greek and Cyrillic) or [SHIFT] . (Also Greek)
;	Semicolon	Unshifted ; (Greek §: Cyrillic [SHIFT] ,)
:	Colon	[SHIFT] ; (Also Greek: Cyrillic [SHIFT] .)
...	Ellipsis	[ALT] V
—	Dash	[ALT] − (Also Greek)
!	Exclamation mark	[SHIFT] 1 (Also Greek and Cyrillic)
?	Question mark	[SHIFT] / (Cyrillic [SHIFT] 4)
	Space	Space Bar (All variations)
&	Ampersand	[SHIFT] 7
'	Apostrophe	[SHIFT] 6
'	Open single quote	[ALT] 6 (Greek: [SHIFT] /)
'	Close single quote	[SHIFT] [ALT] 6 (Greek: [SHIFT] ½; Cyrillic: [SHIFT] 6)
"	Double quote	[SHIFT] 2 (Also Greek and Cyrillic)
"	Open double quote	[ALT] 2 (Greek: /)
"	Close double quote	[SHIFT] [ALT] 2 (Greek: ½)
_	Underline	[SHIFT] −
*	Asterisk	[SHIFT] 8
#	Hash	Unshifted #
/	Slash	Unshifted / (Greek: [ALT] /)
(	Open parenthesis	[SHIFT] 9 (Also Greek and Cyrillic)
)	Close parenthesis	[SHIFT] 0 (Also Greek and Cyrillic)
[	Open square bracket	Unshifted [
]	Close square bracket	Unshifted]
{	Open curly brace	[SHIFT] [

9010

Symbol	Description	Key combination
}	Close curly brace	[SHIFT]]
@	At	[SHIFT] ½
∴	Therefore	[ALT] B
∵	Because of	[SHIFT] [ALT] B
℅	Care of	[SHIFT] [ALT] C
©	Copyright	[ALT] C
®	Registered	[ALT] R
™	Trade mark	[SHIFT] [ALT] R
°	Open circle	[ALT] M
•	Bullet	[SHIFT] [ALT] M
¶	Paragraph (Pilcrow)	[SHIFT] [ALT] −
§	Section	Unshifted §
†	Dagger	[ALT] =
‡	Double dagger	[SHIFT] [ALT] =
		Vertical bar	[EXTRA] §

Continental textual symbols

‹	Single guillemet	[SHIFT] [ALT] §
›		[SHIFT] [ALT] #
«	Double guillemet	[ALT] § (Greek: [SHIFT] §; Cyrillic: [SHIFT] 7)
»		[ALT] # (Greek: [SHIFT] #; Cyrillic: [SHIFT] 8)
„	German open double quote	[ALT] 3
¿	Open query	[SHIFT] [ALT] /
¡	Open shriek	[SHIFT] [ALT] 1
ª	Feminine ordinal	[SHIFT] [ALT] 7
º	Masculine ordinal	[SHIFT] [ALT] 8
·	Greek semicolon	Greek: #

Currency symbols

£	Pound	[SHIFT] 3
$	Dollar	[SHIFT] 4
¢	Cent	[SHIFT] [ALT] 4
¤	Internatl. currency symbol	[SHIFT] [ALT] 3
₣	Franc	[ALT] 4
₤	Turkish pound	[ALT] 9
ƒ	Florin	[ALT] 1
¥	Yen	[ALT] 8
₧	Peseta	[ALT] 5

Mathematical and Technical symbols

Symbol	Description	Key combination
+	Plus	[SHIFT] =
−	Minus	Unshifted −
✳	Multiply	[SHIFT] 8
×	Times	[ALT] X
÷	Divide	[SHIFT] [ALT] X
/	Divide (Slash)	Unshifted / (Greek: [ALT] /)
↑	Exponentiation	Symbol: Q
=	Equals	Unshifted =
I	Modulus	Symbol: §
\	Backslash	[ALT] ½
½	Half	Unshifted ½
⅛	One eighth	Symbol: [
¼	One quarter	[EXTRA] [
⅓	One third	Symbol: =
⅜	Three eighths	Symbol:]
⅝	Five eighths	Symbol: [SHIFT] [
⅔	Two thirds	Symbol: [SHIFT] =
¾	Three quarters	[EXTRA]]
⅞	Seven eighths	Symbol: [SHIFT]]
1/	One upon	[EXTRA] ½
$^0 \ldots ^9$	Superscript 0...9	Symbol: 0...9
^{n}	Superscript n	Symbol: −
•	Decimal point	[EXTRA] .
±	Plus or minus	[ALT] ;
∓	Minus or plus	[SHIFT] [ALT] ;
<	Less than	[SHIFT] §
>	Greater than	[SHIFT] #
≤	Less than or equal	[EXTRA] −
≠	Not equals	[EXTRA] #
≥	Greater than or equal	[EXTRA] =
≃	Approx. equal to	Symbol: P
≈	Nearly equal to	Symbol: [SHIFT] P
≪	Much less than	Symbol: [SHIFT] §
~	Asymptotically equal to	Symbol: [SHIFT] −
≫	Much greater than	Symbol: [SHIFT] #
≡	Equivalent	Symbol: O
≅	Congruent	Symbol: [SHIFT] O
∝	Proportional to	Symbol: [SHIFT] 2

Symbol	Description	Key combination
Ω	Ohms symbol	Greek: [SHIFT] V
°	Degrees	[ALT] 7
′	Minutes	[ALT] G
″	Seconds	[SHIFT] [ALT] G
%	Percent	[SHIFT] 5 (Also Cyrillic)
‰	Per thousand	[SHIFT] [ALT] 5
‖	Parallel	Symbol: #
⊥	Perpendicular	Symbol: [SHIFT] 1
∞	Infinity	Symbol: [SHIFT] 0
√	Root	Symbol: [SHIFT] ;
∟	Angle	Symbol: J
∡		Symbol: [SHIFT] J
∃	Exists	Symbol: [SHIFT] A
∋	Such that	Symbol: [SHIFT] S
∀	Universal	Symbol: A
∨	Logical Or	Symbol: [SHIFT] H
∧	Logical And	Symbol: H
¬	Logical Not	Symbol: [SHIFT] 9
∅	Empty set	Symbol: ;
∩	Intersection	Symbol: G
∪	Union	Symbol: [SHIFT] G
⊂	Proper subset	Symbol: D
⊃	Proper superset	Symbol: [SHIFT] D
⊆	Reflex subset	Symbol: F
⊇	Reflex superset	Symbol: [SHIFT] F
∈	Element	Symbol: S
⌊	Floor	Symbol: K
⌋		Symbol: L
⌈	Ceiling	Symbol: [SHIFT] K
⌉		Symbol: [SHIFT] L
⊕	Circle plus (special operator)	Symbol: [SHIFT] 7
⊗	Circle times (special operator)	Symbol: [SHIFT] 6
∑	Sum	Symbol: M
∏	Product	Symbol: [SHIFT] M
∫	Integral	Symbol: U
∮	Contour integral	Symbol: I
∫	Integral (large)	Symbol: [SHIFT] U
∮	Contour integral (large)	Symbol: [SHIFT] I
∂	Partial differential	Symbol: [SHIFT] 4
∇	Gradient	Symbol: [SHIFT] 3

9010

Symbol	Description	Key combination
/	Slash (large)	[ALT] /
(	Bracket (large)	[SHIFT] [ALT] 9
)		[SHIFT] [ALT] 0
[	Square bracket (large)	[ALT] [
]		[ALT]]
{	Curly brackets (large)	[SHIFT] [ALT] [
}		[SHIFT] [ALT]]

Arrows

↑	Symbol: Q	⇊	Symbol: [SHIFT] E
↕	Symbol: W	⇐	Symbol: [SHIFT] R
↓	Symbol: E	⇔	Symbol: [SHIFT] T
←	Symbol: R	⇒	Symbol: [SHIFT] Y
↔	Symbol: T	▲	Symbol: C
→	Symbol: Y	▼	Symbol: [SHIFT] C
⇑	Symbol: [SHIFT] Q	◄	Symbol: V
⇓	Symbol: [SHIFT] W	►	Symbol: [SHIFT] V

Special Textual Symbols

Symbol	Description	Key combination
⊙	Circle dot (arrow out)	Symbol: [SHIFT] 5
○	Large open circle	Symbol: Z
●	Large bullet	Symbol: [SHIFT] Z
□	Box	Symbol: X
■	Filled Box	Symbol: [SHIFT] X
◊	Diamond	[SHIFT] [ALT] V
✓	Tick	Symbol: N
×	Cross	Symbol: [SHIFT] N
✳	Star	Symbol: [SHIFT] 8
⓪...⑨	Circled digits	[EXTRA] 0...9
☺	Smiling face	Symbol: /
☻	Black smiling face	Symbol: [SHIFT] /
♂	Mars	Symbol: [SHIFT] B
♀	Venus	Symbol: B
♣	Clubs	Symbol: [SHIFT] ,
♦	Diamonds	Symbol: ,
♥	Hearts	Symbol: .
♠	Spades	Symbol: [SHIFT] .
♪	Note	Symbol: ½
♫	Two-note	Symbol: [SHIFT] ½

Special key combinations

As well as the key combinations that produce characters, there are also some special key combinations which modify which characters are produced. These are:

- The Super-Shifts [ALT] [f1], [ALT] [f3], [ALT] [f5] and [ALT] [f7] – which put the keyboard into a different character mode (Normal, Greek, Cyrillic and Symbol, respectively)

- The Caps Lock [ALT] [ENTER] – which sets or clears the conversion of all lower case (small) letters to their upper case counterpart

- The Num Lock [ALT] [RELAY] – which sets or clears the use of the Textual Movement keys and Cursor keys as a numeric keypad

- Indent Tab – [ALT] [TAB]

- Form Feed – [ALT] [RETURN]

- [SHIFT] [EXTRA] [EXIT] – which resets your machine

Characters for names within LocoScript

A number of items within LocoScript have names:

- Documents
- Groups
- Discs
- Layouts
- Paper Types
- Printers
- Character Sets
- Character Styles
- Identity text

The names used for your printers and their Character Sets and for the supplied range of Paper Types are set up for you. However, you get to choose the names for everything else and there are rules about how these names should be constructed – in particular, about the range of characters and the number of characters that can be used. By no means all the characters that you can type using LocoScript 2 can be used in these names.

The items split into two groups, in terms of the range of characters that can be used in their names. The first group comprises Documents, Groups and Discs: the second group comprises Layouts, Paper Types, Character Styles and the Identity text. We list the characters that can be used below – together with a brief outline of the other rules that apply to these names.

9010

Documents, Groups and Discs

The names of Documents, Groups and Discs are restricted to the following range of characters:

- the capital letters A...Z
- the digits 0...9
- the characters " # $ % ' @ _ § { } ½ ◊

No other characters may be used: in particular, you cannot include any spaces in these names.

Note: Document and Disc names have a main part which is between one and eight characters long, to which you can add an extension of up to three characters which you separate from the main part by a full stop. The names for Groups are simply between one and eight characters long.

Layouts, Paper Types, Character Styles, Identity

A very much wider range of characters can be used in the names of Layouts, Paper Types and Character Styles, and for the Identity text. Grouping these in the same way as we have done in the table above, the characters are:

- a...z, A...Z, 0...9, 0 , æ, Æ, œ, Œ
- these accented characters only: á...ú, à...ù, â...û, ãõ, ç, ÄÖÜ, ä...üÿ, Å, å, Ñ, ñ, ġ
- all the Greek characters
- all the 'Other Special Language Characters', except l', L'
- the following Textual Symbols: - , . ; : ... ! ? (space) & ' " _ * # / ( ) [ ] { } @ © ® ™ § ¶ ° • ◊
- the following Continental Textual Symbols: « » ¿ ¡ ª º
- the following Currency Symbol: $
- the following Mathematical Symbols: + – * / = | \ ½ . < > %

The principal groups of characters you can't use are:
- the Cyrillic characters
- many of the special mathematical symbols
- the special textual symbols

Note: Each of these names can be up to 12 characters long.

Appendix IV

Quick reference

The following pages give brief instructions on how to carry out the commonest actions within LocoScript 2.

The instructions are designed to be used as an 'aide-memoire', reminding you of the steps rather than going through the processes in detail. If you need further help on any action, then you should work through the relevant part of the tutorial. The session of the tutorial you want is given in brackets at the top of each set of instructions.

Word-processing is a complex activity, so there is a long list even of the most common actions. To make the instructions you want reasonably easy to find, we have grouped the actions under different sub-headings as follows:

Loading LocoScript 2

Block editing:	Copying text to a block
	Inserting a Block
	Inspecting Blocks
Discs:	Changing Discs
	Formatting a new disc
	Copying a disc
Disc Management:	Copying documents
	Erasing documents
	Moving documents
	Renaming documents
	Running the Disc Manager from the Editor
	Displaying Limbo/Hidden files
Documents:	Creating a document
	Editing a document
	Making an ASCII file
Document Set-up:	Scope
	Gaining access to the Document Set-up
Headers and Footers	Editing the Pagination Layout
(Pagination text):	Setting how the Headers and Footers are used
	Inserting page numbers
	Setting First Page numbers of a series of documents
Inserting text:	Inserting text from another document
	Inserting a whole document

8809

Appendix IV: Quick Reference

Layouts:	Scope
	Using a New Layout
	Using a Stock Layout
	Changing the Layout
	Changing a Stock Layout
	Setting Margins
	Setting Tabs
	Clearing Tabs
	Showing Rulers
Page breaks and Line breaks:	Allowing a line break in the middle of a word
	Preventing a line break at a space or a hyphen
	Starting a new page
	Keeping lines together
	Setting the general rules for Page Breaks
Paper:	Setting Document Paper Type
	Setting Printer Paper Type
	Setting Page Layout
Phrases:	Loading a set of Phrases
	Setting up a new Phrase
	Inserting a Phrase
	Saving a set of Phrases
	Inspecting Phrases
Positioning text:	Centring a line of text
	Moving a line to the right
	Indenting a paragraph
Printing:	Printing one copy
	Printing multiple copies
	Printing selected pages
	Entering Printer Control State
	Reprinting
	Setting Left Offset
	Suspending/Resuming printing
	Print to end of page
Search and Replace:	Find
	Exchange
Text preparation:	Styling text
	Displaying word-processing codes
	Setting character size
	Setting line spacing
	Setting/Clearing Justification
	Moving round the document

8809

Loading LocoScript 2 (page 19)

1 Switch on or reset your PCW
2 Insert your Start-of-Day disc in Drive A
3 If the computer doesn't automatically start reading from the disc, press the Space Bar
4 Wait while the computer reads the LocoScript program off this disc (The light on the disc drive will flash on and off.)
5 Remove the Start-of Day disc from the drive and put it to one side

Block editing

Copying text to a block (Session 6)

- while editing a document

1 Move the Text cursor to the start of the section of text
2 Press COPY
3 Move the Text cursor to the end of the section of text
4 Press COPY to retain the original text; press CUT to delete the original text
5 Type the number of the Block (0...9)

Inserting a Block (Session 6)

- while editing a document

1 Position the Text cursor where the Block is to be inserted
2 Press PASTE
3 Type the number of the Block (0...9)

Inspecting Blocks (Session 6)

- while editing a document or from the Disc Manager Screen

1 Press f1 to bring the Actions menu onto the screen
2 Select Show blocks
3 Press ENTER

A menu showing the first few words of each block is then displayed. Press CAN when you have finished with this menu.

9108

Discs

All the actions described here are carried out from the Disc Manager Screen.

Changing Discs (Session 2)

1 Change the disc in the drive

2 Press ⌐f7⌐

Formatting a new disc (Session 7)

1 Remove all discs from your disc drives

2 Press ⌐f2⌐ to bring the Disc menu onto the screen

3 Select Format disc

4 Press ⌐ENTER⌐

5 Follow the on-screen instructions

Copying a disc (Session 7)

1 Remove all discs from your disc drives

2 Press ⌐f2⌐ to bring the Disc menu onto the screen

3 Select Copy disc

4 Press ⌐ENTER⌐

5 Follow the on-screen instructions

Disc Management

These operations are carried out from the Disc Manager Screen, unless otherwise stated.

Copying a document (Session 7)

Note: The disc on which the copy is to be made must be in the right type of drive.

1 Pick out the document with the File cursor

2 Press ⌐f3⌐ to bring the File menu onto the screen

3 Select Copy file and press ⌐ENTER⌐

4 Pick out the group where the copy is to be stored with the Group cursor

5 Press ⌐ENTER⌐

6 Check and, if necessary, correct the details in the Selection menu

7 Press ⌐ENTER⌐

Erasing a document (Session 7)

Note: The disc holding the document must be in the correct type of drive.

1 Pick out the document with the File cursor

2 Press ⌐f3⌐ to bring the File menu onto the screen

3 Select Erase file and press ⌐ENTER⌐

4 Check and, if necessary, correct the details in the Selection menu

5 Press ⌐ENTER⌐

Moving a document (Session 7)

Note: Both the disc holding the document and the disc to which the document is to be moved must be in the correct type of drive.

1 Pick out the document with the File cursor

2 Press 〔f3〕 to bring the File menu onto the screen

3 Select Move file and press 〔ENTER〕

4 Pick out the group where the document is to be stored with the Group cursor

5 Press 〔ENTER〕

6 Check and, if necessary, correct the details in the Selection menu

7 Press 〔ENTER〕

Renaming a document (Session 7)

Note: The disc holding the document must be in the correct type of drive.

1 Pick out the document with the File cursor

2 Press 〔f3〕 to bring the File menu onto the screen

3 Select Rename file and press 〔ENTER〕

4 Fill in the new name in the Selection menu

5 Press 〔ENTER〕

Running the Disc Manager from the Editor (Session 7)

1 Press 〔f1〕 to bring the Actions menu onto the screen

2 Select Disc manager and press 〔ENTER〕

You can now carry out many of the actions normally carried out from the Disc Manager Screen. However, you can't change any of the information held in the SETTINGS.STD file, you can't open another document for editing and you must not remove the disc holding the document you are editing.

When you have finished using the Disc Manager, press 〔EXIT〕 to return to the Editor.

Showing Limbo/Hidden Files (Session 7)

1 Press 〔f8〕 to bring the Options menu onto the screen

2 Set Show Limbo/Hidden files

3 Press 〔ENTER〕

Documents

The actions described here are all carried out from the Disc Manager Screen.

Creating a document (Session 3)

1 Pick out the group in which the new document is to be stored with the Group cursor

2 Press **C**

3 Replace the name in the Selection menu that LocoScript suggests with the name you have chosen for the new document. Press [ENTER]

The new document is then opened for editing.

Editing a document (Session 5)

1 Pick out the document you want to edit with the File cursor

2 Press **E**

3 Check and, if necessary, correct the details in the Selection menu. Press [ENTER]

Making an ASCII file (Session 14)

1 Pick out the document you want to make an ASCII version of

2 Press [f1] to bring the Actions menu onto the screen

3 Select Make ASCII file. Press [ENTER]

4 Pick out the group in which the ASCII file is to be stored with the Group cursor. Press [ENTER]

5 Fill in the name you want for the ASCII file and check the details in the Selection menu. Press [ENTER]

Document Set-up

Scope (Session 17)

- Printer and character set selected for document (see Printing)
- Paper Type selected for document (see Paper)
- Page Layout (see Paper)
- Header and Footer text (see Headers and Footers)
- Header and Footer Layout (see Headers and Footers)
- Rules for applying Headers and Footers (see Headers and Footers)
- The Stock Layouts (see Layouts)
- Rules for Page Breaks (see Page breaks and Line breaks)
- First Page (and Total Pages) numbers (see Headers and Footers)

Gaining access to the Document Set-up (Session 17)

Note: You can only gain access to the Document Set-up while you are editing the document.

1 Press [f1] to bring the Actions menu onto the screen

2 Select Document setup

3 Press [ENTER]

LocoScript then displays the special Pagination Screen, together with the array of menus that help you change the various aspects of the Document Set-up.

LocoScript 2 User Guide: Appendices

Headers and Footers (Pagination text)

Editing the Pagination Layout (Sessions 16 and 11)

- from the Pagination Screen

1 Press ⌜f2⌝ to bring the Layout menu onto the screen

2 Select Change layout

3 Press ⌜ENTER⌝

This puts you into the Layout Editor. You can now edit the Layout in the normal way.

When you have finished using the Layout editor, press ⌜EXIT⌝ to return to the Pagination Screen.

Setting how the Headers and Footers are used (Session 16)

- from the Pagination Screen

1 Press ⌜f5⌝ to bring the Page menu onto the screen

2 Select Header/footer options and press ⌜ENTER⌝

3 Set the use to which Header/Footer 1 will be put

4 Set those Headers and Footers that will be required on the First and Last pages of the document

5 Set the source of the Footer that will be used on single-page documents

6 Press ⌜ENTER⌝ ⌜EXIT⌝ ⌜ENTER⌝

Inserting page numbers (Session 16)

To insert the current page number:

1 Press ⌜⊞⌝ and type PN

2 Type as many <s, >s or =s as are necessary to reserve space for the page number

To insert the Total Pages number:

1 Press ⌜⊞⌝ and type LPN

2 Type as many <s, >s or =s as are necessary to reserve space for the number

Setting First Page numbers of a series of documents (Session 18)

- from the Disc Manager Screen

1 Pick out the first document of the series with the File cursor

2 Press ⌜f5⌝ to bring the Document menu onto the screen

3 Select Set first pages and press ⌜ENTER⌝

4 Select Set counter=first page and press ⌜ENTER⌝

5 Pick out the next document with the File cursor and press ⌜ENTER⌝

6 Select Set first page=counter and press ⌜ENTER⌝

7 Repeat Steps 5 and 6 until all documents have been selected

8 Press ⌜CAN⌝

8809

Inserting text

The actions described here are carried out while editing a document.

Inserting text from another document (Session 14)

Note: The text to be inserted must have been copied to a Block in a previous edit and not overwritten by other text.

1 Position the Text cursor where the text is to be inserted

2 Press [PASTE]

3 Type the number of the Block holding the text (0 . . . 9)

Inserting a whole document (Session 14)

1 Position the Text cursor where the document is to be inserted

2 Press [f1] to bring the Actions menu onto the screen

3 Select Insert text; press [ENTER]

4 Pick out the Document you want to insert with the File cursor

5 Press [ENTER]

6 Check, and if necessary correct, the details in the selection menu

7 Press [ENTER]

Layouts

The actions described here are carried out while the document is being edited, unless otherwise stated.

Scope (Session 11)

- Position of margins
- Position and type of each Tab
- Justification of paragraphs
- Default character size and styling
- Default line spacing, line pitch and CR extra spacing
- Decimal Point character
- Standard zero character

Using a New Layout (Session 11)

1 Position the Text cursor where you want to start using the Layout

2 Press [f2] to bring the Layout menu onto the screen

3 Select New layout

4 Press [ENTER]

This puts you into the Layout Editor. You can now edit the Layout with the aid of the Layout Editor menus.

When you have finished using the Layout editor, press [EXIT] to return to the document. Delete the extra Carriage Return LocoScript gives you if you don't want this.

8809

Using a Stock Layout (Session 11)

Menu method:

1 Position the Text cursor where you want to start using the Layout

2 Press ⌜f2⌝ to select the Layout menu

3 Select New layout and press ⌜ENTER⌝

4 Press ⌜f5⌝ to select the Stock menu

5 Move the Menu cursor to the required Layout

6 Press ⌜ENTER⌝ and then ⌜EXIT⌝ to return to the document

Delete the extra Carriage Return LocoScript gives you if you don't want this.

Keystroke method:

1 Position the Text cursor anywhere on the line above the first line to be laid out using this layout

2 Press ⌜+⌝ and type LT followed by the number of the Layout

3 Press ⌜ENTER⌝

Changing the Layout (Session 11)

1 Press ⌜f2⌝ to bring the Layout menu onto the screen

2 Move the Menu cursor to Change layout

3 Press ⌜ENTER⌝

This puts you into the Layout Editor. You can now edit the Layout with the aid of the Layout Editor menus. When you have finished using the Layout editor, press ⌜EXIT⌝ to return to the document.

Changing a Stock Layout (Session 17)

- from the Pagination Screen

1 Press ⌜f2⌝ to bring the Layout menu onto the screen

2 Move the Menu cursor to Change stock layouts and press ⌜ENTER⌝

3 Move the Menu cursor to the Stock Layout you want to change

4 Press ⌜ENTER⌝

This puts you into the Layout Editor. You can now edit the Layout with the aid of the Layout Editor menus. When you have finished using the Layout editor, press ⌜EXIT⌝

Setting Margins (Session 11)

The margins are set while the Layout is being edited.

1 Move the Ruler cursor to the new position for the margin

2 Press ⌜f1⌝ to bring the Margins menu onto the screen

3 Select Set Left/Right Margin as appropriate

4 Press ⌜ENTER⌝

Setting Tabs (Session 11)

Tabs are set while the Layout is being edited.

1 Move the Ruler cursor to the position for the new Tab

2 Press ⌜f3⌝ to bring the Tabs menu onto the screen

3 Select the type of Tab you want

4 Press ⌜ENTER⌝

Clearing Tabs (Session 11)

Tabs are cleared while the Layout is being edited.

Menu method:

Clearing one Tab:

1   Pick out the Tab with the Ruler cursor

2   Press ⌜f3⌝ to bring the Tabs menu onto the screen

3   Select Clear tab and press ⌜ENTER⌝

Clearing all Tabs:

1   Press ⌜f3⌝ to bring the Tabs menu onto the screen

2   Select Clear all tabs and press ⌜ENTER⌝

Keystroke method:

Clearing one tab:

1   Pick out the Tab with the Ruler cursor

2   Press ⌜-⌝

Showing Rulers (Session 11)

– while editing a document

1   Press ⌜f8⌝ to bring the Options menu onto the screen

2   Set Rulers

3   Press ⌜ENTER⌝

Page breaks and Line breaks

The actions described here control where LocoScript can break the text of a document between one line and the next and between one page and the next. Unless otherwise stated, these are carried out while the document is being edited.

Allowing a line break in the middle of a word (Session 15)

1   Position the Text cursor where you are willing for the word to break

2   Type the appropriate key sequence for the type of character you want to appear when the word is broken - as follows:

Hyphen   ⌜-⌝ followed by a hyphen

Space   ⌜-⌝ followed by a space

Preventing a line break at a space or a hyphen (Session 15)

1   Delete the existing character

2   Type the appropriate key sequence as follows:

Hyphen   ⌜#⌝ followed by a hyphen

Space   ⌜#⌝ followed by a space

Starting a new page (Session 15)

1 Position the Text cursor where you want the new page to start

2 Hold down ⟨ALT⟩ and press ⟨RETURN⟩

Keeping lines together (Session 15)

Menu method:

1 Position the Text cursor on the first line of the group that you want to keep together

2 Press ⟨f5⟩ to bring the Page menu onto the screen

3 Move the Menu cursor to ?? lines below

4 Type the total number of lines in the group

5 Press ⟨ENTER⟩

Keystroke method:

1 Position the Text cursor on the first line of the group

2 Press ⟨⊞⟩ and type K, followed by the total number of lines in the group

3 Press ⟨ENTER⟩

Setting the general rules for Page Breaks (Session 17)

- from the Pagination Screen

1 Press ⟨f5⟩ to bring the Page menu onto the screen

2 Select Page Break Control and press ⟨ENTER⟩

3 Set the required Page Break rule

4 Press ⟨ENTER⟩

Paper

Setting Document Paper Type (Session 19)

- from the Pagination Screen

1 Press ⟨f5⟩ to bring the Page menu onto the screen

2 Select Paper Type and press ⟨ENTER⟩

3 Set the type of paper - one of the standard Paper Types or the Special Paper Type

4 Set whether the paper is to be used Portrait or Landscape

5 Select Show Paper Type and press ⟨ENTER⟩

6 Make any changes you need to the specification of the Paper Type so that Paper Type describes the paper that will actually be used

7 Press ⟨ENTER⟩ ⟨↑⟩ ⟨ENTER⟩

Setting Printer Paper Type (Session 19)

Setting to match the Document Paper Type:

1 Select the document and tell LocoScript to print this

2 Select Change to Paper intended for document

3 Press ⟨ENTER⟩

LocoScript then sets up the Printer for the same paper as the document you have picked out for printing. The document is then printed.

Setting up for 'drafting' paper - from LocoScript's Printer Control State (see Printing):

1 Press `f3` to bring the Paper menu onto the screen

2 Set the type of paper - one of the standard Paper Types or the Special Paper Type

3 Set whether the paper is to be used Portrait or Landscape

4 Select Show paper type and press `ENTER`

5 Make any changes you need to the specification of the Paper Type so that Paper Type describes the paper that will actually be used

6 Press `ENTER` `↑` `ENTER`

Setting Page Layout (Session 17)

- from the Pagination Screen

1 Press `f5` to bring the Page menu onto the screen

2 Select Page Layout and press `ENTER`

3 Move the Menu cursor to Header/Footer zone and type in the number of lines you want this to be; then press `ENTER`

4 If necessary, set the other zone in the same way

5 Set whether you want a Fixed or a Floating Footer zone

6 Press `ENTER` again

Phrases

Loading a set of Phrases (Session 14)

- from the Disc Manager Screen

1 Pick out the Phrases file you want to load with the File cursor

2 Press `f1` to bring the Actions menu onto the screen

3 Select Load Phrases and press `ENTER`

4 Check, and if necessary correct, the details in the Selection menu

5 Press `ENTER`

Setting up a new Phrase (Session 14)

- while editing a document

1 Move the Text cursor to the beginning of the phrase in your document

2 Press `COPY`

3 Move the Text cursor to the end of the phrase

4 Press `COPY`

5 Type the name for the Phrase (A . . . Z)

Inserting a Phrase (Session 14)

- while editing a document or setting up Pagination text

1 Position the Text cursor where the Phrase is to be inserted

2 Press [PASTE]

3 Type the name of the Phrase (A...Z)

Saving a set of Phrases (Session 14)

- from the Disc Manager Screen

1 Press [f1] to bring the Actions menu onto the screen

2 Select Save Phrases and press [ENTER]

3 Pick out the group in which you want to store the Phrases with the File/ Group cursor

4 Press [ENTER]

5 Check, and if necessary change, the details in the Selection menu

6 Press [ENTER]

Inspecting Phrases (Session 14)

- from either the Disc Manager Screen or the Editor

1 Press [f1] to bring the Actions menu onto the screen

2 Select Show Phrases

3 Press [ENTER]

A menu showing the first few words of each stored Phrase is then displayed. Press [CAN] when you have finished with this menu.

Positioning text

Centring a line of text (Session 8)

Menu method:

1 Position the Text cursor at the beginning of the line

2 Press [f2] to bring the Layout menu onto the screen and select Centre

3 Press [ENTER]

Keystroke method:

1 Position the Text cursor at the beginning of the line

2 Press [⊞] and type CE

Moving a line to the right (Session 8)

Menu method:

1 Position the Text cursor at the beginning of the line

2 Press [f2] to bring the Layout menu onto the screen and select Right Align

3 Press [ENTER]

Keystroke method:

1 Position the Text cursor at the beginning of the line

2 Press [⊞] and type RA

Indenting a whole paragraph (Session 8)

1 Move the Text cursor to the beginning of the paragraph

2 Hold down [ALT] as you press [TAB]

8809

Printing

Note: These instructions don't cover the various Alert messages that LocoScript will display prior to printing your document if, for example, your printer is not set up for the same type of paper as the document. If an Alert message appears, select one of the options offered in the message and press `ENTER`.

Printing one copy (Session 4)

- from the Disc Manager Screen

1 Pick out the document you want to print one copy of with the File cursor

2 Press **P**

3 Check, and if necessary correct, the details in the Selection menu

4 Set `High/Draft` quality

5 Press `ENTER`

Printing multiple copies (Session 4)

- from the Disc Manager Screen

1 Pick out with the File cursor the document you want to print multiple copies of

2 Press **P**

3 Check, and if necessary correct, the details of the document you have picked out

4 Set `High/Draft` quality

5 Select `Number of copies`

6 Type the number of copies you require and press `ENTER`

Printing selected pages (Session 4)

- from the Disc Manager Screen

1 Pick out with the File cursor the document you want to print pages from

2 Press **P**

3 Check, and if necessary correct, the details of the document you have picked out

4 Set `High/Draft quality`

5 Set the number of copies as above

6 Move Menu cursor to `Print Part of document`

7 Press `ENTER`

8 Move the Menu cursor to `From page` and type the number of the first page to be printed; then press `ENTER`

9 Move the Menu cursor `To page` and type the number of the last page to be printed; then press `ENTER`

10 Press `ENTER` again

Entering Printer Control State (Session 4)

Enter LocoScript's Printer Control State by pressing `PTR`. Leave it again by pressing `EXIT`

Note: Loading paper into the built-in printer automatically puts LocoScript into Printer Control State.

8809

Reprinting (Session 4)

- from Printer Control State

1 Press ⌜f7⌝ to bring the Document menu onto the screen

2 Select required Reprint option

3 Press ⌜ENTER⌝ ⌜EXIT⌝ ⌜ENTER⌝

Setting Left Offset (Session 12)

- from Printer Control State

1 Press ⌜f6⌝ to bring the Left Offset menu onto the screen

2 Increase the Left Offset by moving the Menu cursor to `Increase Offset` and pressing ⌜ENTER⌝ as many times as necessary

3 Decrease the Left Offset by moving the Menu cursor to `Decrease Offset` and pressing ⌜ENTER⌝ as many times as necessary

4 Press ⌜EXIT⌝ ⌜ENTER⌝

Suspending/Resuming printing (Session 4)

- from Printer Control State

1 Press ⌜f1⌝ to bring the Actions menu onto the screen

2 Select `Suspend/Resume Printing`

3 Press ⌜ENTER⌝

Print to end of page (Session 4)

– from Printer Control State

1 Press ⌜f1⌝ to select the Actions menu

2 Select `Print to end of page`

3 Press ⌜ENTER⌝

Search and Replace

Find (Session 13)

- while editing a document

1 Check that the Text cursor is higher up the document than the word or phrase you want to find

2 Press ⌜FIND⌝

3 Make the Find text match the word or phrase you want LocoScript to search for

4 Set the Search options you require

5 Press ⌜ENTER⌝

Exchange (Session 13)

- while editing the document

1 Check that the Text cursor is higher up the document than the first instance of the word or phrase that you want to replace

2 Press ⌜EXCH⌝

3 Make the Find text match the word or phrase that you want to replace

4 Make the Exchange text match the word or phrase that you want to insert instead

5 Set the Search and Replace options

6 Either select `Manual Exchange` and press ⌜ENTER⌝ or select `Automatic exchange` and press ⌜PARA⌝, ⌜PAGE⌝ or ⌜DOC⌝ depending on how much you want to change

If you select Manual Exchange, press ⌜⊞⌝ to confirm the exchange, ⌜⊟⌝ to carry on without exchanging or ⌜CAN⌝ to abandon the exchange each time LocoScript picks out an example of the Find text.

8809

Text preparation

The actions described here are carried out while a document is being edited.

Styling text (Session 9)

Note: The methods described here style all the following text until cancelled by another styling instruction.

Menu method:

1 Position the Text cursor where the styling is to changed

2 Press ⌜73⌝ to bring the Style menu onto the screen

3 Set and Clear the options in this menu as appropriate

4 Press ⌜ENTER⌝

Keystroke method:

1 Position the Text cursor where the styling is to be changed

2 Type the appropriate sequence of keystrokes as follows:

	Set	Clear
Bold	⌞⊞⌟B	⌞⊟⌟B
Double Strike	⌞⊞⌟D	⌞⊟⌟D
Italic	⌞⊞⌟I	⌞⊟⌟I
Reverse	⌞⊞⌟RV	⌞⊟⌟RV
Underline	⌞⊞⌟UL	⌞⊟⌟UL
Word underline	⌞⊞⌟W	⌞⊟⌟UL
Superscript	⌞⊞⌟SR	⌞⊟⌟SR
Subscript	⌞⊞⌟SB	⌞⊟⌟SB

Displaying word-processing codes (Session 9)

1 Press ⌜f8⌝ to bring the Options menu onto the screen

2 Set Codes

3 Press ⌜ENTER⌝

Setting character size (Session 10)

Note: The methods described here set the size of characters used for all the following text until the character size is reset either by another sizing instruction or by a change of Layout.

Menu method:

1 Position the Text cursor where the character size is to be changed

2 Press ⌜f4⌝ to bring the Size menu onto the screen

3 Set the required Character Pitch

4 Set the required Character width

5 Press ⌜ENTER⌝

Keystroke method:

1 Position the Text cursor where the character size is to be changed

2 Press ⌞⊞⌟ and type P

3 Type the combination of numbers and letters that define the required pitch and width (for example, 15D or PS)

4 Press ⌜ENTER⌝

Note: The Character Pitch options are:
10, 12, 15, 17 and PS

Setting line spacing (Session 10)

Note: The methods described here set the line spacing used for all the following text until the line spacing is reset either by another spacing instruction or by a change of Layout.

Menu method:

1 Position the Text cursor where the line spacing is to be changed

2 Press ⌐f4⌐ to bring the Size menu onto the screen

3 Set the required Line Spacing

4 Set the required CR Extra Spacing

5 Set the required Line Pitch

6 Press ⌐ENTER⌐

Keystroke method:

1 Position the Text cursor where the line spacing is to be changed

2 Type the appropriate sequence of keys as follows:

Line Spacing: ⌐⊞⌐LS followed by the number of lines

CR Extra Spacing: ⌐⊞⌐CR followed by the number of lines

Line Pitch: ⌐⊞⌐LP followed the required Line Pitch

Finish each code by pressing ⌐ENTER⌐

Note:

The Line Spacing options are:
0, ½, 1, 1½, 2, 2½, 3

The CR Extra Spacing options are:
0, ½, 1, 1½

The Line Pitch options are: 5, 6, 7½, 8

Setting/Clearing Justification (Session 8)

Menu method:

1 Position the Text cursor where the justification is to be changed

2 Press ⌐f2⌐ to bring the Layout menu onto the screen

3 Move the Menu cursor to Set/Clear justification

4 Press ⌐ENTER⌐

Keystroke method:

1 Position Text cursor where the justification is to be changed

2 Set Justification by pressing ⌐⊞⌐ and typing J; Clear Justification by pressing ⌐⊡⌐ and typing J

Moving round the document (Session 5)

To move to a particular page:

1 Press ⌐f5⌐ to bring the Page menu onto the screen

2 With the Menu cursor on Find page ????, type the number of the page you require

3 Press ⌐ENTER⌐

To move to the start of the next word, paragraph, page etc:

- Press the appropriate Textual Movement Key (⌐WORD⌐, ⌐PARA⌐, ⌐PAGE⌐ etc.)

To move to the start of the previous word, paragraph, page etc:

- Hold down ⌐ALT⌐ as you press the appropriate Textual Movement Key

Appendix V

Troubleshooting

This appendix looks at what to do and what might have gone wrong when your system doesn't work in the way you expect. If you can't find the solution to your problem here, consult your dealer.

I: Trouble with the machine as a whole

• The screen doesn't come up bright green after you switch on

Check that the mains socket you are using is working by plugging in and switching on a lamp that you know is working.

Check that the PCW's mains plug is wired correctly and that the fuse hasn't blown.

If neither of these actions show you where the problem is, consult your dealer.

• The screen goes blank or your machine seems 'dead'

Remove the disc(s) from the drive(s). Then try resetting your machine by holding down [SHIFT] and [EXTRA] and pressing [EXIT]. If this doesn't bring your PCW back to life, switch off, wait a few seconds and then switch on again.

Reload LocoScript 2 and then repeat what you were doing when the problem happened. The chances are that it won't happen again but if it does, consult your dealer or write, giving full details, to Locomotive Software (see the Introduction to this User Guide).

II: Trouble using the disc drive

• You can't insert your disc in the drive

Press the Eject button on the drive – to release any disc already in the drive. If this doesn't solve the problem, check that there isn't anything else in the drive – for example, a piece of cardboard. (If your machine is new, you may have forgotten to take the pieces of cardboard packing out of the disc drives.)

Check that you were trying to insert the disc the right way round.

If you still can't insert the disc, consult your dealer – whatever you do, don't force the disc into the drive. You will only succeed in damaging the drive.

• You can't release the disc from the drive

Consult your dealer – don't try poking anything into the drive to 'help' release the disc.

• You insert a disc in the drive and a message appears telling you that the disc is unformatted

The disc either:

- is completely blank; or
- isn't suitable for your computer

Either insert a different disc or use the Format disc option in the Disc menu to mark the disc out correctly.

Note: Check that the disc is either completely unused or doesn't have anything you want stored on it before you format it. Formatting a disc destroys any data that is currently stored on it.

• 'Disc is unsuitable for drive'

You are either trying to use a 720k 'Drive B' 3" disc in Drive A of a PCW8256/8512 or you are trying to write to a 180k 'Drive A' 3" disc in a 720k disc drive.

You should normally only use discs in the type of disc drive for which they were formatted, though you can read a 180k 'Drive A' disc in a 720k 3" disc drive.

III: Trouble during Start-up or while resetting your PCW

• The PCW just bleeps or the screen flashes

The disc in Drive A either:

- doesn't have the LocoScript software on it; or
- has been damaged; or
- isn't suitable for your computer

Check that you inserted the right disc and then reset your machine. If it bleeps again, try to load the Installation program on your LocoScript 2 Master disc. If this fails too, consult your dealer.

• Software is loaded from the disc but you don't see the LocoScript 2 Copyright screen or the Disc Manager Screen

You have inserted a disc with the wrong software on it. Try using a different Start-of-day disc.

IV: Trouble while copying or formatting a disc

• A message appears reporting a 'Disc Error'

Your disc may have been damaged.

Select the Retry option and press [ENTER]: this may well clear the problem. However, if the message simply reappears, select Cancel operation and press [ENTER]. This returns you to the Disc Manager Screen.

Release the disc(s) from the drive, then try copying/formatting the disc again. If this also fails, rescue what files you can from the damaged disc by using the File menu to copy these one by one to a different disc. Then abandon using the disc.

• A message appears saying that the disc is 'Write-protected'

You are trying to copy to or format a disc which has either or both of the Write-protect holes open. Either:

- close the Write-protect hole and select `Disc write enabled: continue`; or

- select `Cancel operation` – if you realise that if you continue, you will destroy information you didn't mean to lose

V: Trouble when you select a document for editing or create a new document

• A message appears telling you that what you have picked out is 'Not a LocoScript 2 document'

You are trying to edit a file that is not a LocoScript 2 document. It could, for example, be one of your Phrases files or an ASCII version you have created of one of your LocoScript 2 documents.

The only documents you can edit using LocoScript 2 are LocoScript 2 documents or LocoScript '1' documents. LocoScript '1' documents are automatically converted as the first step in the process. If you want to edit information that you have prepared under a different computer system, you must create a new document and then 'insert' the file containing this information into your new document – which you can then edit, save and print.

• A message appears telling you that the 'Disc is write-protected'

The disc holding the document you selected to edit is write-protected – so LocoScript won't be able to save the new version you create back on the same disc.

You can now release the disc, close its write-protect holes, return it to the drive and select `Disc write enabled: continue`. But if you have only opened the document for editing so that you can look at it or copy a section of it into a Block, you might prefer to simply select `Send result to Drive M:`.

• A message appears telling you that the 'Directory is full'

You have so many files on the disc that you have filled up the space reserved for filenames. You can't store any more documents on this disc – but you can edit the documents on the disc without any problems.

VI: Trouble while editing

• Your PCW bleeps as you press a key

The key you pressed isn't one of the ones LocoScript was expecting – so it bleeped to tell you that it couldn't process your keystroke.

The likely reasons for this are:

- you have pressed [RETURN] when you should have pressed [ENTER] or vice versa (you tell LocoScript to go ahead in menus by pressing [ENTER] – not [RETURN])

- you are forgetting that LocoScript is currently in Printer Control State – for example, because you have just loaded a piece of paper into the printer

- you are forgetting that you still have a menu or an Alert message on the screen

Think again about the key you should be pressing.

• Typing produces all the wrong characters

If these characters are Greek letters, Cyrillic letters or Symbols, then your keyboard is currently working in one of its alternative modes. Hold down [ALT] and press [f1] to go back to typing the standard range of 'Roman' script characters.

If what you are getting is Capital letters rather than small letters, you are currently working with Caps Lock set. Hold down [ALT] and press [ENTER] to clear this.

• Using the Textual Movement Keys just produces numbers

You are currently working with Num Lock set. Hold down [ALT] and press [RELAY] to clear this.

• LocoScript appears to be working but whatever you type doesn't have any effect

Your keyboard may be faulty. Unplug the keyboard from the Monitor unit and then plug it in again. If LocoScript doesn't respond after this, reload LocoScript. If it still fails to respond, consult your dealer.

• A message appears on the screen telling you that the 'Disc is full'

There is either no longer room on the disc to store your new version of the document or no longer room on Drive M for the temporary files LocoScript has created while editing your document.

Look at the message to see which Drive has run out of space; then select Run Disc Manager. You can then move documents off the affected disc onto another disc or delete them – until you make enough room. If you run out of space on Drive M, another option is to use the Show blocks option in the f1 Actions menu and the [+] key to remove Blocks that you no longer need. The steps are similar to the ones used to clear Phrases (see page 148).

When you believe you have done enough, press [EXIT]. If you haven't made enough room, the message will appear again, giving you another chance to sort the problem out – but if all is well, you can just continue editing.

Note: It is possible that when you try to erase certain files on Drive M, all you will see is a Alert message telling you that the file is 'in use'. The reason for this is that LocoScript generally keeps the printer file containing the character set you are currently using open on Drive M. (Where you are only using the built-in printer and just one typestyle on this printer, no file will be 'in use' but space on the disc will be taken up by an extra hidden (system) file.)

If you need to free the space occupied by this printer file, you must 'close' the file as follows. First finish any printing you are currently doing. Then press [PTR] to go into Printer Control State; press [f5] to display the Printer menu, select the Remove Current Set option and press [ENTER]. This leaves your system with a printer but no Character Set to work with. Press [EXIT] to leave Printer Control State and you will now be able to erase the printer file. (The extra hidden file used by the built-in printer will have gone of its own accord.)

Note, however, that the Print document and Direct print options will now have been withdrawn. If you later want to print a document, first restore to Drive M all the relevant Printer files for the printer and character set you want to use (.PRI file, .#*xx* file – plus INSTALL.DRV/LQ24.DRV if you are using an external printer). If the printer, Character Set etc. you intend to use are the Intended ones for the document, you can now go ahead and print. But if you want to use some other printer or Character Set, you must go into Printer Control State and use the f5 Printer menu to select these first. (Alternatively, you could re-load LocoScript.)

• A message appears telling you that there is a 'Data error' or a 'Missing address mark'

The document you are editing has been damaged.

The option to take when this message first appears is Retry – because this may well make the problem go away.

If the message just returns, which option you take depends on how much editing you have done:

- If you have made a lot of changes up to the point you are currently working, select the Ignore option. You will then see another message warning you that you are working with a damaged document. Save this document and recover the previous version from Limbo.

- If you haven't made any changes up to this point, select Cancel operation. This returns you to the Disc Manager Screen – as if you hadn't started editing the document.

If you don't have a back-up copy of this document on another disc, you should now try using the Copy file option in the File menu to copy the original document to another disc. However, this may fail.

9010

Re-edit the original document and the new version (if you saved this) and copy undamaged sections of these documents into Blocks. Paste these sections into a new document. Use this technique to 'rescue' as much of the damaged document as you can.

• A message appears on the screen telling you that the 'Editor data buffer is full'

The page you are working on is either excessively large or excessively complicated. Simplify it, for example by reducing the number of tabs you are using.

VII: Trouble when trying to print a document

• There is no 'Save and Print' option in the Exit menu

There is no printer currently connected to your PCW – or the printer is already busy. Save the document, press [PTR] and then use the Document menu to see if the printer is printing anything.

If this menu gives details of a document, then LocoScript is in the middle of printing this document: perhaps you haven't fed in enough paper to finish that last document you asked LocoScript to print. If the menu doesn't give give details of a document, switch your PCW off and check that the printer is connected properly. Then reload LocoScript 2.

Look at the Information lines on the Disc Manager Screen. If these show the P=Print Document and D=Direct Printing options, then all is well and your printer is now correctly attached. If not, your printer may well be faulty – so consult your dealer.

• You press P or D and you see a message telling you that the printer is absent

There is no printer currently connected to your PCW. Switch your PCW off and check that the printer is connected properly. Then reload LocoScript 2.

Look at the Information lines on the Disc Manager Screen. If these show the P=Print Document and D=Direct Printing options, then all is well and your printer is now correctly attached. If not, your printer may well be faulty – consult your dealer.

• The Printer Actions menu just has the one entry – Reset Printer

Your printer has been left in a strange state. Press [ENTER], so that LocoScript resets the printer.

• A message appears telling you that what you have picked out is 'Not a LocoScript 2 document'

You are trying to print a file that is not a LocoScript 2 document. It could, for example, be one of your Phrases files or an ASCII version you have created of one of your LocoScript 2 documents.

The only documents you can print using LocoScript 2 are LocoScript 2 documents. If you want to print information that you have prepared under a different computer system, you must create a new document and then 'insert' the file containing this information into your new document – which you can then edit, save and print.

• You pick out a document for printing and you see a message telling you that you have picked out a LocoScript '1' document

The document you picked out was prepared using the earlier version of LocoScript. Before you can print this, you must edit it. Then LocoScript 2 can carry out the necessary conversion to produce a document that can be printed using LocoScript 2.

• The built-in printer doesn't autoload

You have pushed the sheet of paper too far in before turning the Paper Load Knob. Turn this knob back (so that the bail bar is back against the platen), take the sheet of paper out of the printer and try again. This time, just rest the paper in the printer.

• The printer doesn't start to print

First check that there is paper in the printer and the bail bar is holding the paper against the platen. If there isn't any paper in the printer, load a sheet of paper and press [EXIT]: your document will probably print now.

If this doesn't solve the problem, press [PTR] to put LocoScript into Printer Control State and see whether the printer is waiting for paper or otherwise currently suspended. Use the [f1] Actions menu to 'resume printing'. Press [EXIT] to leave Printer Control State.

If your document still doesn't print, press [PTR] again. This time use the [f5] Printer menu to check which printer LocoScript is expecting to print on and, if necessary, change it. If it was set up for the printer you expected, check that this printer is properly plugged into your PCW. Press [EXIT] again.

If the document still doesn't print, consult your dealer.

• The printer appears to work but nothing is printed

Check that you have a ribbon in the printer.

9010

• The printer suddenly stops printing

Press [PTR] to put LocoScript into Printer Control State and see if the current printer state is No Paper. If it is, then the printer has detected the end of the paper you are feeding into the printer.

Don't load fresh paper yet. First use the [f1] Actions menu to 'print to end of page'. When printing stops again, load fresh paper and then use the menu to 'Resume printing'.

This problem typically only happens when you are using continuous stationery.

• The printer prints rubbish

You haven't set up LocoScript correctly for the printer you are using. Press [PTR] so that the printer stops printing as soon as possible. (Unfortunately, if the printer keeps a large store of characters to print, this may take a while!)

Use the Printer menus to set up LocoScript correctly (see Session 20) and to restart printing the document (see Session 4).

• The paper jams in the printer

Press [PTR] so that the printer stops printing as soon as possible. (Unfortunately, if the printer keeps a large store of characters to print, this may take a while!)

Clear out the damaged paper, reload with fresh paper and then use the Printer menus to restart printing the document (see Session 4).

• The text is poorly positioned on the page

Press [PTR] to put LocoScript into its Printer Control State and then use the [f6] Left Offset menu to adjust the start position of each line of text. Then use the Document menu to restart printing the document (see Session 4).

Locomotive Software

Important Notice

THE SOFTWARE CONTAINED IN THE DISKETTE PACKAGE IS SUPPLIED TO YOU ON THE TERMS AND CONDITIONS INDICATED BELOW. THE OPENING OF THIS PACKAGE INDICATES YOUR ACCEPTANCE OF THESE TERMS AND CONDITIONS. IF SUCH TERMS AND CONDITIONS ARE NOT ACCEPTED BY YOU, YOU MUST RETURN THE UNOPENED PACKAGE TO THE PLACE OF PURCHASE AND YOUR MONEY WILL BE REFUNDED. NO REFUNDS WILL BE GIVEN WHERE THE PACKAGE HAS BEEN OPENED UNLESS THE PRODUCT IS FAULTY AND SUCH REFUND BECOMES PAYABLE UNDER CLAUSE 7 BELOW

In this notice, the terms:

'Locomotive' means Locomotive Software Limited

'The Program' means the program known as LocoScript 2 on the diskette supplied in the diskette package.

1. Copyright

Material within The Program is copyright Locomotive.

Locomotive grants to the purchaser of this package a non-exclusive right to use The Program in accordance with these terms and conditions. Such Licence may be transferred only in accordance with Clause 3 below. Any other use or dealing not expressly authorised by these terms and conditions is strictly prohibited.

2. Use

The Program may only be used on a single machine or terminal at any one time but may be copied in support of that use. Any such copying is subject to there being no modification of The Program and in particular to the copyright notices of Locomotive being preserved in the copy. Save for copying as aforesaid, any other operations (including modification or translation from machine readable form) are expressly prohibited.

3. Transfer

The Program may be transferred to a third party provided the original Program and all copies are transferred or otherwise destroyed and provided further these terms and conditions are produced to that third party and prior to the transfer that party agrees and undertakes to observe and continue to observe the same. Without such transfer

LocoScript 2 User Guide

and undertaking any application of The Program or copies thereof by any other person will not be authorised by Locomotive and will be in breach of Locomotive's copyright and other proprietary rights.

4. Documentation

The documentation accompanying The Program is copyright Locomotive. However, no right to reproduce that documentation in part or in whole is granted by Locomotive. Should additional copies of the documentation be required for whatever reason, application must be made in writing to Locomotive which will be considered in its discretion.

5. Breach

If the user for the time being acts in breach of any of these terms and conditions it shall indemnify Locomotive against all loss suffered (including loss of profits) and the licence granted hereunder shall be deemed to be terminated forthwith. On termination the user shall deliver up to Locomotive all infringing and lawful copies of The Program.

6. Exclusions

Neither Locomotive nor any person authorised by it gives warranties or makes representations that The Program is error free or will meet functions required by the user. It shall be the responsibility of the user to satisfy itself that The Program meets the user's requirements. The Program is supplied on an 'as is' basis and save as expressly provided in these conditions all warranties of any nature (and whether express or implied) are excluded.

7. Liability

Locomotive warrants that the diskette on which The Program is stored is free from material defect and through normal use will remain so for a period of 90 days after purchase. In the event of any breach of this warranty (or statutory warranty or conditions incapable of exclusion by these conditions) the responsibilities of Locomotive shall be limited to replacing the enclosed program or to returning the price paid for the same as they shall determine.

As the sole exception to the foregoing Locomotive will accept liability for death or personal injury resulting from its negligence. In no circumstance shall Locomotive be liable for any indirect or consequential costs damages or losses (including loss of business profits, operating time or otherwise) arising out of the use or inability to use the enclosed program and diskette and whether or not the likelihood of damage was advised to Locomotive or its dealer.

This notice does not affect your statutory rights.

INDEX

LocoScript 2 User Guide

LocoScript 2 User Guide

LocoScript 2 User Guide

Index

LocoScript 2 User Guide

Index